D0871928

INTERMODERNISM

For George, Helen and Vera

INTERMODERNISM

Literary Culture in
Mid-Twentieth-Century Britain

Edited by
Kristin Bluemel

EDINBURGH UNIVERSITY PRESS

© in this edition Edinburgh University Press, 2009
© in the individual contributions is retained by the authors

Edinburgh University Press Ltd
22 George Square, Edinburgh

www.euppublishing.com

Typeset in Sabon and Gill Sans
by Servis Filmsetting Ltd, Stockport, Cheshire, and
printed and bound in Great Britain by
CPI Antony Rowe, Chippenham and Eastbourne

A CIP record for this book is available from the British Library

ISBN 978 0 7486 3509 2 (hardback)

CONTENTS

ACKNOWLEDGEMENTS

I would like to thank Jackie Jones of Edinburgh University Press for exceptional editorial vision, guidance and patience. She was an integral part of the intellectual and institutional processes that led to *Intermodernism*. I'd also like to thank Nicola Wood, the copyeditor for the book, and James Dale, the Press's managing editor, for their careful work on the manuscript during later stages of its production. The book's origins are in Tulsa, Oklahoma, where members of the MSA panel on Intermodernism, Phyllis Lassner, Faye Hammill, myself and Bernard Schweizer began to imagine what a book on intermodernism would look like. To Bernard I owe a special debt of gratitude for organising that panel and advocating vigorously for extending its arguments into a broader public sphere.

I would also like to thank members of The Space Between Society for providing an acutely attentive, supportive audience for scholarship – both my own and others – that I now think of as part of an emergent field of intermodernist studies. Thanks also to Nick Hubble and Philip Tew for hosting me at the 2008 Literary London conference at Brunel University where I enjoyed many stimulating, challenging conversations about intermodernism, and to Brycchan Carey and Susan Ash for valuable discussions about neglected intermodern genres. Thanks also to Aileen Christianson for last-minute help with the appendix. I'm also grateful to the graduate students at Monmouth University who participated in my 2007 seminar on Intermodernism. Their curiosity, enthusiasm, insights and healthy scepticism provided an ideal context for testing out my ideas and for attaining the real goal of the intermodern enterprise: to teach in a coherent and sustained way the literature of the interwar and war years that otherwise makes only superficial appearances in courses on British and Irish modernism. Michelle Giles, my graduate assistant at Monmouth University, deserves special thanks for her careful help with the appendix. Also, a heartfelt thank-you to Phyllis Lassner for years of shared reading, conversations, emails and even arguments about all of the beautiful, terrible things in and of intermodernism that, spell-like, have kept our imaginations fixed on the history and people of the interwar and war years. Finally and as always, I'd like to acknowledge the love, patience and support of my family members, George, Helen and Vera Witte, to whom this book is dedicated.

INTRODUCTION: WHAT IS INTERMODERNISM?

Kristin Bluemel

This collection of critical essays on intermodernism challenges readers to accept a new term, new critical category and new literary history for twentieth-century British literary culture. *Intermodernism* takes as its primary subject the fascinating, compelling and grossly neglected writing of the years of Depression and World War II. These are the novels, memoirs and essays of writers like George Orwell, Storm Jameson, William Empson, Harold Heslop and Stella Gibbons that emerged from, anticipated and influenced perceptions of two world wars and their aftermaths. In contrast to T. S. Eliot, who argued in 'The Social Function of Poetry' that the 'responsibility of the poet is not, primarily, to the people', but 'to his *language*, first to preserve, second to extend and improve' (qtd in Shiach 29), the writers featured in this volume saw their responsibilities, as writers, primarily to 'the people'.[1] *Intermodernism* explores the manifestations and implications of such intermodern responsibility, focusing on three defining features: cultural features (intermodernists typically represent working-class and working middle-class cultures); political features (intermodernists are often politically radical, 'radically eccentric'); and literary features (intermodernists are committed to non-canonical, even 'middlebrow' or 'mass' genres). Researching, defining and theorising intermodernism, the contributors to this volume do not believe that academic publishers' backlists and university courses on the thirties and the forties, modernism and post-modernism or postcolonialism, can do justice to the web of sometimes subtle, sometimes obvious associations between the writers, institutions and cultural forms of the middle years of the twentieth century. They all are committed to the long-term goal of making intermodernism as familiar to twenty-first century readers as modernism is to twentieth-century critics. *Intermodernism: Literary Culture in Mid-Twentieth-Century Britain* marks the first collective, co-ordinated effort towards realising this goal.

This introduction attempts to define intermodernism, the motives for inventing it and the ways of incorporating it within literary critical discourse. My effort to represent a complex theoretical enterprise in concise and coherent terms is supported by ten chapters that are divided into four sections, the first section on work, the next on community, the third on war and the last on documents. These four concerns – work, community, war and documents – emerge out of intermodern writing itself; they seem to force themselves upon our imaginations and demand that theme, as well as cultural, political and literary features, be taken into consideration in formulations of this new field. To a certain extent, they serve as structuring axes along which early intermodern conversations can be organised, awaiting replacement when scholars feel confident proposing more subtle or complex frames of analysis. While each chapter may be read as an intermodern case study, the more ambitious theoretical aims of this project will be realised once a given chapter is read in terms of the other chapters in its section and when chapters in different sections are read in terms of each other. To encourage this 'intersectional' approach, I conclude the introduction with an analysis of the book's key qualitative relationships – of literary history, genre, language and audience – that help sustain my claims for intermodernism.

WHY INTERMODERNISM?

This project assumes that any proposal or advocacy of intermodernism will have to take place in relation to the discourse of modernism. Within the last ten years, and particularly in America, the apparent colonisation of virtually all areas of study of twentieth-century literary cultural activity by the 'New Modernist Studies' has ensured that whatever is not modernism will function as modernism's other, an other that is measured against and known in terms of the same: the same iterations of modernism (or more generously, 'modernisms').[2] Of course the term intermodernism invites such comparison, containing within it reference to the very dominant cultural and critical movement it seeks to disturb. 'Intermodernism' thus anticipates, resists and depends on this inevitable process of comparison.[3] The modernism/intermodernism binary, which I did not invent but rather discovered, ready and waiting for me, functions as a call to deconstruction. I've tried to anticipate or facilitate such deconstruction through the word intermodernism itself. 'Inter-' means 'between' so a modernism that is between should be regarded as something more than a simple binary term. I want intermodernism to locate a cultural and critical bridge or borderland whose inhabitants are always looking two ways. Nick

Hubble has argued elsewhere that 'It is precisely this dual perspective which sets intermodernist narrative free from the association of high or low (or middlebrow) culture and gives it the potential to make things happen in the world' ('Origins' 167). Working out the implications of Hubble's idea, I'd argue that intermodernism deconstructs *multiple* binaries, not just the highbrow/lowbrow opposition. So while intermodernism might initially function as modernism's other in academic practice, it has the *potential* to be the concept or space that inserts itself between modernism and its many structuring oppositions, reshaping the ways we think about relations between elite and common, experimental and popular, urban and rural, masculine and feminine, abstract and realistic, colonial and colonised. Within an institutional context, this is one of the good things that it could make happen in the world. If the academic institutions that regulate and reproduce cultural knowledge begin to shift in response to a critical discourse about intermodernism, revisionary theoretical movements that challenge the dominant, structuring oppositions of modernism/postmodernism and modernism/modernity will gain much needed momentum.[4]

I am sceptical about institutional practices that assume modernism can function as a label that organises or disciplines study of literary texts and cultures from 1860 (or earlier) to 1960 (or later), from the traditional American and European centres (New York, Paris, London, St Petersburg) to just about anywhere in the globe and everywhere in between. Other scholars share this scepticism and have been urging us for a decade or more to find new ways of describing and understanding the forces and forms that produced non-modernist, mid-twentieth-century literature. In 2000, Nancy Paxton argued in her leading chapter of *Outside Modernism: In Pursuit of the English Novel, 1900–30*, that scholars need to rethink the values that have made literary Modernism the 'privileged expression of the "modern" in this period' (4). She considers the ways realism was integral to canonical modernism and, along with her co-editor Lynne Hapgood, directs us to read neglected realist novels by writers like John Galsworthy, Radclyffe Hall, Frederic Manning and Patrick Hamilton. Around the same time, Tyrus Miller published *Late Modernism: Politics, Fiction, and the Arts between the Wars*. While Paxton and Hapgood focus on recovering English novels that had been eclipsed by the 'unexamined nationalism' influencing the modernist canon (5), Miller tries to theorise a new period, treating late modernism as 'a problem' of literary history and ideology.

Drawing on Astradur Eysteinsson's *The Concept of Modernism*, among other studies, Miller reminds readers that conceptions of modernism go well beyond aesthetic concerns and that modernism, in all its ideological forms, has generated dozens of stories about itself and its making. As an alternative to the familiar stories of modernism which he describes as a kind of 'academic folk wisdom' (4), Miller poses his own story by looking at modernism 'from the perspective of its end', the modernism of the late twenties and early thirties (12). This is valuable and exciting work, but like many contributions to the New Modernist Studies, Miller's dominant literary examples, theoretical sources and aesthetic criteria make the kind of writing I consider intermodernist no more visible than, say, Bradbury and McFarlane's traditional account of modernism.[5]

For those interested in recovering writers stuck in what Miller calls 'the no man's land' between the camps of modernism and postmodernism, two of the most valuable studies to appear in recent memory are Marina MacKay's closely argued monograph, *Modernism and World War II*, and her collection, co-edited with Lyndsey Stonebridge, *British Fiction after Modernism: The Novel at Mid-Century*. The latter study, in particular, establishes a theoretical and critical approach to British writing that supports the intermodern project. Like Paxton and Hapgood's book, it considers only British fiction and is preoccupied with questions of realism's (or 'realisms'') relations to experimental modernism. But unlike the other studies recuperating the 'in between' period and texts of mid-century, MacKay and Stonebridge's anthology emphasises the literature of World War II and its aftermath, seeking continuities among texts that adopt an aesthetic of anxiety generated by the violence of not two, but three wars (World Wars I and II, and the Cold War) (7).

Ten years on from Miller's *Late Modernism*, the mid-century literature of 'the back bedroom' has been dusted off (MacKay and Stonebridge 1), earning treatment in ambitious new studies that attempt to redefine its relation to modernism and Britishness in aesthetic, as well as social, ideological and historical terms. In addition to the studies I've already mentioned, the twenty-first century has brought us Peter Kalliney's *Cities of Affluence and Anger: A Literary Geography of Modern Englishness* (2006), John Marx's *The Modernist Novel and the Decline of Empire* (2005), and Jed Esty's *A Shrinking Island: Modernism and National Culture in England* (2004). There are also numerous studies of the literature of the interwar and war years that examine specific kinds of historical periods, writers, genres and regions: there are separate studies on British literature of the 1930s or the 1940s; on literature by women, working-class intellectuals, civilians on the home front and colonial writers; mid-century novels, World War II poetry, BBC propaganda or children's literature; literature of England, the colonies, the shires.[6]

The concerns and claims of *Intermodernism* build on and then exceed those of the studies mentioned here. Its excess is evident in its claim to be able to describe diverse literary forms (not just novels and short stories), more populist genres (not just elite or 'difficult' texts) and multiple kinds of media (not just literature but also radio and film and journalism) over a period of time that overlaps with all those periods described as 'late modernist', 'outside' or 'after' modernism. In particular, the web of personal, literary and institutional relations it traces suggests that regardless of the extent to which writers of the mid-century 'wilfully positioned themselves on the outside' (MacKay and

Stonebridge 9), they were just as much as the modernists involved in literary groups. Attention to intermodern communities, networks and institutions manifests itself not only in the two chapters included in 'Part II: Community', but also in a chapter on Storm Jameson and the European P.E.N. that appears in 'Part I: Work', chapters on Elizabeth Bowen or Rebecca West and the Nazi trials in 'Part III: War', and a chapter on William Empson and Mass-Observation in 'Part IV: Documents'. These and other chapters often emphasise intermodern writers' eccentric political alliances and identifications (with communists, socialists and feminists) or their contributions to genres of writing that fall far outside formal markers of modernism (documentaries, historical and suburban novels, spy-detection thrillers, radio and film scripts or pamphlet journalism). *Intermodernism*, like many of the mid-century texts it analyses and celebrates, is not especially concerned with the critical vocabulary of high modernism or with tracing the relations between intermodern and modernist texts. This means that while other studies of mid-century British writing are compatible with – or even exemplify – the New Modernist Studies, *Intermodernism* is not so well behaved.

WHAT IS INTERMODERNISM?

1: Intermodernism, like modernism, is a category that alludes to both period and style. On the one hand, it designates the interwar, wartime and immediately postwar years, and thus offers itself as a 'new' historical period, one that separates certain years from the accepted, and supposedly known periods of modernism and postmodernism. Of course intermodernism is only a 'new' period to the extent that within the discourse of modernist studies it inscribes lines around new dates and thus suggests a reorganisation of values. This means that intermodernism, like any other movement category such as romanticism or modernism or Futurism is blatantly, self-consciously, ideological. In other words – and this is important – intermodernism is an ideology. This understanding of intermodernism as ideology underlies and subsumes all other debates about intermodernism's status as period or style. Insofar as it is intended to challenge an equally ideological scholarly discourse about modernism, or at least to challenge the process by which modernism has expanded to take over the field of twentieth-century cultural studies, intermodernism is revisionary, 'radically eccentric'.[7]

It is important *not* to define intermodernism primarily or only as a period, since all efforts of periodisation are open to critique for being arbitrary – of claiming beginning and ending dates that have no inherent meaning, of excluding someone or something crucial from the period. Intermodernism must therefore also be thought of as a *kind of writing* (by which I mean it is an aesthetic category), a *social formation* (an institutional, materialist category), and an expression of *shared values* (an ideological category). And this brings me to my next point.

2: Above all, intermodernism should be functional. It should provide scholars with a literary-critical compass, analytical tool, or useful guidepost for finding and valuing vital figures and cultural forms that disappear in discussions of modernism or postmodernism.

3: Intermodernism is a postmodern invention. It is a retroactive, after the fact intervention in twenty-first century critical discourse about modernism. By stating a so-obvious-seeming fact I am attempting to defend against the notion that the writers who inspired my coining of the term intermodernism thought of themselves as intermodernists. *Intermodernism* announces itself as an opportunity for scholars and critics working more than fifty years after 'intermodernism' itself to talk in new ways about artists, writers, journalists and architects who were active during the interwar and war years and who, until now, have been treated as modernism's others, if they were treated at all. So there is a kind of inversion or doubling in the use of this category, as with other similar categories. Twenty-first century scholars of intermodernism are the 'real' intermodernists. Yet the term as it is used in this volume signifies people who are all dead, never heard of intermodernism, and would never consider themselves intermodernists if asked to do so. This leads to the observation that inventing intermodernism is a dynamic process that involves both *discovery* – research on artists, writers and other members of the intelligentsia who invite us to think of them in new terms – and *theorising* – the intellectual activity of adjusting our conceptual, critical categories, including the categories of literary history, to accommodate new knowledge.

4: Intermodernism is not just for literary scholars. While this discussion of intermodernism finds its point of origin and many points of reference in the critical vocabulary of literary studies, it depends on interdisciplinary theories that have shaped notions of modernism and postmodernism, culture and literacy, the national and transnational, the aesthetic and ideological. Even more importantly, it suggests that in the future, the places intermodernism ought to investigate include texts, cultural forms and figures from many disciplines: art and design, film, geography, architecture, urban studies, working-class studies, Jewish studies, gender studies – not to mention the cultural and social spaces between these disciplines.

5: Intermodernism is not just for scholars of twentieth-century British literature and culture, even though it is scholars who are experts in this field who have initiated the process of intermodern discovery and theorisation. These scholars recognise that amid all the writing and theorising of transnational, global modernism, it would be naive to define intermodernism as a manifestation of a supposedly consistent or autonomous British national culture. Cultural theorists Simon Gikandi and Ian Baucom, among others, have argued persuasively that constructions of British national culture can only be understood in relation to other constructions (for example Englishness) and in the context of the histories of empire and imperialism. The British bias or basis of intermodernism is not meant to isolate the writers from the colonial or international scene that so influenced their writings. (The importance of Mulk Raj Anand for my earlier formulation of intermodernism demonstrates my scholarly investment in understanding 'British' literature in precisely the relational way Gikandi recommends.) One reason I associate this volume's examples of intermodernism with something called British literature and British culture is because I work within institutional structures that accept that category as meaningful; I teach classes in British, not English, literature. The second reason this volume claims to examine British as opposed to English literature, is that my focus on the writing of the 1930s, 1940s and early 1950s was produced by those who had to contemplate the end of the British Empire and thus the end of the 'Great' 'British' global imagined community. As scholars like Kalliney, Marx and Esty have shown, at this particular historical moment, the label 'British' became especially important because it was especially vulnerable. In the 1930s, the usual threats of imperial disintegration from rebellious colonies were multiplied by threats of world-wide economic failure and world-wide Soviet-style revolution. In the 1940s, the British contemplated the even more dire threat of national dissolution from the world-wide imperialist military movement inspired by German, Italian and Japanese fascism. The 'greater' British nation did matter to the intermodernists. Though they might have contested its boundaries, meanings and claims upon their allegiance, they did not regard it as arbitrary. Hitler made sure of that.

The next section of this introduction looks at a writer whose response to fascist threat and British national dissolution in large part defines the nature of his contribution to intermodern literature. Richard Hillary's memoir of his student days at Oxford and his work as an RAF pilot in the Battle of Britain, followed three years later by his death while training at night in a Blenheim twin engine plane, suspended him in the intermodernist period, unrecognised by scholars of modernism or postmodernism. His story functions as a kind of parable pointing toward the kinds of materials, methods and meanings of intermodern scholarship.

RICHARD HILLARY AND THE PROBLEM OF THE POPULAR

Richard Hillary's account of his life in the RAF, *The Last Enemy*, became an instant classic of war literature and made him a national hero. Hillary became famous as much for his writing as his fighting; of the latter he'd done relatively little, having been shot down in his Spitfire on 3 September 1940 after only three weeks of active missions. His description of his recovery from the crash and torturous reconstruction in the 'beauty shop' of plastic surgeon A. H. McIndoe is as compelling as it is horrifying. Read in conjunction with Hillary's justly famous flight sequences, the chapters on life amid and after hospitalisation can be seen to foreground the typical intermodern concerns of work (of pilots, nurses and surgeons), of community (of students, pilots and patients), of war (the Battle of Britain, the Blitz) and of documents (of fiction-alised memoir).

Beyond *The Last Enemy*'s contributions to discussion of the dominant intermodern themes noted above, I am interested in the ways that Hillary's narrative of his transformation from a celebrated golden boy of Oxford to the last of the long haired boys of the Battle of Britain is saturated with meanings and myths of intermodern England. Crucial to these meanings are the dictates of gender and more specifically the powerful force of masculine ideals upon manly and military conduct. Surprisingly, no other critics have asked about the implications of Hillary's loss of mobility, grace and beauty upon his gendered identity or the relation of that identity to his narrative forms and their reception by different kinds of audiences. These now strike me as intermodern questions, that is to say, questions that become possible or at least valuable once Hillary is regarded as an intermodernist. Approaching Hillary through the fiction of Orwell and other intermodernists, he 'looks' different to me from the way he looks to other readers who measure him against the World War I combatant writers, or the dominant literary voices of his undergraduate days, Eliot and Pound, or against what Hillary disparagingly referred to as 'the Auden group'. In other words, I can already provide a compelling answer to the question: 'What does intermodernism do for Hillary?' It makes him an immensely satisfying subject for feminist and cultural study. What follows is a more expansive answer to a corollary question: 'What might Hillary do for intermodernism?'

In 1950, seven years after Hillary's death, R. Lovat Dickson, Hillary's editor at Macmillan, published a memoir about the young author, describing his first meeting with Hillary in March 1941. Dickson confesses that he found himself feeling repulsed by Hillary's looks – his lidless, watering eyes and 'thin skeleton fingers, horribly raw in colour, without nails and permanently bent' (115, 116). He also recalls how Hillary took advantage of his discomfort, insisting that Dickson listen to him read aloud from his work. Dickson remembers that

> [he] was shy, and the nervousness underneath his domineering manner made the skin on his face flush, so that all the marks of the burns stood out like weals. . . . And underneath the bad reading, overcoming the distraction of his burns, were the words of the first chapter of *The Last Enemy*. (116)

This first chapter, which Dickson praises as 'first-class' and 'all action' (116) and Koestler later acclaimed as having 'all the qualities of first-rate reportage – precision, vividity, brilliancy, economy, excitement' (65) – I admire for its spare, documentary prose style inherited from the writing of the previous decade.

Asking again, 'What does Hillary do for intermodernism?', I can answer: 'He makes visible and real the connections between World War II literature and 1930s literature.' In other words, Hillary supports the first point in my definition of intermodernism: that it can be both style and period. If we take Hillary's writing seriously, it suggests that despite a literary history that imagines a total break between the 1930s and 1940s, there are continuities of style – or rather, styles – between these decades that construct an intermodern literary period extending from the interwar through war and immediately postwar years.

Insofar as *The Last Enemy* encourages us to move from analysis of a kind of writing characteristic of the intermodern period – documentary, fictionalised autobiography, in Hillary's case – to analysis of institutions and ideologies, it also reinforces my second defining characteristic of intermodernism. The institutions Hillary asks us to consider are not those of Auden's Oxford or Eliot's or Pound's or Woolf's London, but the Oxford Hillary knew, that was populated by 'intelligent philistines' who became the raffish, sardonic, insouciant young fliers in the RAF. Like Hillary or Anand or Orwell, they might have come from the colonies, and, were it not for the war, would have ended up working in the so-called outposts of empire. Instead, their off-centre orientation toward the dominant institutions of their day led them to adopt oppositional ideologies that expressed themselves in their literature either as an anti-establishment attitude, as in Hillary's case, or as active dissenting politics, as in Anand's.

Finally, the dialectical process I mention in the third point of my definition of intermodernism, the process of *discovering* intermodern works and then *theorising* about their impact upon existing critical discourse, allows us to see how Hillary's memoir supports the other defining points I have made about intermodernism. I have described intermodernism as a *postmodern* invention: only a contemporary attention to popular culture, legitimised through institutionalisation of cultural studies, makes Hillary visible as an intermodernist. My fourth point was that intermodernism is potentially interdisciplinary. Hillary is helpful here, too. At the very least, his narrative is embedded in histories of war and gender, inviting analysis from scholars associated with diverse disciplines and in relation to non-literary texts and artefacts. Lastly, my fifth point was that while intermodernism may have British origins, it is not necessarily exclusively British. Hillary's status as an Australian-born, English-trained RAF pilot engaged in an air battle of epic national and international implications, not to mention his book's initial status as an American text published by the New York house of Reynal and Hitchcock, and ultimately international bestseller, points to the ways *The Last Enemy* is both typically and problematically 'British'. In the best of all possible worlds, intermodernism would bring Hillary back into academic literary history, but Hillary would bring intermodernism into the academy. Ironically, it is Hillary's success, his popularity, that makes it difficult for me to realise either of these goals.

Literary scholars rarely treat Hillary as a serious writer in part because they assume he was too popular to be good. However, Jameson, Phyllis Bottome, Rebecca West and Koestler did believe in him as a writer. In April 1943, three months after Hillary's death, Koestler published in Cyril Connolly's *Horizon* an influential essay on Hillary titled 'The Birth of a Myth'.[8] Here he describes *The Last Enemy* as 'the most promising book that came out of [Hillary's] generation' (54). In pages that ostensibly probed the sources of the Hillary myth – the social and psychological forces that, in Koestler's words, made Hillary's name 'one of the symbolic names of this war' (51) – Koestler did more than any other critic to *create* the Hillary myth. He achieved this in part by framing his essay with the following passage from a love letter Hillary wrote from a RAF Staff College to the London socialite, Mary Booker, with whom he was having a passionate affair. Tormented by doubts, desperately lonely and still in pain, Hillary describes himself as the 'man who is left', the 'last' man:

> I feel a little sick, for I have learned today that Colin Pinckney [one of his closest friends during flight training] has been killed in Singapore. You do not know him, but you will, and, I hope, like him, when you read the book. His death makes an apt postscript and it raises in my mind yet again the question which I have put in the book and attempted to answer, of what is the responsibility of the man who is left. I say man and not men, for I am now the last. (qtd in Koestler 52)

Embedded in Koestler's April 1943 essay, this fragment of a letter written in March 1942 seems to collapse history, announcing at one and the same moment Hillary's living sense of his own sublime status as the last man, but also an eerie sense of his own impending death and its future literary function as an 'apt postscript' to *The Last Enemy*. As 'the man who is left', 'the last' man, Hillary anticipates Orwell's working title for *Nineteen Eighty-Four* (1949), which was *The Last Man in Europe*. The attraction of both writers to the image of 'the last man' points to personal, thematic and ideological concerns that make Hillary and Orwell quintessential intermodernists.

The status Orwell and Hillary achieved even before their deaths suggests the mythical power of the image of the last man, an image that guided their interpretations of their own lives and won them astonishingly huge readerships. Yet the myths that surround them, myths that were forged out of their deep investment in and commentary on the historical forces of their time, have had the perverse effect of isolating them in literary history. Both Orwell and Hillary emerge in critical writings as uniquely autonomous writers: in Orwell's case, the common-man genius; in Hillary's, as the beautiful boy wonder. To quarantine them in this fashion cheats us out of a vibrant literature that testifies to the writers' engagement with diverse figures and institutions in Britain during an understudied period of twentieth-century literary history.

READING *INTERMODERNISM*

Regarding Hillary and Orwell as fully engaged members of intermodern communities prepares readers to discover in the following chapters the shared themes, vocabulary and concerns of intermodernism. *George Orwell and the Radical Eccentrics* also participates in this conversation. In the introduction to that book, I attempted to describe a network of intermodern relations, drawing more tentative conclusions about the distinguishing characteristics of intermodernism due to my more limited scope: instead of the diverse figures examined in the following chapters, I looked closely at only four writers whom I termed the radical eccentrics – Orwell, Stevie Smith, Inez Holden and Mulk Raj Anand, and only one region, London. There, as here, I did not claim all writers of the interwar and war years for intermodernism or claim that all critical projects on Orwell, Smith, Anand and Holden should be advanced in terms of intermodernism. But I did claim that intermodernism would solve practical problems for scholars who found themselves stymied by theoretical and institutional priorities that made it difficult to have sustained discussions about figures whose work and working conditions were different from or eccentric to those of the modernists. The chapters that comprise *Intermodernism* introduce new strands into the intermodern web I first described in *George Orwell and the Radical Eccentrics* in an effort to strengthen its claim upon readers' critical imaginations.

Elizabeth Maslen's chapter on Storm Jameson frames this book because its key concerns point to dominant intermodern forms and concerns discussed in other chapters and in existing scholarship on intermodernism.[9] As I've already mentioned, one of the most important of those concerns is work – work as a constant pressure, a subject for investigation and an influence upon political belief and action. Jameson never stopped working, either as a writer or as advocate for war refugees, and her fiction and non-fiction is full of representations of people working. We see attention to work, workers and the way class mediates the experience of work in other chapters, too, most notably Janet Montefiore's analysis of the Marxist Sylvia Townsend Warner's novel *The Corner That Held Them* and T. H. White's historically nuanced *The Once and Future King*, and John Fordham's chapter on the literary and political work of the '*miner* writer' Harold Heslop. These three scholars associate the theme of work with another defining intermodern concern: community. The community of value in Heslop's fiction is that of his fellow miners and trade unionists of 'the North'; in Warner's, the nuns of her fictional convent, Oby; and in White's, the knights of King Arthur's Round Table. We also see Stella Gibbons's concern with suburban community in Faye Hammill's analysis of *Miss Linsey and Pa*, *My American* and *The Bachelor* and J. B. Priestley's preoccupation with English and later British community in Lisa Colletta's analysis of his travel narratives of the mid-1930s, *English Journey* and *Midnight on the Desert*.

Priestley's sense of community, of 'the people', was established during a youth spent in the industrial region of Bradford. This points to another intermodern quality: a provincial, countryside or regional landscape as site of origins or identity. Unlike many of the modernist writers who were associated with London and the home counties, Jameson was from the coastal town of Whitby in northern Yorkshire; Heslop from New Hunwick, County Durham, and later, South Shields; Warner spent the war in a state of rural privation in Dorset; and the pacifist White was miserably settled in the countryside of neutral Eire. Other authors treated in this volume were also geographical 'outsiders'. Elizabeth Bowen was famously of Bowen's Court, County Cork; and Helen MacInnes and John Grierson came from Scotland.

According to Maslen, Jameson's concerns with 'the matter of contemporary community' led to her conviction that 'matter' could not be separated from 'the manner of expressing it'. While many writers of the 1930s, including those associated with the Auden Generation, were also attempting to work out a style of commitment, a political aesthetic, 'manner' is an especially fraught issue for the women intermodernists treated in this volume. Many, like Jameson, tried to speak to and for community, in the language of the people, but thereby risked the period's dismissive label of 'middlebrow'. Winifred Holtby, Rosamond Lehmann, Rose Macaulay, Phyllis Bottome, E. H. Young, Elizabeth Bowen, Sylvia Townsend Warner, Stella Gibbons, Storm Jameson – all can be regarded as intermodernists who for years were placed beyond the pale of scholarly study, even during the heyday of academic feminism, due to the legacy of interwar debates over brows.

Faye Hammill, in her chapter 'Stella Gibbons, Ex-Centricity and the Suburb', engages most directly with contemporary implications of the period's middlebrow debate. She argues that the suburb, a place associated with the middlebrow and like it, feminised and despised, is 'a crucial site for the development of an intermodern aesthetic'.[10] Intermodernism, a larger category than middlebrow in its naming of a period and style, but smaller in its reference to a few twentieth-century decades, provides one means of 'redeeming' literature like Gibbons's. It provides a similar kind of recuperative energy to Phyllis Lassner's project, an analysis of the successful spy detective novelists Margery Allingham and Helen MacInnes in the context of Britain's war against Nazism.

Lassner points out that Allingham and MacInnes, who were regarded as entertaining genre writers, did not even 'rise' to middlebrow status. Approaching these two women writers as intermodernists, Lassner finds in their fictions a complex interweaving of political and cultural concerns with narrative experiment. She explores the diverse paths that prompted Allingham and MacInnes to send their fictional spies into enemy territory, demonstrating their shared concern with what Jameson called 'England in Europe'. She also analyses implications of the novelists' decision to bring their spies back to

Britain after the war ended. Such retreat leaves readers with questions about the 'future' in which Britain would realise the end of empire.

The fantastic terrain of the immediately postwar world as it is explored in British intermodern writing is most thoroughly charted in Allan Hepburn's chapter on Elizabeth Bowen, 'Trials and Errors', and Debra Rae Cohen's chapter, 'Rebecca West's Palimpsestic Praxis'. Hepburn reads Elizabeth Bowen's *The Heat of the Day* (1948) against a backdrop of Bowen's postwar East European travels on behalf of the British Council and as an example of the 'intermodern narrative mode of the trial'. This intermodern mode is also evident in the postwar writing of Rebecca West, whose reporting on the Nuremberg Trials is one of Cohen's subjects. Cohen invites readers to see as characteristic of intermodernism West's qualities of language (reportage), her fraught narrative stance (witness), and immediately postwar theme (the trial).

The compulsion to record facts evident in West's postwar reportage is more famously manifest in the Mass-Observation movement that Nick Hubble examines in his chapter on the exemplary intermodernist, William Empson. Hubble identifies Mass-Observation as the most important expression of Empson's type of intermodernism. He finds support for this position in Empson's correspondence with Charles Madge and his literary criticism, in particular his works on pastoral and 'proletarian literature'. Analysing what he sees as a massive shift in public notions about the possibility of a future mass society brought about by the intermodern confrontation with pressures of war, Hubble tempts readers to test his theory against the claims of other contributors to the volume who also address the role of the masses and mass media in literary culture.

With the exception of Priestley as BBC broadcaster, Allingham and MacInnes won larger audiences than any of the other writers discussed in this volume. Lassner's textual analysis demonstrates that these two popular writers, who were presumed to have nothing to say that mattered and no manner of saying it, actually thought hard about the formal qualities of their writing. Warner, too, cared deeply about the crafting of fiction, writing in 'The Historical Novel' that 'the novelist's rendering of history should use present-day language in the truth-telling speech of working class characters who "fill the role of the commentator, the analyst, the person who sums things up"'(Warner 54). Equally concerned with narrative stance and language but less influenced by Marxism than Warner, Jameson declared in a lecture of her own that '[t]he more deeply [the novelist] has felt, the harder he must work to detach himself'. She went on to demand 'new and unexpected combinations of words to bring out the meaning – as sharply as it is brought out in a documentary film by choice of significant detail and the angles from which the picture is made' (Jameson 27). This comment again points to Jameson's work as a useful frame for debates about an intermodern aesthetic, here understood not in terms of a dialectical sense of history or the fruitful ambiguities of pastoral but through narrative stance, diction and documentary style.

Documentary style and mass media are two defining qualities of intermodernism, so it is fitting that this collection ends with a chapter by Laura Marcus on documentary cinema and film journalism. Focusing on films produced by John Grierson, including *Coal Face* and *Night Mail*, Marcus explores what could be called an intermodern sense of the complexity of 'actuality'. Marcus's chapter leads us full circle, pointing us back to the volume's first chapter through her discussion of Jameson's journal, *Fact*, and forward, to the possible interdisciplinary future for studies of intermodernism.

Jameson had something to say about our future, too. When approached by Koestler in 1943 with a request to submit a story for a collection on the world in 1975, she replied, 'All my visions of the future are nightmares. I think we are in for a Dark Age. I don't think it is the end of the human race, I think it is just another interregnum, unpleasant while it lasts, and it might last a couple of centuries. Or more' (1 March 1943; qtd in Maslen in this volume, p. 33). In the context of the letter, Jameson's statement reads not as a sign of despair or cynicism, but rather hope; she declines the invitation to contribute because she thinks Koestler's book should aspire to 'eagles and the trumpets'. In this nod to fanfare, romance and myth, there is the germ of that same hope in 'the people' expressed by many intermodernists who wrote about diverse, beleaguered interwar and wartime communities. Only history books published in the future will be able to judge whether Jameson was right both to hope and to judge. Perhaps they will determine that now, in the twenty-first century, we are writing and reading in an extended Dark Age. Then amid accounts of the long interregnum of the warring twentieth, twenty-first and twenty-second centuries, the short interregnum – or in between space – of intermodernism will vanish to nothing. Or perhaps it will stand as the core reference for later decades of darkness. Persuaded by the intermodernists that hope is still worth writing about, however, I'll conclude on an optimistic note. I'd like to see intermodernism become as sustaining and inspiring a myth as the myth of modernism, pointing to alternative subjects for and approaches to scholarly study of the twentieth century. And for this to take place I need others to join the contributors to this volume, going to the archives and preparing the histories and critical analyses that can recreate the web of personal and professional relations that sustained Britain during the dark years of 1930s Depression, 1940s war and 1950s reconstruction. Only after this hard work of discovery can theorists of intermodernism challenge the familiar names, audiences and ideologies that constitute traditional twentieth-century British literary history.

NOTES

1. Morag Shiach's comparison of the language reform efforts of T. S. Eliot on the one hand, and C. K. Ogden and I. A. Richards on the other, begins to measure this intermodern difference.

2. The history of the New Modernist Studies is usefully traced in a *PMLA* article written by two vigorous and prominent contributors to that movement, Douglas Mao and Rebecca Walkowitz. The primary quality they associate with the New Modernist Studies is 'expansion'.

3. It is important to note that from an alternative perspective, intermodernism is postmodernism's other. See Brian Richardson's 'Remapping the Present' for a provocative, insightful, but seemingly ignored call to rewrite literary history through exploration of the origins of postmodernism (what Richardson calls 'expressionist fiction') – origins that in some ways could be called intermodernist.

4. This is not to say that critics' use of conceptual pairs is intended to enforce binary logic (clearly the opposite is the case, for example, Gikandi's treatment of Modernism and postcolonialism), but that such logic inevitably organises institutional responses to such pairings. See my 'Not Waving or Drowning' for a more thoroughgoing analysis of the ways multiple critical binaries have limited the terms of access and aesthetic valuation for intermodern texts. By way of contrast, see Susan Stanford Friedman's articles 'Definitional Excursions' and 'Periodizing Modernism', which advocate further expansion of modernism – 'modernisms on a planetary landscape' – as a way of achieving deconstructive ends ('Periodizing' 430).

5. Miller's exemplary late modernists, Wyndham Lewis, Djuna Barnes, Samuel Beckett and Mina Loy, support his characterisation of late modernist writing as 'not particularly successful in either critical or commercial terms', with each work tending toward 'formal singularity, as if the author had hit a dead end and had to begin again. In content, too, these works reflected a closure of the horizon of the future' (13). Intermodernism, in contrast, describes works that struggle with different problems: the problem of popularity (not unpopularity), of perceptions of reproducibility (not singularity), of engagements with a future felt to be dynamically manifest in the present (not doomed to closure, to 'decline and fall').

6. See for example Faye Hammill's *Women, Celebrity and Literary Culture between the Wars* (2007), Chris Hopkins's *English Fiction in the 1930s* (2007), Owen Dudley Edwards's *British Children's Fiction in the Second World War* (2007), Nick Hubble's *Mass-Observation and Everyday Life* (2006), Victoria Stewart's *Narratives of Memory* (2006), Chiara Briganti and Kathy Mezei's *Domestic Modernism, the Interwar Novel, and E. H. Young* (2006), Jennifer Poulos Nesbitt's *Narrative Settlements* (2005), Phyllis Lassner's *Colonial Strangers: Women Writing the End of Empire* (2004), Lisa Colletta's *Dark Humor and Social Satire in the Modern British Novel* (2003), Ann L. Ardis's *Modernism and Cultural Conflict, 1880–1922* (2003), John Fordham's *James Hanley* (2003), Elizabeth Maslen's *Political and Social Issues in British Women's Fiction 1928–1968* (2001), Margaret Stetz's *British Women's Comic Fiction, 1890–1990* (2001), Bernard Schweizer's *Radicals on the Road* (2001), and Mark Rawlinson's *British Writing of the Second World War* (2000). Valuable edited collections that have come out in the same ten-year period include Danielle Hipkins and Gill Plain's *War-Torn Tales* (2007), Antony Shuttleworth's *And in Our Time* (2003), Stella Deen's *Challenging Modernism* (2002), Rod Mengham and N. H. Reeve's *The Fiction of the 1940s* (2001), and Gustav Klaus and Stephen Knight's *British Industrial Fictions* (2000).

7. Almost twenty years ago, Neil Larson began his very different kind of oppositional critique of modernism's cultural hegemony by noting, 'Modernism's breakup is now openly declared under the sign of the postmodern – a still volatile, contested, and uncertain epochal marker but one that nevertheless has the advantage of making it more difficult for modernism to avoid ideological detection' (xxii).

8. Koestler's essay was reprinted as 'In Memory of Richard Hillary' in his 1965 collection, *The Yogi and the Commissar*.

9. In addition to Bluemel, see Nick Hubble on 'The Origins of Intermodernism in Ford Madox Ford's Parallax View' and 'Intermodern Pastoral'.
10. I would add Jews to the list of degraded subjects associated, like women, with the suburbs. See my *Radical Eccentrics* and 'The Urban Geography of English Antisemitism and Assimilation'.

WORKS CITED

Ardis, Ann L. *Modernism and Cultural Conflict, 1880–1922*. Cambridge: Cambridge University Press, 2003.

Baucom, Ian. *Out of Place: Englishness, Empire, and the Locations of Identity*. Princeton: Princeton University Press, 1999.

Bluemel, Kristin. *George Orwell and the Radical Eccentrics: Intermodernism in Literary London*. New York and Basingstoke: Palgrave Macmillan, 2004.

—. 'Not Waving or Drowning: Refusing Critical Options, Rewriting Literary History'. *And In Our Time: Vision, Revision, and British Writing of the 1930s*. Ed. Antony Shuttleworth. Lewisburg: Bucknell University Press, 2003. 65–94.

—. 'The Urban Geography of English Antisemitism and Assimilation: A Case Study'. *Antisemitism and Philosemitism in the Twentieth and Twenty-First Centuries: Representing Jews, Jewishness, and Modern Culture*. Ed. Phyllis Lassner and Lara Trubowitz. Newark: University of Delaware Press, 2008. 175–95.

Bradbury, Malcolm and James McFarlane, eds. *Modernism 1890–1930*. New York: Penguin, 1976.

Briganti, Chiara and Kathy Mezei. *Domestic Modernism, the Interwar Novel, and E. H. Young*. Burlington: Ashgate, 2006.

Colletta, Lisa. *Dark Humor and Social Satire in the Modern British Novel: The Triumph of Narcissism*. New York: Palgrave, 2003.

Deen, Stella, ed. *Challenging Modernism: New Readings in Literature and Culture, 1914–1945*. Burlington: Ashgate, 2002.

Dickson, Lovat. *Richard Hillary*. London: Macmillan, 1950.

Edwards, Owen Dudley. *British Children's Fiction in the Second World War*. Edinburgh: Edinburgh University Press, 2007.

Esty, Jed. *A Shrinking Island: Modernism and National Culture in England*. Princeton: Princeton University Press, 2004.

Eysteinsson, Astradur. *The Concept of Modernism*. Ithaca: Cornell University Press, 1990.

Fordham, John. *James Hanley: Modernism and the Working Class*. Cardiff: University of Wales Press, 2003.

Friedman, Susan Stanford. 'Definitional Excursions: The Meanings of Modern/ Modernity/Modernism'. *Modernism/Modernity* 8 (2001): 493–513.

—. 'Periodizing Modernism: Postcolonial Modernities and the Space/Time Borders of Modernist Studies'. *Modernism/Modernity* 13 (2006): 425–43.

Garrity, Jane. *Step-Daughters of England: British Women Modernists and the National Imaginary*. New York: Manchester University Press, 2005.

Gikandi, Simon. 'Modernism in the World'. *Modernism/Modernity* 13 (2006): 419–24.

Hammill, Faye. *Women, Celebrity and Literary Culture between the Wars*. Austin: University of Texas Press, 2007.

Hapgood, Lynne and Nancy Paxton, eds. *Outside Modernism: In Pursuit of the English Novel, 1900–30*. New York and Basingstoke: Palgrave Macmillan, 2000.

Hillary, Richard. *The Last Enemy*. 1942. Short Hills: Burford Books, 1997.

Hipkins, Danielle, and Gill Plain, eds. *War-Torn Tales: Literature, Film and Gender in the Aftermath of World War II*. New York: Peter Lang, 2007.

Hopkins, Chris. *English Fiction in the 1930s*. London: Continuum, 2007.

Hubble, Nick. 'Intermodern Pastoral: William Empson and George Orwell'. *New Versions of Pastoral: Post-Romantic, Modern, and Contemporary Responses to the Tradition*. Ed. David James and Philip Tew. Madison: Fairleigh Dickinson University Press; London: Associated University Press, 2009. 125–35.

—. *Mass-Observation and Everyday Life: Culture, History, Theory*. London: Palgrave, 2006.

—. 'The Origins of Intermodernism in Ford Madox Ford's Parallax View'. *Ford Madox Ford: Literary Networks and Cultural Transformations*. Ed. Andrzej Gasiorek and Daniel Moore. Amsterdam and New York: Rodopi, 2008. 167–88.

Jameson, Storm. *The Novel in Contemporary Life*. Boston: The Writer, 1938.

Kalliney, Peter J. *Cities of Affluence and Anger: A Literary Geography of Modern Englishness*. Charlottesville: University of Virginia Press, 2006.

Klaus, H. Gustav and Stephen Knight, eds. *British Industrial Fictions*. Cardiff: University of Wales Press, 2000.

Koestler, Arthur. 'In Memory of Richard Hillary'. 1943. *The Yogi and the Commissar*. New York: Macmillan, 1965. 51–70.

Larson, Neil. *Modernism and Hegemony: A Materialist Critique of Aesthetic Agencies*. Minneapolis: University of Minnesota Press, 1990.

Lassner, Phyllis. *Colonial Strangers: Women Writing the End of Empire*. New Brunswick: Rutgers University Press, 2004.

MacKay, Marina. *Modernism and World War II*. Cambridge: Cambridge University Press, 2007.

— and Lyndsey Stonebridge, eds. *British Fiction after Modernism: The Novel at Mid-Century*. New York: Palgrave Macmillan, 2007.

Marx, John. *The Modernist Novel and the Decline of Empire*. Cambridge and New York: Cambridge University Press, 2005.

Maslen, Elizabeth. *Political and Social Issues in British Women's Fiction 1928–1968*. London: Palgrave Macmillan, 2001.

Mengham, Rod and N. H. Reeve, eds. *The Fiction of the 1940s: Stories of Survival*. New York: Palgrave Macmillan, 2001.

Miller, Tyrus. *Late Modernism: Politics, Fiction, and the Arts between the Wars*. Berkeley: University of California Press, 1999.

Nesbitt, Jennifer Poulos. *Narrative Settlements: Geographies of British Women's Fiction between the Wars*. Toronto: University of Toronto Press, 2005.

Orwell, George. *Nineteen Eighty-Four*. New York: Harcourt Brace,1949.

Paxton, Nancy. 'Eclipsed by Modernism'. Hapgood and Paxton 3–21.

Rawlinson, Mark. *British Writing of the Second World War*. Oxford: Clarendon Press, 2000.

Richardson, Brian. 'Remapping the Present: The Master Narrative of Modern Literary History and the Lost Forms of Twentieth-Century Fiction'. *Twentieth-Century Literature* 43 (1997): 291–309.

Schweizer, Bernard. *Radicals on the Road: The Politics of English Travel Writing in the 1930s*. Charlottesville: University of Virginia Press, 2001.

Shiach, Morag. '"To Purify the Dialect of the tribe": Modernism and Language Reform'. *Modernism/Modernity* 14 (2007): 21–34.

Shuttleworth, Antony, ed. *And in Our Time: Vision, Revision, and British Writing of the Thirties*. Lewisburg: Bucknell University Press, 2003.

Stetz, Margaret. *British Women's Comic Fiction, 1890–1990: Not Drowning, But Laughing*. London: Ashgate, 2001.

Stewart, Victoria. *Narratives of Memory: British Writing of the 1940s*. Basingstoke: Palgrave Macmillan, 2006.

Walkowitz, Rebecca L. and Douglas Mao. 'The New Modernist Studies'. *PMLA* 123 (2008): 737–48.

Warner, Sylvia Townsend. 'The Historical Novel'. 1940. *Journal of Sylvia Townsend Warner Society* (2007): 53–5.

PART I
WORK

I

A CASSANDRA WITH CLOUT: STORM JAMESON, LITTLE ENGLANDER AND GOOD EUROPEAN

Elizabeth Maslen

Literary labels, even if we deplore them, exist and are in constant play. It is therefore crucial that they perform a useful semantic function, which is why the term 'intermodernism' is promising. It could encourage more subtle classification of a number of mid-century narrative texts, including texts by Storm Jameson, that are at present neglected because they are identified with the ideologically-charged, blanket term 'middlebrow'. My main objection to the term 'middlebrow' is that it brings with it an agenda from the past; it is *backward* looking. Although many people associate the 'middlebrow' with the protests of Virginia Woolf and Q. D. Leavis and the debate in the popular press that they helped inspire, it drags into the twentieth century phrenological debates of the nineteenth century, where high, middle and low physical brows were taken as measurable evidence of intelligence and intellectual capacity, and were linked with other debates, most memorably those concerning the relative intellectual capacities of different races.[1] It is hard to shake that distasteful legacy. When applied to writers, the classifying 'brow' terms continue to suggest a league table of intellectual ability, with the highbrow seen as innovative, experimental in language and form and having a vision and dynamism beyond the reach of the middlebrow who, while serious-minded, is seen as unadventurous in style, content with old-fashioned ways, worthy but plodding.

While the term 'modernist' has largely replaced the term 'highbrow' in literary discourse, giving both terms, by semantic implication, a privileged link with modernity, the term 'middlebrow' has functioned (or malfunctioned) as a catch-all term for a group of writers that includes those who, while remaining serious-minded, fail to qualify for inclusion under 'modernist' or 'postmodernist'. Yet many of the writers so unhelpfully labelled 'middlebrow' are passionately involved with their modernity, the issues of their time and place, and wrestle articulately, both in theory and practice, with how best to express their involvement, how to communicate their vision to their readers. One of the strengths of the term 'intermodernism' is its linking of a number of twentieth-century writers, many of whom are women who have been labelled 'middlebrow', with their contemporaries, many of whom are men who are acknowledged to be concerned, in a rapidly changing world, with issues of content, expression and over-arching vision. By exploring where such writers stand in relation to 'modernism', it becomes clear that a large number are not timid and backward-looking, but are moulding their medium in all sorts of ways to cope with the increasing complexities and confusions of twentieth-century modernity.

When we look, for example, at the social and cultural roles of thinking women who could be labelled intermodernists, writers like Storm Jameson, Elizabeth Bowen, Rebecca West and Naomi Mitchison, all active in the 1930s and 1940s, the sheer diversity is impressive, both in what they do, what they say, how they write and where they publish. In a period of accelerating change, many women made their voices heard in the key debates of the time, and many were right in the public eye when action was needed. After the granting of universal suffrage at the end of the twenties, they debated women's rights and their roles in society in such periodicals as *Time & Tide*, and in the women's pages of the daily press; and these debates were increasingly linked with the case for pacifism, at least until 1938. However, the emergence of fascism disrupted pacifist movement, and an anti-fascist lobby was strengthened as more and more refugees fleeing Nazi atrocities arrived. Britain's part in the now infamous Munich treaty of 1938, and her declaration of war in 1939 made further demands on thinking women – what should their role be? And, if they were writers, how should they write? They did not, by any means, all take the same route: Vera Brittain, for instance, would remain a committed pacifist throughout, Edith Pargeter (better known by her pen-name, Ellis Peters) would become passionately pro-war after hearing of the atrocities committed during the invasion of Czechoslovakia, while Virginia Woolf famously declared in *Three Guineas* (1938) that women should stand aside from matters for which she held men responsible. Storm Jameson took yet another route, while being closely involved in all the main issues of her time. She wrote persuasively on how writers should respond to a changing world, both in supporting causes and in shaping their own fiction; she played an active role in helping refugees throughout the thirties and forties – and she is a valuable example, throughout these two crucial decades, of how different concerns could impinge on each other, setting problems for the thinking man or woman, as social animal and as writer, which had no easy solution. She thus produces work which can test the value of the term 'intermodernism' in historical, ideological and aesthetic contexts, and because she is both honest and eloquent, we can follow the developments in her theory and practice throughout all the complex interactions of this period.

Jameson brings a perspective to her writing very different from her Oxbridge and home-county contemporaries. She is from the provinces, born on the northeast coast of Yorkshire in 1891, in the little town of Whitby, for centuries a proudly ex-centric town, backed by moors and looking out to sea, its people virtually isolated from the rest of England, having little time for the outsiders they termed 'run-a-countries'.[2] This background is in itself important, for while Jameson claims to be a 'little Englander' who is trying to be a 'good European',[3] her definition is profoundly affected by the ex-centric standards of her birthplace, and differs strikingly from, say, Bloomsbury ways of depicting English life as essentially that of the south or, even more narrowly, as that of a comfortably placed middle class. Provincialism is a key factor in her writing, in that her yardstick for Englishness is the Yorkshire of her childhood, its moors, its ferociously vital seas, and the tough characters produced by this environment.

Jameson was the first in her family to go to university, but not to Oxford or Cambridge. She took a first in the English BA at Leeds, and studied for an MA in London. She married young, had a child, and suffered the stresses and humiliations endemic in early twentieth-century divorce proceedings before marrying again. She worked at different times as advertising copywriter, editor and literary agent, doing a considerable amount of reviewing and journalism when financial worries were pressing. She was continually out of pocket, as she was all too often generous beyond her means, and, until she was verging on seventy, was continually on the move. She was never a member of any of the major literary groupings of the interwar years, though she was well acquainted with, and respected by, many writers who were. She was on the Left in politics, and a passionate supporter of anti-war and anti-fascist causes. But crucially she was, throughout her life, an iconoclast, always asking questions of society, of causes and groupings she approved of and those she distrusted, and of herself, wrestling with the problems of a writer's role in society and how that should affect ways of presenting their work, never comfortably accepting any of the sacred cows of her time. As she urges in her introduction to *Civil Journey*, written on 22 and 23 September 1939, a week before the Munich agreement: 'A writer should not in any circumstances or for any cause surrender his duty to criticise and to enquire freely into the soundness of any idea, faith, doctrine, delivered to him by the mouth of authority' (Jameson, *Civil Journey* 11). Jameson does not renounce social and political commitment, either in her life or, importantly, in her writing; but she is always equally concerned to stress the importance of how a writer shapes material. The way she voices this concern links her with her Marxist friends of the thirties, with critics like Ralph Fox who state the Marxist line that 'neither form nor content are separate and passive entities. Form is produced by content, is identical and one with it, and, though the primacy is on the side of content, form reacts on content and never remains passive' (Fox 32).[4] But Jameson is never other than her own woman; it is too easy to see her 1937 essay 'Documents', for instance, as simply stating the socialist line on how to write. Crucially, she is always asserting that the way the writer writes springs from his (and we would add 'her') own personality, his own 'take' on society, as she says as early as 1932:

> The form of any novel is not so much the way in which the novelist has chosen to write, as the way which has been chosen for him – by his attitude to experience. It is our first means of knowing how sensitive, how conscious, how uncompromising towards himself, and how aware of his time a writer is. (Jameson, *The New English Weekly* 235)

Throughout the thirties, Jameson had not just been writing about her views. Alongside commitments to a range of anti-war and anti-fascist organisations, she was also an increasingly active member of the P.E.N. Club, where we see her priorities in action. Founded by Amy Dawson Scott in 1921, originally as a literary dining club but soon to champion freedom of expression,[5] the P.E.N. quickly spawned branches throughout the world at a time when free speech was increasingly under threat and when writers in many countries were being persecuted for their views. Jameson became a member in 1922. In her close links with a number of anti-war and anti-fascist groupings in the thirties and as a member of the P.E.N., she listened and learned, both in her travels abroad and in her encounters with refugees fleeing repression. Jameson had always been drawn to the literature of Europe: before WWI she redirected her MA to explore the largely uncharted territory of European drama; she took part in the translation of de Maupassant's short stories in the early twenties, and she read continental works voraciously, with a particular but not exclusive love of French literature. During the thirties, as the P.E.N. was increasingly involved in striving to find sanctuary for refugee writers (and the term 'writers' became more and more widely interpreted as the European crisis deepened), she was meeting many of these refugees face to face, discussing their experiences, and the political and cultural problems of their home countries. Her travels took her to France on a regular basis, but also to Berlin in 1932, and memorably in 1938 to the P.E.N. conference in Czechoslovakia, followed by a fact-finding journey to Austria and Hungary. So European affairs, whether political, cultural or literary, as well as increasing problems in Britain, spark the questions she raises in her writing. Her focus is never narrow, she is always probing and questioning, while the theories she evolves for communicating the complex matters she confronts are lucidly and passionately expressed as her writing develops in the thirties and forties. In her increasing insistence that matter – especially the matter of contemporary communities – and the manner of expressing it should not be seen as separate, she is showing what may be termed her intermodernist colours.

In her fiction, she rattles the cage doors of those members of her society who choose to turn away from European problems. In 1936 she publishes the novel *In the Second Year*, set in England, but offering a disturbingly vivid English version of Hitler's second year in office, in the three-month period leading up to the Night of the Long Knives. The Nazi progress and its major participants are matched in her narrative by native equivalents, but this is no simple transliteration of material; this is translation at its most sensitive in catching the essence and naturalising its presentation so as to entangle the reader in a recognisably English plot. Written as Mosley's supporters were growing increasingly assertive, and while a good number of well-placed British people were more prepared to admire what Hitler had done to restore German social order and discipline than to note the appalling human cost of this achievement, Jameson presents what the human cost would be in an English social and natural landscape, strikingly placing her concentration camp in her much loved northern moors. Her novel moulds its realism admirably so that the England she describes is vividly contemporary, the characters convincingly drawn, the betrayals chillingly but quietly done. And, significantly for the way Jameson's ideas are developing, her narrator, a peace-loving liberal who has been living in Norway, is shown as retreating from the fray, very much adopting the role of Woolf's later outsider, grieving but opting out. Jameson here seems to be already confronting where a pacifist stance might lead in the event of war, either civil or international.

It is revealing to note reactions to the novel at the time, as a number of critics could not cope with matter (especially in a woman's work, one is tempted to think) which privileged community in all its complex intricacy. A number of critics pronounced that the book was well done but not really what art should be about; the shaping of an aesthetic which could engage with the crises of its time clearly made some uneasy. Sean O'Faolain, for example, writes, 'In effect *In the Second Year* is a thriller by a first-class pamphleteer. It makes one furiously to think; stirs the mind; and is like a rod poked into the nerves. What more would you have? . . . But I fear this effort to make literature *useful*' (O'Faolain 226). The latter critique in particular demonstrates a conservative resistance to an increasing leftist urge to 'make literature useful', while the writer is categorised as a pamphleteer, not an artist. However, Philip Henderson puts this work among what he approvingly terms 'revolutionary' writings by, for example, Henri Barbusse, and Heinrich and Thomas Mann – it is noteworthy that most of these are European. He says of Jameson's novel:

> Accounts of conditions in other countries, however vivid, always remain something of a picture, remote from the actualities of one's own life . . . Storm Jameson's achievement is that she has made such a state of things terribly real . . . On the surface England still remains gentlemanly and urbane. There is no need for England to adopt the theatrical methods of Mussolini or Hitler. Atrocious things are done with perfect manners. (Henderson 223–24)

Jameson had every reason to be concerned that such things could happen in England; the economic crisis and massive unemployment meant that there was growing resentment about governmental paralysis, while the far Right was increasingly active in its demonstrations of strength. The press on the whole remained ambivalent or diversionary, yet on 2 May 1936 the *Saturday Review*, at that time under a flamboyantly right-wing editor, Lady Houston, printed an article ending: '[I]t is cheap claptrap to say that England would not tolerate a dictator. Of course she would if that dictator were a great and determined ruler' ('Kim' 551–52). When such attitudes existed, it is hardly surprising that writers like Jameson turned away from literary priorities which they saw as privileging aesthetics over social concerns. There is no way that she, given her close involvement with so many refugees from Europe, could separate her role as writer from the social and cultural upheavals of her time, both at home and abroad.

As the 1930s progress, we find Jameson increasingly concerned about the role of the writer, and the kind of fiction that she felt important, both in content and style. Too often scholars write as though only the modernists had a monopoly on style, innovation and an overarching vision. Jameson, while stressing, as we have seen, the links between content and form, shares many of the concerns that supposedly preoccupied only members of the literary elite. She is one of those who are deeply exercised as to where the fiction of their time should be going. By 1937, in her well-known article, 'Documents', and in an important lecture given at Leeds University, *The Novel in Contemporary Life*, she draws comparisons with the skills developing in film documentary for what she wants fiction to achieve.[6] She says in her lecture: 'The more deeply [the novelist] has felt, the harder he must work to detach himself'; and she repeatedly stresses the importance of innovative language: 'We need . . . new and unexpected combinations of words to bring out the meaning – as sharply as it is brought out in a documentary film by choice of significant detail and the angles from which the picture is made' (Jameson, *Novel* 27). When it comes to subject matter, she says the novelist 'must wrestle faithfully . . . with the life of his age until he knows what is essential in it, what is living and what is dead and done for. When he knows this he can give the things he is able to write about a significance they owe to being a part . . . of a larger world'. And crucially she adds, 'If he cannot deal with the whole contemporary scene he can take soundings in it' (Jameson, *Novel* 23–24).

Taking 'soundings' is a key idea which Jameson develops with increasing skill in the novels of the late thirties and forties. 'Soundings', as she interprets the term, offer her readers a chance to measure the depths of a contemporary crisis through close inspection of a sample community containing all the critical elements. As a result, these 'soundings' allow what would otherwise be an unwieldy mass to be honed into articulate aesthetic structures, and by their agency Jameson produces some wonderfully varied experiments.

She has already begun to feel towards this theory of 'soundings' before her 1937 essays. In her trilogy, 'Mirror in Darkness', exploring the links between character and context, Jameson obeys her own rule of letting characters think and speak with as little interference from the author as possible, offering a range of men and women as 'soundings' for a cross-section of English society, revealing each as a product of their background, and how, as a result, each reacts to and is affected by the world they inherit. In the late forties, she will return to this particular method again, taking a daring look at the hot topic of how victors and vanquished behave in *Before the Crossing* (1947) and *Black Laurel* (1947), two starkly honest books which take us from Britain to the ruins of Berlin. Alongside many new characters, some of the key characters from 'The Mirror in Darkness' series will reappear as 'soundings' for the disturbing commercial, political and cultural issues of the immediate postwar world. But Jameson's protagonist will not be Hervey, her alter-ego who presides over the earlier trilogy, but the male Renn. Crucially, Renn provides the depersonalised eye which she advocates in 'Documents'.

Also in the thirties, she publishes a novel set in a town based on her beloved Whitby, *The Moon Is Making*,[7] which celebrates a noted local people's champion, and analyses what has gone into the making of her provincial brand of Englishness. Characters in *The Moon is Making* were not always recognised by southern critics as drawn from real life; the *Times* reviewer, for instance, sees 'the mirror' of the novel as

> deliberately distorted, the two Wikker sisters and their brother Ezekiel are shamelessly enlarged in their greed, cruelty and egotism, and one must search for Miss Jameson's reason for discovering in the mirror what is not visible to the naked eye. (*Times*, 27 Aug. 1937, 6d)

Yet, allegedly, the novel had to be removed from the shelves of the Whitby public library, because of none too complimentary comments in the margin identifying these very characters.[8] These responses are valuable reminders that 'Englishness', which is one of the factors in her writing which may be termed intermodernist, should not be defined solely according to London and home county experience as is done too often by critics; there never has been a single 'English way of life'.

All these novels of the thirties have a striking social and cultural identity, deliberately adopted and cultivated, as Jameson's essays demonstrate. This does not mean, of course, that she was unaware of what the high modernists were doing. Her review of Virginia Woolf's *The Waves* is instructive. Jameson admires the novel, exploring why to label it 'a novel in the "stream of consciousness" method . . . is inadequate'. She sees Woolf as 'striving – without the concessions made in her earlier books – to convey a *whole* vision, the essence of life, not a story – full of scattered and fragmentary forms', and to have achieved much. But ultimately and revealingly, Jameson says,

> Mrs. W has made enormous sacrifices. She is like a woman who has turned her back on life and watches it passing in a mirror, so that nothing shall shake the steadiness of her glance, none of those distractions, those sudden blindings, that come from touching what one sees. (Jameson, Rev. of *The Waves* 677–78)

This image may not correspond to the one most critics have of Woolf, but it does suggest what ideal Jameson had for herself; she is increasingly convinced that novelists must engage with contemporary culture and community in all their works.

In the autumn of 1938, however, Jameson's writing career met a series of challenges. For just after the Munich pact handed the Czechoslovakian Sudetenland to Germany (an area where, by a cruel irony, many of those fleeing Nazi oppression had found refuge), she was elected president of the English section of the P.E.N.; she had been an increasingly active member since the 1920s, but the demands now grew dramatically, and arguably affected decisions she took about the direction of her fiction. Within the P.E.N., she wasted no time in enlarging the membership, lobbying government departments, collaborating with other refugee-friendly organisations, and raising public awareness by letters to papers, articles and meetings. When, straight after the declaration of war, many refugees were interned, often quite arbitrarily, a good number in appalling conditions, regardless of how long they had been in Britain or what role they had played against the Nazis, she and the P.E.N. general secretary Hermon Ould were tireless in fighting for their release, hounding Government departments and rallying the support of eminent social figures. Jameson and Ould helped writers and their dependents who were often living in utter poverty, as the club's funds, like those of other organisations, were exhausted, faced with the sheer scale of the need. This rescue mission was in itself a Herculean task, but Jameson did not only look to present need (though the letters which had to be written, the people who had to be seen, the visits to the destitute that had to be made were all but overwhelming her). She planned, with Ould's help, a world conference of writers in London for 1941, its theme being the need to ensure a just peace at the end of the war (an aim close to the heart of many, after the problems resulting from the treaties at the end of World War I). The theme is encapsulated in Jameson's message printed in the *Adam International Review*, of September 1941:

> Here we are and here we intend to remain, Europe in England and England in Europe. This war is being fought, among other reasons, so that writers can meet and talk without expecting the Gestapo to put its filthy hand over their mouths. The agony of this war must give birth to a new and better Europe, and it is up to writers to create the vision of this better Europe, to keep it before the eyes of the men and women who are fighting and enduring, so that they don't lose faith and in losing faith lose heart, and in losing heart lose England, lose Europe, lose the future. Our community of writers, our twenty nations of writers, here this day, has enough to do. [Frontispiece]

The conference, not to mention its aim, was, on the face of it, almost outrageous, given the apparently unstoppable advance of the Nazi forces throughout Europe at that time, yet many came to it. Indeed, as the above quotation shows, many of the European writers invited were already in England, and many of the European branches of the P.E.N. had resettled in London. The conference had government approval, and Jameson's personal reputation in the corridors of power was enhanced. The P.E.N. was increasingly consulted on issues concerning the treatment of foreign writers, and other matters affecting writers and their work, as the British government belatedly realised the importance of writers as communicators.

Yet Jameson never felt that she was doing enough. When, in the spring of 1940, Harold Macmillan, one of the directors of the Macmillan publishing company, was appointed a member of Churchill's new government, Jameson wrote to him as a friend, asking if he could suggest her for an appropriate job. Macmillan replied:

> I can well understand your desire to help at this difficult moment by doing something which you feel will be of immediate service to the country. Help of every kind is needed. On the other hand, I am certain myself that you and a few other of our leading authors can serve the country in no better way than by continuing with your work as writers. The written word coming from a trained writer with a clear mind is of vital importance. (Macmillan MLB 466)

His comments, while urging her away from the direct action she craved at the time, correspond with Jameson's sense of a writer's responsibilities. Indeed, from the Munich crisis, she changes direction dramatically, basing all her novels of the 1940s in Europe, and using the techniques she has been spelling out through the 1930s.[9] This is to be a major part of her war-work as a writer, extending into the early years of the peace, as she takes on disturbing and at times controversial subject matter.

Europe to Let (1940) is a series of four portraits of Europe, 'seen in this and that light, from this and that angle, as a painter might go on trying to get at the truth of a man or a woman, looking for it both in himself and his model' (Jameson, *Journey*: II 14). So Jameson describes the work which she formally terms 'portraits, long *nouvelles* or *récits*' (*Journey*: II 14). In these four *récits* Jameson tries out the theories about documents that she offers in her more famous 1937 essays; the three set in Budapest, Czechoslovakia and Vienna (written though not published in that order) offer bleak revelations of the growing threat posed by Nazism in central and eastern Europe, its corrosive effect on the societies it menaces, while the first *récit* gives us a sketch of German youth in 1923 as the roots of the later conflict develop. Jameson's first-person narrator is a male English journalist, a World War I veteran, and he offers, I think, the key to this work which is the closest in execution to her theories about documents, since the following three *récits*, while skilfully shaped as individual tales with different emphases, draw heavily on material she noted down after her visits to Czechoslovakia, Austria and Hungary in 1938. Intriguingly, Jameson names her narrator Esk after a Yorkshire river, which surely implies a link with Eric Blair's East Anglian river pen-name, Orwell,[10] especially as she had taken issue with the handling of the narrator of *The Road to Wigan Pier* in a review for *Fact* on 15 May 1937. Through her narrator, Jameson explores different ways of employing the observer of events. In the book's first *récit*, he is lightly sketched as a young Englishman of peasant stock, fleeing his north-country village roots after his alienating World War I experiences, coming to Germany to explore the truths which defeat may have unveiled, but quickly realising his role is as observer of other men's crises after the French incursion into the Ruhr and the subsequent brief separatist uprising. He is unable to intervene in his German friend's personal tragedy, while seeing all too clearly the growth of violence, hatred and betrayal. In the second *récit*, based in Vienna, he is all but anonymous, a fly on the wall as Jewish siblings and a German socialist refugee act as soundings for victims of the *Anschluss*. In the third *récit*, exploring the Czechoslovak crisis, he is much more implicated with his Czech friends, and acts himself as a sounding for left-wing English opinion as the crisis unfolds, registering guilt and helplessness as the French and English leaders go back on their promises of support, and charting a range of Czech, German and French reactions through vividly realised characters. But it is in the book's final *récit* (the first she wrote), set in Budapest, that Jameson offers the most deliberately shocking sketch of her Esk. Here, she shows compassion as a finite thing, as Esk reaches the limit of what he can absorb of someone else's tragedy. She has him record, on three visits from 1936 to 1938, the inexorable increase in anti-Semitism as registered both

by the Jew he is fond of and by the right-wing family he visits. He shows how
the creation of Czechoslovakia after World War I has left festering wounds
among young Hungarians with Slovakian roots; he sees the inevitable outcome
as Hitler's ideas take hold. He is shockingly honest about his psychological
need to distance himself from the tragedy, as he admits to himself: 'I am resistant and irresponsible. What is happening to the men and women clinging to
Europe as to a raft does not move me. There have been too many disasters: too
many bad jokes' (*Europe to Let* 237). And the nightmare vision that dominates
this section is captured in such details as the surreal imagery conjured up by his
subconscious. As he listens to his right-wing hosts, he imagines

> a round white Easter egg, rolling across Europe, left on the roads traces
> of blood: Warsaw, Berlin, Vienna, Budapest. Rome, Prague, tomorrow.
> To be devoured with the mind's salt. Shall I say, 'your chatter disgusts
> me'? No, I am not that man. I listen. I am consenting to the business of
> jackals. When it is finished, from a safe place I shall condemn what has
> been done. Do I hear a cock crow? (258)

Full of self-disgust but unable to play the hero, he finds himself unwilling to see
too much of his Jewish friend because: 'He made me feel responsible for all the
cruelty in the world' (260). This does not make for uplifting or easy reading,
and yet as she wrote it, Jameson was working desperately to help refugees in
England and those trying to get out of Europe. The emotional, nervous cost
of involvement is huge, and for many too much to bear. Like Stevie Smith in
Novel on Yellow Paper, Jameson has her narrator share the shortcomings of
her own kind, the shortcomings we prefer not to explore, while avoiding the
personal involvement with the private lives of others which she diagnosed and
disliked in *The Road to Wigan Pier*. Esk can be seen as a development of the
narrator of *In the Second Year*, maturing after Munich.[11]

In her next novel, *Cousin Honoré*, Jameson abandons the extremes of documentary writing, using a different form of 'sounding'. In this superb novel,
the inhabitants of a village in Alsace encapsulate all the divisions and conflicts
leading to the outbreak of war, and indeed, as she says in her *Journey*, mirror
many of the main players in the deadly drama played out in 1938–9 (II 58–59).
These vividly drawn characters all have their different priorities; the protagonist, for instance, has a temperament and values which place his vineyards
above all political considerations, while his grandson, child of the old man's
illegitimate daughter, little regarded by his grandfather and resenting his casual
contempt, is an easy convert to Nazism.[12] Most reviewers described the novel
as set in France, failing to see the significance of its being set in Alsace, which
over the past century had been French, German and again French by turns,
while its population had roots and links with many countries. Also, many
reviewers could not bring themselves to praise the novel because they found

most of the characters 'unpleasant'. Jameson, however, uses this 'sounding' method again, in *Cloudless May* (1943), set in a French town on the Loire. Here she compresses major dilemmas of the moment into one vividly drawn community, with all the elements of resistance, appeasement, collaboration, fraternisation and treachery fleshed out in strong, three-dimensional characters, to draw English readers into an understanding of how conflicting motives and loyalties emerge under the threat of occupation.

Jameson may be delivering lucid reminders of the truths of this war, but she is constantly varying her method while reacting with extraordinary speed to events as they happen; she may write fast, but she revises ruthlessly, and is always experimenting with form, with ways of conveying 'soundings' of her contemporary world, with lucid expression, with characters whose roots and experiences inevitably shape the ways in which they develop. She writes *The Fort* (1941), structured rigorously on the model of a Greek tragedy, with French and British soldiers holed up in a French cellar as the Germans advance, debating the origins of this new war, and revealing the tensions in France as to whether to resist or appease. Her next short novel, *Then We Shall Hear Singing* (1942), is, by contrast, cast in a popular form, as a folktale-cum-fable with ingredients of science fiction, but it is clearly a poignant little elegy for the invasion of Czechoslovakia, the suppression of its way of life, about a people who are 'most resilient under poverty and richest in inner resources, sceptical, enduring' (*Then We Shall Hear* 5). By using many of the techniques of folktale and fable, Jameson is able to tap into the tradition whereby the lowly-born triumph over all hazards to suggest that the future will bring release. But one suspects Jameson is doing rather more than that. She must have been aware of a readership made up of refugees as well as native English; fable was a favourite form for political statement throughout Eastern Europe, so her offering, while again treated coolly by a number of reviewers, was sensitively apt in concept. And for the Czechoslovak connoisseur there is a further link. Jameson was a great admirer of the Czech writer, Karel Capek, whom she last saw at the P.E.N. conference in June 1938, and who died at the end of the same year. Capek himself was renowned for his moulding of folktale, fable and science fiction elements into sophisticated but readily accessible literary mirrorings of contemporary issues, and for his championing of the Czech language as a literary medium, where contemporaries like Kafka used German. So Jameson's little book can be read as a tribute to his way of presenting sensitive material in a deceptively simple form, while her poignant exposure of a people whose culture and language is suppressed by their invaders stresses an aspect of the tragedy which goes beyond the physical. Jameson shows her skill at adapting a European method to deal with a devastating European situation, in this instance offering a cry of pain and solidarity controlled by the abandonment of realism.[13]

By 1943 the prospects for the future were, in the view of many writers in Britain, steadily darkening. In that year, Arthur Koestler wanted to edit an anthology of short stories by leading P.E.N. writers, all to give their vision of the future world of 1975. However, when he invited Jameson to contribute, she warned him that:

> although you say contributions may be nightmares, I don't think you really want nightmares in such a book. Surely, nightmares defeat the first intention of the book, which is to provide the eagles and the trumpets? // All my visions of the future are nightmares. I think we are in for a Dark Age. I don't think it is the end of the human race, I think it is just another interregnum, unpleasant while it lasts, and it might last a couple of centuries. Or more. In thirty years' time, we should thus be just jolting down another level or two. // I can't help feeling that to offer such a vision would be all wrong – in your book. (Jameson to Koestler, 1 March 1943)

The story she wrote for him is indeed grimly bleak, set in a totalitarian world where all must conform, where friendships and loves are unsparingly scrutinised, and where punishment, under a pretence of 'a generalised fellowship and brotherhood', is a subtle leaching of all that is thought of as democracy, all liberal values, all personal freedoms (Jameson, 'Young Prisoner' 115). The story looks forward to a world after World War II of 'an ineffectual fascism, a sham air of order, with violence, hypocrisy, cruelty given the status of virtues.' ('Young Prisoner' 122).[14] The anthology never materialised, but, given the peculiarly grim vision Jameson offers and the aspects of totalitarianism she chooses to highlight, it is extremely tempting to recall that Koestler was a close friend of George Orwell, who was about to embark on a narrative that would become *Nineteen Eighty-Four*, a novel that shares most of Jameson's concerns. Did they discuss Koestler's project, or indeed Jameson's contribution? At the very least we can see that Orwell and his circle were not the only writers in 1943 with what can usefully be termed intermodernist anxieties about a postwar world of ever increasing bleakness, restriction and controlling government.

In all her work, Jameson offers and expects no easy answers, striving to show human nature in its complexity and diversity, and how it responds in myriad ways to the crises it confronts. Her novels of this period use all the experience she brings from her own travels and from the many conversations she has had or has heard amongst European friends and colleagues. What she gives us in her novels of the forties, alongside the short stories and articles she continues to write, is an exceptional insight into the conflicts and tragedies of her time. Put these alongside her writings of the thirties, and it becomes very clear that we have in Jameson a powerful writer with an 'ex-centric' perspective indebted to her provincial origins, seen by many of her contemporaries as a brilliant depicter of the life and views of her age, responding honestly and with great generosity to the bewilderingly chaotic changes in her world, concerned above all to evolve a style that communicates without self-aggrandisement. The qualities of her works can truly be termed intermodernist, and we miss a great deal if we ignore her Cassandra-like vision, formal innovations and her lucid prose.[15]

NOTES

1. See, for example, Robert Knox, *The Races of Men: a Fragment*, London: Renshaw, 1850.
2. Hugh P. Kendall, in his *Ten Reprints of Local History from the 'Whitby Gazette'* tells in the essay 'The Streets of Whitby and their Associations' how

   while we welcome visitors to-day it was not always so; for, we are told, shortly after Alfred Tennyson had joined the married state, it was his intention to settle in Whitby. . . . To assist him in his quest the poet approached the chairman . . . of the Street Commissioners, but that worthy had no time to bother with "run-a-countrys" as all strangers were styled, and received the great man coldly, not to say rudely.

   In her novels based in the Whitby area, Jameson's characters often demonstrate this same outspokenness, not always appreciated by her home county critics.
3. Storm Jameson, in an untitled essay. In *What is Patriotism?* she says: 'I am a Little Englander on one side (the left – the side of the heart), and on the other I try to be a good European.' Jameson uses the term 'Little Englander' meaning, as it did originally, someone who was against Empire and for England to be contained within the United Kingdom; it has later come to suggest someone who is xenophobic and narrowly patriotic.
4. Fox was an influential Marxist critic, but not a hardliner, and he was much admired by Jameson. He was killed in the Spanish Civil War.
5. P.E.N., originally P.P.E.N., stands for 'poet, playwright, editor, novelist'. However, its membership has not been entirely inflexible as regards writers of non-fiction.
6. Jameson's approach in this lecture, which may be termed 'liberal Marxist', shows her affinity with writers like Fox and Stephen Spender in the middle thirties.
7. Jameson has a series of novels based in and around the Whitby of her childhood, which she names Wik in *The Moon is Making*, and Danesacre in the series of works based on her own family history: the trilogy 'The Triumph of Time' (which includes *The Lovely Ship*, *The Voyage Home* and *A Richer Dust*), *That Was Yesterday*, the trilogy 'Mirror in Darkness' (which includes *Company Parade*, *Love in Winter* and *None Turn Back*) and *Farewell, Night; Welcome, Day*. Danesacre is a telling pseudonym, since it recalls not only the Viking past of North Yorkshire but also the strong European links of the little port.
8. Told to me in conversation with a retired Whitby schoolmaster as one of his grandmother's anecdotes about Jameson. It is interesting to set this against Jameson's own late comment on what she terms this 'Breughel-like novel about the violently individual men and women . . . whom my mother remembered from her childhood' (*Journey* 1 346).
9. Jameson's *The Journal of Mary Hervey Russell* (1945) is an exception, but Jameson frequently refers to this book in correspondence as non-fiction, even though her publishers do not make the distinction.
10. Jameson is playing with pseudonyms and with references to her contemporaries at this time. She has just completed novels using the pen-names William Lamb

and James Hill, while in Hill's novel *No Victory for the Soldier* she names a number of her characters after contemporaries, for example, Priestley, Auden, Greenwood, Eyles and Neumann. In *Europe to Let*, the playfulness is a little different: Sheerwater certainly has much in common with Wells.

11. For a differently focused reading of *Europe to Let*, see Jennifer Birkett, 'The Work of Storm Jameson in the Inter-War Years'. In contrast to Birkett, I interpret Esk's proclivity for street scenes and architecture rather than people's private spaces in light of Jameson's own frequent assertions that she likes to concentrate on these things when in an alien environment. Maybe this is a way of avoiding the sense of intrusion she dislikes in *The Road to Wigan Pier*, and asserting her preference for a detached narrator.

12. Jameson is clearly fascinated as to how a Goebbels could come into being. In *Cousin Honoré*, the old man's grandson, Henry Eschelmer, explores one possible provenance; in *Europe to Let*, Otto Wiedemann offers another.

13. Orwell's *Animal Farm*, also written during World War II, uses fable in ways comparable to East European political satirists, just as Naomi Mitchison had done in her short story 'The Fourth Pig'. At the same time, Clemence Dane also produced her idiosyncratically vivid fable, *The Arrogant History of White Ben*.

14. Her story, 'The Young Prisoner', was finally published in 1944. Koestler had thought it 'outstandingly brilliant', as he wrote to Hermon Ould, 7 June 1943 (P.E.N. Archive at P.E.N. Headquarters).

15. For discussions of other writers who can usefully be seen as intermodernist, see, for instance, Jenny Hartley, *Millions Like Us*; Phyllis Lassner, *British Women Writers of World War Two*; Elizabeth Maslen, *Political and Social Issues in British Women's Fiction, 1928–1968*; Janet Montefiore, *Men and Women Writers of the 1930s*; Gill Plain, *Women's Fiction of the Second World War*; *British Fiction after Modernism*, eds, Marina Mackay and Lindsey Stonebridge; *Women in Europe between the Wars*, eds, Angela Kershaw and Angela Kimyongür; *The Fiction of the 1940s*, eds, Rod Mengham and N. H. Reeve. For additional discussion of Jameson, see *Storm Jameson: Writing in Dialogue*, eds, Jennifer Birkett and Chiara Briganti and Birkett's biography, *Margaret Storm Jameson*.

WORKS CITED

Birkett, Jennifer. *Margaret Storm Jameson: A Life*. Oxford: Oxford University Press, 2009.

—. '"The Spectacle of Europe": Politics, P.E.N. and Prose Fiction. The Work of Storm Jameson in the Inter-War Years'. *Women in Europe between the Wars: Politics, Culture and Society*. Eds Angela Kershaw and Angela Kimyongür. Aldershot and Burlington: Ashgate, 2007. 25–38.

Birkett, Jennifer and Chiara Briganti, eds. *Storm Jameson: Writing in Dialogue*. Newcastle: Cambridge Scholars Publishing, 2007.

Dane, Clemence. *The Arrogant History of White Ben*. London: William Heinemann, 1939.

Fox, Ralph. *The Novel and the People*. London: Lawrence and Wishart, 1937.

Hartley, Jenny. *Millions Like Us: British Women's Fiction of the Second World War*. London: Virago, 1997.

Henderson Philip. *The Novel Today: Studies in Contemporary Attitudes*. London: John Lane The Bodley Head, 1936.

Jameson, Storm. *Before the Crossing*. London: Macmillan, 1947.

—. *The Black Laurel*. London: Macmillan, 1947.

—. *Civil Journey*. London: Cassell, 1939.

— *Cloudless May*. London: Macmillan, 1943.

—. *Cousin Honoré*. London: Cassell, 1940.

—. 'Documents'. *Writing in Revolt*. Spec. issue of *Fact*. July 1937: 9–18.

—. *Europe to Let: The Memoirs of an Obscure Man*. London: Macmillan, 1940.

—. *Farewell, Night; Welcome, Day*. London: Cassell, 1939.

—. *The Fort*. London: Cassell, 1941.

—. *In the Second Year*. 1936. Ed. Stan Smith. Nottingham: Trent, 2004.

—. *The Journal of Mary Hervey Russell*. London: Macmillan, 1945.

—. *Journey from the North*. Vol. I, 1969. Vol. II, 1970. London: Virago, 1984.

—. Letter to Arthur Koestler. 1 March 1943 (2399/1). Koestler–Jameson Correspondence. Koestler Archive, University of Edinburgh Library.

—. The 'Mirror in Darkness' trilogy:
> *Company Parade*. 1934. London: Virago, 1982.
> *Love in Winter*. 1935. London: Virago, 1984.
> *None Turn Back*. 1936. London: Virago, 1984.

—. *The Moon is Making*. London: Cassell, 1937.

—. 'New Novels'. *The New English Weekly* 23 June 1932: 235–36.

—. *The Novel in Contemporary Life*. Boston: The Writer, 1938.

—. Rev. of *The Waves*, by Virginia Woolf. *Fortnightly Review* Nov. 1931: 677–78.

—. *That Was Yesterday*. London: Heinemann, 1932.

—. *Then We Shall Hear Singing: A Fantasy in C Major*. London: Cassell, 1942.

—. The 'Triumph of Time' trilogy. 1932:
> *The Lovely Ship*. London: Heinemann, 1927.
> *A Richer Dust*. London: Heinemann, 1931.
> *The Voyage Home*. London: Heinemann, 1930.

— Untitled essay. *What is Patriotism?* Ed. N. P. Macdonald. London: Thornton Butterworth, 1935. 123–33.

—. Untitled essay. *Adam International Review*. September 1941. Frontispiece.

—. 'The Young Prisoner'. *Modern Reading* 9 (1944): 111–26.

— as Hill, James. *No Victory for the Soldier*. London: Collins, 1938.

Kendall, H[ugh]. P. 'The Streets of Whitby and their Associations'. *Ten Reprints of Local History from the 'Whitby Gazette'*. Privately printed by the Whitby Literary and Philosophical Society, undated.

Kershaw, Angela and Angela Kimyongür, eds. *Women in Europe between the Wars: Politics, Culture and Society*. Aldershot and Burlington: Ashgate, 2007.

'Kim'. 'England Wants a Dictator'. *Saturday Review* 2 May 1936: 551–52.

Knox, Robert. *The Races of Men: A Fragment*. London: Renshaw, 1850.

Lassner, Phyllis. *British Women Writers of World War Two: Battlegrounds of Their Own*. London: Macmillan, 1998.

MacKay, Marina and Lindsey Stonebridge, eds. *British Fiction after Modernism*. London: Palgrave Macmillan, 2007.

Macmillan, Harold. Letter. 119, MLB 466. Publishers' Archive, British Library.

Maslen, Elizabeth. *Political and Social Issues in British Women's Fiction, 1928–1968*. London: Palgrave Macmillan, 2001.

Mengham, Rod and N. H. Reeve, eds. *The Fiction of the 1940s: Stories of Survival*. London: Palgrave Macmillan, 2001.

Mitchison, Naomi. 'The Fourth Pig'. *The Fourth Pig*. London: Constable, 1936.

Montefiore, Janet. *Men and Women Writers of the 1930s: The Dangerous Flood of History*. London: Routledge, 1996.

O'Faolain, Sean. Rev. of *In the Second Year*, by Storm Jameson. *The Spectator* 7 Feb. 1936: 226.

Orwell, George. *Animal Farm: A Fairy Story*. London: Gollancz, 1945.

—. *Nineteen Eighty-Four*. London: Gollancz, 1949.

—. *The Road to Wigan Pier*. London: Gollancz, 1937.

Plain, Gill. *Women's Fiction of the Second World War: Gender, Power and Resistance*. Edinburgh: Edinburgh University Press, 1996.

Woolf, Virginia. *Three Guineas*. 1938. *A Room of One's Own and Three Guineas*. Ed. Morag Shiach. Oxford: Oxford University Press, 1992.

2

ENGLANDS ANCIENT AND MODERN: SYLVIA TOWNSEND WARNER, T. H. WHITE AND THE FICTIONS OF MEDIEVAL ENGLISHNESS

Janet Montefiore

Explicit liber Regis Quondam, graviter et laboriose scriptus inter annos MDCCCXXXVI et MDCCCXLII, nationibus in diro bello certaintibus. Hic etiam incipit, si forte in futuro homo superstes pestilenciam posit evadere et opus continuare inceptum, spes Regis Futuri. Ora pro Thoma Malory Equite, discupuloque humili ejus, qui nunc sua sponte libros deponit ut pro specie pugnet.

Here ends the book of the Onetime King, written with much toil and effort between the years 1936 and 1942, when the nations were striving in fearful warfare. Here also begins – if perchance a man may in future time survive the pestilence and continue the task he has begun – the hope of the Future King. Pray for Thomas Malory, Knight, and his humble disciple, who now voluntarily lays aside his books to fight for his kind. (White, *King: Complete* 812)[1]

Having applied to join the Royal Air Force Volunteer Reserve in the late autumn of 1941, T. H. White wrote and translated this Latin *envoi* to 'The Book of Merlyn', the fifth and intended final book of his Arthurian romance *The Once and Future King*.[2] Shortly afterwards, his future biographer Sylvia Townsend Warner began her decidedly un-romantic novel about a fourteenth-century convent, *The Corner That Held Them*. Her diary for 21 February 1942 records 'Our pipes freeze, and I begin to write a story about a medieval nunnery: to be entirely taken up with their money difficulties' (*Diaries* 117).

What is the significance of these two writers independently undertaking a *magnum opus* set in the English Middle Ages during the Second World War? Probably the immediate cause, as for Tolkien constructing Middle-Earth in wartime Oxford, was the desire for a sustained imaginative alternative to a dreary civilian present: for Warner, the frozen plumbing and stolid provinciality of wartime Dorset; for White, the lonely tedium of neutral Eire. Certainly, their wartime origins are visible in the perpetual anxieties that haunt Warner's nuns (her epigraph runs 'But neither might the corner that held them keep them from fear' (*Corner* iii)) and in the ineradicable aggression that fuels and ultimately destroys Arthur's Round Table. Both books put into question the patriotic fantasy of an ideally unchanging England through their unconventionally fictionalised histories. But such intense engagements with history have not won Warner and White critical attention. Both are missing from Avrom Fleishman's *English Historical Novel* and more recent studies of history and fiction by Steven Connor, Helen Hughes and A. S. Byatt. (White's Arthur book, overshadowed by its offspring the musical *Camelot* and the cartoon *Sword in the Stone*, seems virtually to have dropped out of the canon of serious writing, in which Warner's status as a provincial lesbian communist has always been equivocal.) Yet both point forward to the postwar development of what Connor calls 'historicised' fiction – that is, 'fiction about its own historically relative construction of history' (143). Drawing on discourses typically associated with modernism such as psychoanalysis (White) and Marxism (Warner), these playful and/or ironic fictions by eccentric writers whose habitats, political allegiances and sexual preferences differed from the norm, direct us to themes and forms that may come to define intermodernism.

As I have argued elsewhere, Sylvia Townsend Warner had much in common besides homosexuality with her biographee.[3] Although they never met, each admired the other's books, Warner mourning White when he died as 'a friend I never managed to have' (STW, *Diaries* 284, 290). They were born into an English administrative elite: Warner's father was the head of the 'Modern Side' at Harrow, a leading public school; White's parents were respectively a district superintendent of police in India and a daughter of an 'Indian Judge' (i.e. an English judge in colonial India) (STW, *White* 25). Each was a close friend of David Garnett, whose encouragement was important to both their careers. He launched Warner as a writer in 1925 by getting Ian Parsons of Chatto and Windus interested in publishing her work, and his friendship with White began with his enthusiastic reception of *England Have My Bones* (Garnett 12, 218; STW *White* 85).

Another link unknown to either until Warner began researching her biography, came through White's friend and mentor L. J. Potts, his tutor in English Literature at Queen's College, Cambridge, Potts being an admiring former pupil of Warner's beloved father, 'the greatest schoolmaster there has ever been and a man of unerring judgment' (Gallix 118). White himself was educated at the militaristic public school Cheltenham College and at Queen's College, Cambridge, where he discovered Malory's *Morte D'Arthur* through writing an essay on it. When drafting his 'Arthur' books, he consulted both Sydney Cockerell, director of the Fitzwilliam Museum, and Potts, with whom he often resorted to public school idiom: thus Potts complains that Malory's Sir Launcelot is 'rather too head of the house' and White replies, 'Little boys believe that they wont be able to bowl well in the 1st XI match tomorrow, if they abuse themselves today, and Lancelot was captain of the 1st XI. Guenever, whom he could not stop, was stopping his bowling (feats of arms) and his miracles' (Gallix 109, 111). Warner herself was surprisingly at ease with the world of public school and Oxbridge. Educated at home where she 'read everything', she was taught with informal brilliance by her father the historian George Townsend Warner: 'By the age of seventeen or so, Sylvia's erudition was both phenomenal and perfectly natural . . . She was regarded [at Harrow] as "the cleverest fellow we had"' (Harman 20). That Warner for all her political radicalism continued to feel at home in this milieu can be seen from her description of White's exile from the charmed life of a Queen's undergraduate: 'And then it was all over: the dipping willows, the talk and stimulus, the old brick of Erasmus' tower and his portrait in Hall looking like Voltaire, the bicycles and the Mathematical Bridge: however often he saw them again, he would not take them for granted' (*White* 48). Her tone is far removed from the narrator's anger in Woolf's *A Room of One's Own* when she is shooed away from precisely that world of taken-for-granted male privilege.

So far, these educational, social and literary links make White and Warner sound just the sort of 'Bloomsbury' insiders that Q. D. Leavis attacked for writing cosily privileged 'fantasy fiction' (Leavis 320). Yet their homosexuality and differently dissenting politics in fact put both outside the English literary establishment. As a lesbian and a Marxist revolutionary, a political activist in the 1930s and a committed member of the Communist Party until the early 1950s, Warner was a radical whose writings 'challenge a patriarchal, phallocentric world-view' (Bingham 41). White was drawn to conservatism yet cheerfully sent up the codes of foxhunters in *Burke's Steerage* (1938), while his love of youth radicalised him to rebel against the routine subjection of schoolboys to repression by 'Dr Prisonface' the headmaster, and despite his abortive volunteering for the RAF, his pacifism led him to spend the war years in neutral Eire.

Such dissenting politics inflect the different ways in which these two novels engage both with English history and with the notion of the continuity of English landscape which is so powerful in mid-century cultural thinking. Politically, the idea of traditional England was frequently invoked in debates about landscape preservation and organicist culture, as in Stanley Baldwin's 1935 statement 'To me England is the country and the country is England' (Matless 30). The unchanging English countryside was celebrated in topographical literature (an interwar publishing growth area) such as H. V. Morton's *In Search of England* (1927), or H. J. Massingham's *English Downland* (1936). Englishness appears in interwar landscape art from McKnight Kauffer's modernist railway posters to the Bewickian wood engravings of Joan Hassall or Reynolds Stone and the neo-romantic landscapes of John Piper and Graham Sutherland. Rural England is invoked or directly represented in books, anthologies and essays about the traditional countryside and the lives of countrymen, often illustrated with wood engravings in the fashion of Bewick, celebrating traditional skills and crafts, as in Claire Leighton's *The Farmer's Year* (1933), or George Sturt's explicit memorial to obsolete skills of carpentry and to a vanished way of life, *The Wheelwright's Shop* (1923). Adrian Bell's 1936 anthology *The Open Air* likewise praised the old countryman's traditional 'knowledge of process and natural law . . . something that, in a word with him on the commonest subject, gives you a vista of generations' (10).

Such nostalgia for traditional rural life is usually bound up with the conservative politics which invoked England's everlasting landscape as a site of patriotism, spirituality and authenticity (Jacobs 62), justifying and romanticising England as the centre of empire and dominion – as in the 1940 patriotic song 'There'll always be an England / While there's a country lane / Wherever there's a cottage small / Beside a field of grain / . . . The Empire too / We can depend on you'. Yet such representations, as David Matless has rightly emphasised, imply a complex dialectic of conservative pastoral and conscious modernity (even that patriotic song invokes the urban England of the 'busy street' and 'turning wheel'). And there was an obvious contradiction in the way that travel writers deplored motor-cars for causing arterial roads and ribbon development, while depending on them to traverse the countryside they wrote about. White himself began his celebration of rural pleasures (including learning to fly an aeroplane) in *England Have My Bones* by deploring the prospect of 'loop-ways and mustard-yellow touring signs and gentlemen from the A.A.' and ended the book with his own car crash (White, *England* 15).

Warner's writings about rural England draw attention to the fracturing effects of modernity and of pervasive social injustice. Her early poems about ancient presences in the countryside emphasise the death of old ways: 'Ghosts at Chaldon Herring' are 'dead long ago' and in an ancient village, 'Churchyard and church and inn / . . . Are all very old. / Even the beer they draw there / Seems to taste of mould' (STW, *New Poems* 37, 40). Her 1939 essay 'The Way I Have Come' describes her gradual understanding that 'the English Pastoral was a grim and melancholy thing' (5); she denounces the 'unpaid overtime filched from the labourer (he knows it right enough, but he daren't speak)' ('Way' 8). Her tales of rural life emphasise the poverty, insecurity, pinched narrowness, ignorance and frequent malice of country people.

T. H. White's attitude to rural England was less critical. A conservative sportsman with a conscience, he wrote of the countryside as a sensuously alert consumer of its pleasures, acknowledging that his England was 'the country of a leisured class' (*England* 6). Like other historical romances whose 'image of Englishness . . . showed a society of free individuals in which rulers and ruled were bound together by mutual respect' (Hughes 80) his 'Arthur' books idealise feudal society in their rosy picture of 'mediaeval villeins', as contented as the modern labourer who accepts a low wage 'because he does not have to throw his soul into the bargain – as he would have to do in a town' (*England* 137). Yet he was well aware of the cruelty of the blood sports he described so lovingly, and was distressed by a glimpse of an impoverished ploughman with 'a toiling face' (*England* 50); *The Once and Future King* is very far from being a patriotic re-creation of 'Merrie England'. His most impassioned writing about the English countryside is the lyrical paean to its moonlit beauty which in the 1941 'Book of Merlyn' inspires the disillusioned Arthur to courage and purpose:

> He began to love the land under him with a fierce longing, not because it was good or bad, but because it was: because of the shadows of the corn stooks on a golden evening . . . because the stars were brighter in puddles than in the sky; because there were puddles, and leaky gutters, and dung hills with poppies on them; because the salmon in the rivers suddenly leaped and fell . . . All the beauty of his humans came upon him, instead of their horribleness. (*King: Complete* 788–89)

Those corn stooks, gutters and dunghills shaped by invisible labour yet innocent of ownership or social conflict, could in 1941 still represent the continued identity of medieval England with the familiar countryside of 'today'. Arthur's vision of 'his beloved, his sleeping, his defenceless English' (789) is close in feeling to Powell and Pressburger's film *A Canterbury Tale* (1944) whose opening shot of Chaucerian pilgrims turns into an idealised wartime Kentish village where an American soldier can discuss timber with an English blacksmith.

'MALORY AND I ARE BOTH DREAMING'

Landscape may link past and present, but it is not history. White's own engagement with the English Middle Ages came principally through legend. He was well aware of writing not a historical novel but a romance, as is clear when he explains his techniques of double perspective and deliberate anachronism in a 1939 letter to Sydney Cockerell after the latter suggested 1290–1310 as a setting:

> I am trying to write of *an imaginary world which was imagined in the 15th century*. Malory did not imagine the armour of your century (he imagined his own, and I will stick to him through thick and thin), but he did imagine dragons, saints, hermits etc. I state quite explicitly that we all

know that Arthur, and not Edward, was on the throne in the latter half of the 15th century, at the beginning of my second vol . . . By that deliberate statement of an untruth I make it clear to any scholar who may read the book that I am writing, as I said before, of an imaginary world imagined in the 15th cent. . . . I am taking 15th cent. as a provisional *forward* limit (except where magic or serious humour is concerned – for instance, it is a serious comment on chivalry to make knights-errant drop their g's like huntin' men) and often darting back to the positively Gaelic past . . . Malory and I are both dreaming. We care very little for exact dates, and he says I am to tell you I am after the spirit of Morte d'Arthur (just as he was after the spirit of those sources collated) seen through the eyes of 1939. He looked through 1489 (was it ? – can't trouble to verify) and got a lot of 1489 muddled up with the sources. I am looking *through* 1939 *at* 1489 itself looking *backwards*. (STW, *White* 133–34)

In its awareness of historical relativity, fictionality and multiple perspectives, this declaration of conscious anachronism by a modern writer re-inventing a Malory who himself imagined a legendary past in terms of his own medieval 'present', makes the projected work sound like proleptic post-modernism. Even White's allegiance to 'the spirit of Morte D'Arthur' which seemingly appeals to an old-fashioned Romantic essentialism, allowed him to rewrite Malory as a modern fable about finding an antidote to war. This playfully modernist historicism in *The Once and Future King* surfaces when White resorts to the catalogue, as in the long survey of England in the Middle Ages in 'The Candle in the Wind', or the description in 'The Ill-Made Knight' of an armoury whose furniture includes

the inventory of a harness-barrel . . . which recorded, among other articles: a salade garnessed with golde, iij peire gantelez, a vestment, a mesbooke, an auter clothe, a peir of brigandines, a pyssing basin of silver, x schertes for my Lorde, a jakete of leather and a bagge of chessmen. . . . On the desk there were splattering quill pens, blotting sand, sticks for beating Lancelot when he was stupid, and notes, in unutterable confusion, as to which jupons had been lately pawned – pawning was a great institution for valuable armour – and which helms had been brought up to date with a glancing surface, and whose vambrace stood in need of repair, and what had been paid to whom for fforbeshynge which when. Most of the accounts were wrongly added up. (White, *King: Complete* 344)

It is impossible to imagine this being written before the advent of T. S. Eliot, whose work White would have encountered as an undergraduate attending I. A. Richards's lectures. The flaunted scholarship of the reproduced inventory, the 'sand for blotting', the throw-away information about the economics of armour supply, the archaisms 'gantletez', 'fforbeshynge' and 'iij' for 'iv', the armourers' terms 'vambrace' and 'jupon' ('forearm protection' and 'surcoat'), the unlikely jumble of weapons, church furnishings, silver 'pyssing basin' and 'salade garnessed with golde' (without explaining that 'salade' means 'helmet') – all these details stand out from the narrator's modern present in a cheerfully lightweight version of that modernist consciousness of history which is argued for in 'Tradition and the Individual Talent' and informs *The Waste Land*. This playfulness marks the difference between White and those contemporary poets like David Jones or Charles Williams who invoked Arthurian myth. In White's book the anachronisms are reversed: knights betray their basically frivolous attitude to war by dropping their g's like huntin' gentlemen; Arthur's new chivalry is opposed by reactionary barons 'who would have written to *The Times* about it, if there had been such a paper', and the sadistic Sir Turquine whose 'friends would certainly have urged him to be psycho-analysed' if he had lived now, imprisons knights and beats them with thorns in a castle described as 'a sort of concentration camp' (White, *King: Complete* 383, 367, 379).

This conscious fictionalising evidently came to White in the process of composing his Arthur books. White began *The Sword in the Stone* in 1937 as 'a preface to Malory' (Gallix 98), and there is no indication that he originally planned to take Arthur's story further than his coronation. But when writing *The Witch in the Wood* in the summer of 1939, he was already explaining his tetralogy to Potts:

> *The Witch in the Wood*, which Collins will send you, is book II of a projected 4 books about the doom of Arthur. Book III will give the Lancelot–Guenever tangle (it will be romantic) and Book IV will bring the three tragic themes together for the final clash . . .
> I want eventually to publish all 4 books in one volume, and then they will be
>> The Sword in the Stone (Poetry)
>> The Witch in the Wood (Farce, smuggling in the tragic theme under a
>>> cloak of it)
>> The Idea in the Mind (Romance)
>> The Candle in the Wind (Tragedy) (Gallix 98)

White's conception of the work's central tragedy shifted as he wrote from the 'Nemesis of Incest' to the destruction of chivalry through its own aggression (in psychoanalytic terms, the ineradicability of the death drive). Publication in one volume was delayed until 1958 because of a quarrel with his publisher Collins in 1942 arising from White's last-minute desire for the sequence to include a fifth 'Book of Merlyn' in which Arthur, on the eve of the last battle with Mordred, rejoins Merlyn and his animal friends of *The Sword in the Stone* to debate a solution to the curse of war.

'The Book of Merlyn''s stated purpose of finding an antidote to war points up Arthur's real tragedy: the failure of his attempt to reconcile 'Might and Right', Mordred's Oedipal hatred being the means by which the tragedy is worked out. As Warner points out, White was disabled from effective handling of the Arthur/Morgause incest theme, which he originally saw as central, by his own unresolved relationship with his possessive mother. One might expect that his sadism, so sympathetically analysed in Warner's biography, would leave his handling of 'Might and Right' similarly bedevilled by a personal unresolved investment in aggressive fantasy, but this is not at all the case. Certainly, White is ambivalent about war and violence. In 1941 he told Garnett that 'I have written an epic about war, one of whose morals is that Hitler is the kind of chap one has to stop. I believe in my book, and in order to give it a fair chance in life, I must show that I am ready to practise what I preach' (STW, *White* 185). But it is not surprising that he did not go to war to defend the reputation of a book whose principal moral is that war is wicked. The argument starts in Book 2, with Merlyn's sharp response to young Arthur's pleasure in battle:

> 'What is all this chivalry anyway? It simply means being rich enough to have a castle and a suit of armour, and then you can make the Saxon people do what you like . . . Look at the barns burned, and dead men's legs sticking out of ponds, and horses with swelled bellies by the road-side, and mills falling down, and money buried, and nobody daring to walk abroad with gold or ornaments on their clothes. That is chivalry nowadays . . . And then you talk about a battle being fun!' (*King: Complete* 237–38)

The innocent Arthur laboriously works out a different idea of chivalry:

> 'The knights in my order will ride over the world, still dressed in steel and whacking away with their swords – that will give an outlet for wanting to whack, you understand . . . but they will be bound to strike on behalf of what is good, to defend virgins . . . and to help the oppressed and so forth'. (*King: Complete* 263–64)

For a time, Arthur's idea works, much of the sequence being taken up with showing how brute force becomes real chivalry. This theme is dramatised in White's portrait of his most complex and sympathetic figure Sir Lancelot, a man tormented all his life by spiritual longings which his sensual nature and his love for Guenever prevent him from living up to, and by his own sadism. In a sense, White's psychological portrait is a long gloss on the final lament for Lancelot from Malory's *Morte d'Arthur*, quoted at the end of 'The Book of Merlyn':

> 'Thou were the courtliest knight that ever bare shield. And thou were the truest friend of thy lover that ever bestrode horse. And thou were the truest lover, of a sinful man, that ever loved woman. And thou

were the kindest man that ever strake with sword. And thou were the goodliest person that ever came within press of knights. And thou were the meekest man and gentlest that ever ate in hall among ladies. And thou were the sternest knight to thy mortal foe that ever put a spear in rest'. (*King: Complete* 808–09)[4]

'The truest lover, of a sinful man . . . the kindest man that ever strake with sword': White develops these paradoxes into a study of a man whose word of honour 'was valuable to him not only because he was good, but also because he was bad. It is the bad people who need to have principles to restrain them' (White *King: Complete* 365). Both White's empathy with his contradictory hero and his narrative skills can be seen in one of Lancelot's adventures as the first and best of Arthur's knights putting Might in the service of Right, when he meets a lady in flight from her armed husband:

> Lancelot rode between them and said: 'Really, you must not go for a woman like that. I don't care whose fault it is, but you can't kill women.'
> 'Since when?'
> 'Since King Arthur was king.'
> 'She is my wife,' said the knight. 'She is nothing to do with you. Get out! And she is an adulteress, whatever she says.'
> 'Oh no, I am not,' said the lady. 'But you are a bully. And you drink.'
> 'Who made me drink, then? And besides, it is no worse to drink than to be an adulteress.' (White, *King: Complete* 388)

This nursery squabble turns lethal when the knight tricks Lancelot into looking away:

> Lancelot reined in his horse and looked over his shoulder. At the same moment the knight leaned over his near side and swapped off the lady's head. When Lancelot looked back again, without seeing any soldiers, he found the lady sitting beside him with no head on. She slowly began to sag to the left, throbbing horribly, and fell in the dust. There was blood all over his horse.

He then threatens to kill the knight, who to Lancelot's horror begs for mercy:

> He began to shudder, not at the knight but at the cruelty in himself. He held his sword loathingly, and pushed the knight away.
> 'Look at all the blood,' he said.
> 'Don't kill me,' said the knight. 'I yield. I yield. You can't kill a man at mercy.'
> Lancelot put up his sword and went away from the knight as if he

were going back from his own soul. He felt in his heart cruelty and cowardice, the things that made him brave and kind.

'Get up,' he said. 'I won't hurt you. Get up, go.' (389)

This passage displays a striking mastery of different kinds of realism: the brilliant naturalistic staging of movement and behaviour, which shows vividly just how a decapitated person would 'sag' and fall slowly sideways, and the sophisticated depiction of Lancelot's inner struggle, which applies a post-Freudian psychology of sublimated instincts to a medieval knight who leaves off an intended murder 'as if he were going back from his own soul'. (As ever, White writes extraordinarily well about violence.) The obviously anachronistic modernity of the dialogue works in tension with the medieval, Christian setting, to produce a romance that is also a psychological study of sadism and self-mastery. Elsewhere, White's characters move strangely yet convincingly between modern dialogue and medieval English: '"Madam, so ye be pleased, I care not. As for my part, ye shall soon please." He always fell into the grandeur of the High Language, when he was moved' (545). White insists that Lancelot's medieval nature must be understood in its own terms (here strongly resembling Victorian idealism): 'He had not buried his love for Arthur in his passion for Guenever, but still felt for him. To a medieval nature like Lancelot's, with its fatal weakness for loving the highest when he saw it, this was a position of pain' (418).

But Lancelot the 'kindest man that ever strake with sword' is not typical of Arthur's knights. The problem with Arthur's Round Table is that its sub-limation of 'Might' into 'Right' succeeds too well. His knights bring peace to England, but the aggression which the Round Table was invented to tame doesn't go away. He tries sending his knights on the quest of the Holy Grail; this produces romance, adventure and even holiness, but no solution. Only a few perfect knights can attain the Grail, and then they die; meanwhile, the long peace makes Arthur's court decadent and dangerous, in the dynamic described by W. H. Auden in the 1939 sequence 'In Time of War'. Like a much more successful 'Book of Merlyn', this situates a contemporary conflict (here, the Sino-Japanese war) within a series of meditations on humanity's age-old addic-tion to violence. In Sonnet XII, giants and dragons are slain or moribund, and 'they were safe'. Or so the humans think, but

> The vanquished powers were glad
> To be invisible and free: without remorse
> Struck down the sons who strayed into their course,
> And ravished the daughters, and drove the fathers mad. (Auden 256)

Arthur's pacified England is likewise destroyed by its own demons. Arthur himself attempts to solve the problem of 'Might' by fixing his hope on abstract

Justice. He explains to Lancelot and Guenever that justice is an absolute value when he warns them not to compromise themselves or him (which they promptly do). This rigid allegiance to the law leads him to endless mistakes of judgement in 'The Candle in the Wind', where he is constantly manipulated by his treacherous son Mordred. Easily blackmailed by appeals to his own guilt and love, he is trapped by his principles into besieging his friend and wife in Lancelot's French castle while Mordred stages a fascist coup in London. Even though Mordred is fought off, Arthur's Round Table is ended, though in White's book it still lives on through the innocent page 'Tom' Malory to whom Arthur entrusts his story in a final tender moment of metafictional romance.

'NOT A HISTORICAL NOVEL'?

Warner wrote to her friend Paul Nordoff in the early stages of writing *The Corner That Held Them* that her project was 'not in any way a historical novel; it hasn't any thesis' (STW, *Letters* 79). This sounds a strange thing to say of a novel so clearly the work of a historian who explains the increased consumerism of her Oby convent in terms of a market economy stimulated by labour shortage:

> The rise in the cost of living brought a rise in the standard of living. When difficulties with the manor resulted in less home-grown produce the deficiency was made up in buying at fairs and markets. What is produced for sale is naturally more luxurious than what is produced for home consumption. The nuns ate more delicate foods, wore finer wool, drank wine and cider when their home-brew ran out . . . Pins were bought freely, gone were the days when a nun searched on all-fours through the floor-strewn rushes saying: Where is my pin? (*Corner* 70)

The analytical language might almost come from George Townsend Warner's own *Tillage, Trade and Invention* (1912), apart from that last vivid glimpse of the crouching nun searching for her lost pin. Warner most characteristically embodies history in material objects which are handled, touched and smelt, like the inherited fine clothes worn at a feast

> which preserved the bulges of dead and gone wearers . . . just as though the de Stapledon effigies had come south from their freezing chapels; and at the end of the holiday my uncle's boots, my grandfather's hat, Lady Edith's gown faced with wild-cat, would have the dust of travel switched out of them and be put back in chests and presses, or hung in wardrobes where the stink of healthy de Stapleton piss would keep the moths away. (*Corner* 139)

The effect of this dry list, far removed from the flaunted knowingness of White's 'pyssing basin of silver', shows Warner's feeling for how people lived, the pinch and scrape and stink of even a well-to-do medieval family. Similarly with her grasp of her convent's financial difficulties. She explained in a late conversation that 'if you were going to give an accurate picture of the monastic life, you'd have to put in all their finances; how they made their money, how they dodged about from one thing to another and how very precarious it all was' ('Conversation' 36). Unlike White's knights who never think twice about paying for their armour or their castles, Warner shows in detail 'how they made their money'. Economics, class tensions and religion are compounded in Prioress Matilda's apprehensions when threatened with 'God's vengeance' on her priest's open fornication:

> First the cook goes, and then the scullions follow the cook; piously removing themselves from the neighbourhood of an avenging God the workers begin to leak away, the hind leaves the plough, the thatcher makes excuses not to come and mend the roof; the harvest is not gathered, sheep are not shorn, calves are not gelded; and presently dues are not paid, novices are diverted elsewhere, and moneylenders demand their capital. (166)

Such reflections are typical of Warner's ecclesiastical administrators; the convent whose 'life is hid with Christ who is above' (7) is in practice as much of the world, worldly as the great art that so astonishingly flourishes here: the primrose spire that 'whether it brightened or waned . . . seemed to be flying . . . against the scudding sky' (190); the altar-hanging of *opus Anglicanum* embroidery stolen by Dame Adela; the exquisite Machaut polyphony sung by lepers. All have their roots in material existence – 'out came the music, as the kingfisher flashes from its nest of stinking fishbones' (205).

Yet despite its historical materialism, *The Corner That Held Them* differs politically from Warner's previous historical novels *Summer Will Show* (1936) and *After the Death of Don Juan* (1938) which I analysed in an earlier study.[5] Like the novels of Naomi Mitchison and Jack Lindsay, these belong to the genre of the politicised historical novel in which contemporary writers engaged with present conflicts through a semi-allegorical return to the past. As Chris Hopkins observes:

> The tradition of the historical novel and the allegory as political forms in the thirties is rooted in a sense of the explanatory power of broad historical frameworks. History, and historical novels, could help to understand the politics of the present because the present arose from the past, and because there was a pattern to history which meant that valid parallels could be drawn between different periods. In this dual view of history, the past exists both for itself and as a 'type' of another period in the present. (Hopkins 132)

But this 'Aesopian' mode of oblique political commentary can hardly exist in a chronicle that 'hasn't any thesis'. True, the nuns' boredom and insecurity match the experience of civilian life in wartime England, and Jenny Hartley argues for a deliberate parallel between Warner's rendering of the advance of the Black Death and Hitler's blitzkrieg in 1940: 'Warner herself made the . . . analogy explicit, commenting in 1940, "people here would be much more frightened if the Germans were the Black Death. Then the news the Black Death has arrived in Rouen, is in the Channel Ports, has appeared in Paris, would set people thinking: 'Soon I may catch it and die'"'(Hartley 47). Yet the Black Death occupies just one chapter out of fourteen. The Peasants' Revolt likewise appears mainly as an anticipated threat, and the Third Crusade is briefly glimpsed at the end as a host of departing pilgrims. As Wendy Mulford says, the great events 'are seen, as the nuns would see them, through a slit window, or as the peasants might hear them, as snatches repeated from mouth to mouth' (Mulford 200). The book is not a political allegory.

Warner herself wrote about Marxist understanding of the relation between the past and the present in her short 1939 lecture 'The Historical Novel', which argues that the novelist's rendering of history should use present-day language in the truth-telling speech of working-class characters who 'fill the role of the commentator, the analyst, the person who sums things up' because 'when it comes to a piece of plain common sense, it is the ruled who speak' (54). Thus the peasant Ramon in *After the Death of Don Juan* believes that 'as we have hands given us to work with so we have wits given us to think with. There should be justice for the poor . . . Neighbour should stand by neighbour' (349). But no comparable figure speaks from or to the Oby convent. True, a beggar denounces the nuns who 'will stir your white fingers for God's altar, but when did you ever prick your fingers for God's poor? We go in rags . . . Where are the words of Christ when he said, Clothe the naked?' (249). But we are told that this rant is only

> the noise one hears in every alehouse . . . It is not hunger and nakedness that worst afflict the poor, for a very little thieving or a small alms can remedy that. [Their] wretchedness . . . lies below hunger and nakedness. It consists in their incessant incertitude and fear . . . the labouring in quicksand where every step that takes hold of the firm ground is also a step into the danger of condemnation. Not cold and hunger but Law and Justice are the bitterest afflictions of the poor. (257)

Although this sharp perception of 'Law and Justice' as mechanisms of oppression is politically opposed to White's description of King Arthur 'groping towards Right as a criterion of its own – towards Justice as an abstract thing which did not lean upon power' (521), in both books it is not the character but the narrator who in the tradition of George Eliot is 'the commentator, the analyst, the person who sums things up'. It is impossible that one of the characters whom Warner called 'innumerable and insignificant' (STW, *Letters* 91) should play this role, not least because of the great gap between their medieval minds and the historically aware narrator who interprets them. Warner's lecture insists on the novelist's need to understand though not to share the mind-set of the past. 'The historical novelist cannot dodge the obligation . . . of knowing pretty accurately how people clothed their minds. Human nature does not change, etc., but human thinking alters a great deal, is conditioned by what it has been taught, what it believes, or disbelieves; what it admires in art or nature; at what age it marries . . . what careers are open to it; whether it reads Aristotle or Plato; whether it believes in witches or planets' ('Novel' 55). Deeply perceptive about human feeling, Warner understands very well how passions are conditioned by beliefs. The distance between the writer and her characters is made stark when Ralph Kello, who will become the fraudulent priest Sir Ralph, first meets an Oby nun:

> 'Yes, we are all shut up here like knights in a castle. The enemy has broken in, but we aren't overcome yet.'
> Later he was to find Dame Blanche's military fantasies as tedious as everyone else did. But now the contrast between the piping voice and the warlike words touched his heart . . . (21)

The analytical modern voice mocking Dame Blanche's 'military fantasies' is very far removed from the nun's own image of the besieged castle, while Ralph Kello's urbane response to the simile's unconscious pathos comes somewhere between the modern narrator's knowledgeable irony and the medieval Dame Blanche's naivety. This sceptical writer convincingly creates a world in which experiences are shaped by beliefs that she doesn't share and, unlike White, is certainly not drawn towards. There is no irony or animus in her portrayal of Sir Ralph the fraudulent priest living from day to day in the pleasures of the table, knowing his own damnation and intermittently in terror at that knowledge. More ambivalent is her handling of the dying Bishop Walter Dunford, obsessed by his hatred of Oby where he senses 'something quite unusually baleful . . . a wickedness so wicked that it transcended his diagnosis' (221). This class-conscious bishop is shown as a credulous, spiteful fool, 'a man with neither meat nor mercy in him' as Ralph sourly thinks (182), readily believing the lying gossip that the tithes which paid for Oby's spire have been the aristocratic prior 'Thomas Foley['s] price for the carnal pleasures he had enjoyed with his cousin' (221). Deaf to the melancholy well-born Dame Lilias, he listens avidly to the spiteful murderess Dame Alice who like him is of the 'common folk' (165). Yet Dunford's distrust of Oby is, *in his own terms*, absolutely right. As Rachel Willcocks rightly insists in her account of Warner recreating the medieval *mentalité*, '[D]amnation is certain for the nuns of Oby because their priest Sir Ralph is an impostor' (Willcocks 43). On one level, Warner's narrative is a materialist chronicle; on another, it is a tale of demonic haunting.

When Sir Ralph blurts out in delirium that he is no priest, Dame Susanna who overhears him tells herself that 'Heaven would not allow such a thing . . . There would have been a sign. A dream would be sent, a toad would jump from the chalice, the spire would fall.' She tells no one for fear of ruining the convent: 'How could Oby recover from such a scandal?' (88–89). But the spire does fall, and Dame Susanna rushes shrieking to die unshriven beneath the falling blocks. (The mortar had dried unevenly, according to the masons.) In this convent 'as full of spite, lechery, boredom and fantasy as a girls' boarding school' (Mulford 200), Dame Alicia deliberately drowns Magdalen Figgis, the mistress of Sir Ralph, and frightens into silence the prioress who witnesses the deed.

The fraudulent Sir Ralph becomes an ever more sympathetic aesthete enjoying hawking, sexual pleasure, fishing and above all the poem 'Mamillion' which he gradually recognises as a masterpiece. Yet while he is destined 'to live into an old age serene and bright and die without a pang of conscience' (STW, Letters 88),[6] an ambivalent note is struck by the figure of the weasel 'sporting around' him as he lies dying in a field (Corner 280). When Ralph perjured himself to Dame Blanche with a false claim of priesthood, 'a weasel reared up and studied him . . . there is no beast of worse omen than a weasel' (20–1). He later reflects nervously how 'Satan, weasel-shaped behind him, had watched him cross the threshold' (26) and 'for a quiet ante-room to hell he had engaged himself to Oby: a bargain with a weasel' (55). The appearance of the weasel playing around Ralph as he dies suggests that Satan had come to claim his soul. Not that the sceptical ironist who had invoked Satan the 'loving huntsman' in the title of her first novel Lolly Willowes (1926) and would write admiringly in her diary of the 'weasel grace' of her lover Valentine's long slim body would think this cause for worry (Diaries 359). Her Machaut Kyrie sounds as 'the blessed might sing, singing in a duple measure that ran as nimbly on its four feet as a weasel running through a meadow' (Corner 204). This quietly disturbing simile (weasels live by sucking other animals' blood, and the price of the Machaut song-books has been stolen from starving paupers who will shortly murder one of the singers and burn the music-books), underlines the point that beauty financed by squeezing surplus value out of the poor has nothing to do with morality or virtue.

Fleishman argues that 'what makes a historical novel historical is the active presence of a concept of history as a shaping force – acting not only upon the characters of the novel but on the author and readers outside it' (15). Although The Once and Future King, a novel of mythical chivalry and The Corner That Held Them, a 'strictly capitalist' chronicle of nuns and clergy (STW, 'Conversation' 35), differ so widely in form and content, they share their understanding of history as not just a 'shaping force' in Fleishman's post-Lukacsian sense, but as narratives constructed and reconstructed, through the uncompromisingly contemporary narrators who understand and tell the experiences of their medieval characters in the terms of Marxism (Warner) or post-Freudian psychology (White). Their omniscient narration reveals intimately how Sir Lancelot or Prioress Matilda think – and even if Warner doesn't explore the complexities of her characters' feelings as White does Lancelot's, they are very much more than 'humours', each being given an interior life. Byatt argues convincingly in her account of postwar English novelists' engagement with history that the knowledgeable narrator in the tradition of George Eliot, can 'creep closer to the feelings and inner life of characters . . . than any first-person mimicry' because she can 'tell us what we can't know' (56). Entering the world of medieval thought and experience from explicitly twentieth-century viewpoints, these landmark intermodernist novels splendidly pioneered the postwar mode of 'historicised fiction' which disconcerts the reader through a sophisticatedly ironic awareness of what we can't know.

NOTES

1. In a letter to L. J. Potts dated 14 January 1938, White says that he rediscovered Malory and started writing 'last autumn' (i.e., 1937), not 1936 (Gallix 86); and Warner says the manuscript of the five-book 'Arthur' was sent to Collins in November 1941, not 1942 (STW, *White* 186).
2. White never did persuade his publishers to include 'The Book of Merlyn' in *The Once and Future King*; nor did he join the RAF.
3. See Montefiore 'Sylvia Townsend Warner and the Biographer's Moral Sense'.
4. White here quotes from Malory's *Morte D'Arthur*, Book XXI, Chapter 13.
5. See Montefiore *Men and Women Writers of the 1930s*.
6. Warner is mischievously quoting Wordsworth's 'Ode to Duty': 'An old age serene and bright / And lovely as a Lapland light / Shall lead thee to thy grave'.

WORKS CITED

Auden, W. H. *The English Auden: Poems, Essays and Dramatic Writings 1927–1939*. Ed. E. Mendelson. London: Faber, 1977.

Bell, Adrian. *The Open Air: An Anthology of English Country Life*. London: Faber 1936; illustrated edition 1949.

Bingham, Frances. 'The Practice of the Presence of Valentine'. Davies, Malcolm and Simons 29–44.

Brewer, Elisabeth. *T. H. White's Once and Future King*. Cambridge: D. S. Brewer, 1993.

Byatt, A. S. (Antonia Susan). *On Histories and Stories: Selected Essays*. London: Chatto, 2000.

Connor, Steven. *The English Novel in History 1950–1995*. London and New York: Routledge, 1996.

Davis, Gill, David Malcolm and John Simons, eds. *Critical Essays on Sylvia Townsend Warner, English Novelist 1893–1978*. Lampeter: Edwin Mellen Press, 2006.

Fleishman, Avrom. *The English Historical Novel: Walter Scott to Virginia Woolf*. London and Baltimore: Johns Hopkins University Press, 1971.

Gallix, François. *T. H. White: Letters to a Friend: The Correspondence between T. H. White and L. J. Potts*. London: Alan Sutton, 1984.

Garnett, Richard, ed. *Sylvia & David: The Townsend Warner/Garnett Letters*. London: Sinclair-Stevenson, 1994.

Harman, Claire. *Sylvia Townsend Warner: A Biography*. London: Chatto and Windus, 1989.

Hartley, Jenny. *Millions Like Us: British Fiction of the Second World War*. London: Virago, 1997.

Hopkins, Chris. 'Sylvia Townsend Warner and the English Historical Novel 1936–1948'. Davies, Malcolm and Simons 117–44.

Hughes, Helen. *The Historical Romance*. London: Routledge, 1993.

Jacobs, Mary. 'Sylvia Townsend Warner and the Politics of the English Pastoral'. Davies, Malcolm and Simons 61–82.

Leavis, Q. D. *Fiction and the Reading Public*. London: Chatto and Windus, 1932.

Leighton, Claire. *The Farmer's Year: A Calendar of English Husbandry*. London: Collins, 1933.

Lukacs, Georg. *The Historical Novel*. 1961. Trans. Hannah and Stanley Mitchell. London and Lincoln: University of Nebraska Press, 1983.

Massingham, H. J. *English Downland*. London: Batsford 'Face of Britain' series, 1936.

Matless, David. *Landscape and Englishness*. London: Reaktion Books, 1998.

Montefiore, Jan. 'Sylvia Townsend Warner and the Biographer's Moral Sense'. *Imitating Art: Essays in Biography*. Ed. David Ellis. London: Pluto Press, 1993.

—. *Men and Women Writers of the 1930s: The Dangerous Flood of History*. London: Routledge, 1996.

Morton, H. V.. *In Search of England*. London: Methuen, 1927.

Mulford, Wendy. *This Narrow Place: Sylvia Townsend Warner and Valentine Ackland: Life, Letters and Politics 1930–1951*. London: Pandora, 1988.

Sturt, George. *The Wheelwright's Shop*. Cambridge: Cambridge University Press, 1923.

Warner, Sylvia Townsend. *After the Death of Don Juan*. London: Chatto and Windus, 1938.

—. *The Corner That Held Them*. 1948. London: Chatto and Windus, 1977.

—. *Diaries of Sylvia Townsend Warner*. Ed. Claire Harman. London: Chatto and Windus, 1994.

—. *Dorset Stories*. Ed. Judith Stinton. Norwich: Black Dog Books, 2006.

—. 'The Historical Novel'. 1940. Reprinted in *Journal of the Sylvia Townsend Warner Society* (2007): 53–5.

—. *Letters*. Ed. William Maxwell. London: Chatto and Windus, 1982.

—. *Lolly Willowes: Or the Loving Huntsman*. London: Chatto and Windus, 1926.

—. *New Collected Poems*. Ed. Claire Harman. Manchester: Carcanet, 2008.

—. *Summer Will Show*. London: Chatto and Windus, 1936.

—. 'Sylvia Townsend Warner in Conversation'. *PN Review* 23 (Nov–Dec. 1981): 35–7.

—. *T. H. White: A Biography*. London: Jonathan Cape and Chatto and Windus, 1967.

—. 'The Way I Have Come'. 1939. Reprinted in *Journal of the Sylvia Townsend Warner Society* (2007): 1–9.

White, T. H. (Terence Hanbury). *The Book of Merlyn: The Unpublished Conclusion to the Once and Future King*. Austin and London: University of Texas Press, 1977.

—. *Burke's Steerage: The Amateur Gentleman's Introduction to Noble Sports and Pastimes*. London: Collins, 1938.

—. *England Have My Bones*. London: Collins, 1936.

—. *The Ill-Made Knight*. London: Collins, 1941.

—. *The Once and Future King*. London: Collins, 1958.

—. *The Once and Future King: The Complete Edition* (including 'The Book of Merlyn' and an 'Afterword' by Sylvia Townsend Warner). London: Harper Collins, 1996.

—. *The Sword in the Stone*. London: Collins, 1938.

—. *The Witch in the Wood*. London: Collins, 1940.

Willcocks, Rachel. 'Re-Imagining the Middle Ages'. *Journal of the Sylvia Townsend Warner Society* (2006): 39–54.

3

'A STRANGE FIELD': REGION AND CLASS IN THE NOVELS OF HAROLD HESLOP

John Fordham

For Harold Heslop and other working-class writers who emerged during the interwar years the 'strange field' they entered was that of literary production itself: unfamiliar territory to those who, despite having little formal education or time for intellectual work, collectively contributed to what became known as 'proletarian literature'.[1] The nature and quality of such a new form was within a developing culture of the Left a constant subject of debate, encouraged and extended during the 1930s by the growth of small periodicals and magazines, to which both bourgeois and working-class intellectuals contributed.[2] Here, the emerging critical consensus about proletarian literature was that, in returning to the socially and politically engaged forms of realist writing, it constituted a rejection of the experimental, less accessible modes of modernism; but this does not take into account the extent to which the writers themselves were adopting the new modernist techniques. In Heslop's work, for instance, we can identify a symbolic vocabulary of space that enhances and extends a chronicler's concern with memory or historical moment, but the narrative structure lacks the clearly discernible 'spatial turn' that defines any fully developed postmodern cultural form (Jameson 154). This chapter traces the components of a form that is not strictly speaking modernist nor in any way that has heretofore been defined, 'postmodernist'. It exists, as do its principal figures, in the liminal space of *the between*: the intermodern that emerges *after modernism* and which is defined by a constant textual struggle to elaborate the experience of an emergent historical condition.

MODERNISM: THE GREAT SEPARATION

As Raymond Williams has argued, the modern movement was from the outset characterised by a spatial convergence: a gravitation towards the focal space of the city by disparate individuals who, without a sense of any common social or even national ground, became part of a community of the intellect and of the 'medium' in which they worked (Williams 154). Membership of a modernist loose assembly of exiles resulted in an amorphous sense of social identity characterised more by what separated it from the cultures of origin than by any common factor among exiles. At the same time, however, an anxiety was felt about what, in the process of separation or renunciation, had been lost. The feeling of isolation, not wholly compensated for by the new exilic relations of the city coterie, led to a casting around for what might provide that sense of being rooted: a new source of rootedness was discovered in a set of cultural realignments with, or idealisations of, class, nation, region or province. Place then in the intermodernist text becomes the locus of conflict between the priorities of settlement or community and those of movement or mutability. In spatial terms, there is a process of convergence as well as one of dispersion, of return and re-vision, which marks out a space within which old affinities and affections are reaffirmed. It is particularly during the interwar years that such conflicts are overdetermined by a third factor: namely, as a result of a widening of the public and political spheres of activity, and of the possibilities of travel, the development of interests and allegiances beyond the nation state and its restrictive boundaries.

The 'production' of an intermodern cultural space is traceable to modernism's seeming interruption of the flow of cultural and social continuity: first codified by Nietzsche as the intellectual exile's breaking of the ties of social obligation, the overcoming of youthful 'diffidence and delicacy before all that is time-honoured and dignified, [and of] gratitude for the ground out of which [he or she] grew'. This is 'the great separation [which] comes suddenly, like the shock of an earthquake . . . a rebellious despotic, volcanically jolting desire . . . to become alienated, cool, sober, icy' (Nietzsche 6). The overwhelming 'desire' to be free of the bonds of home is the initial impulse that will eventually produce Nietzsche's ideal 'free spirit' of the future; its seismic impact was in turn felt by the working-class provincial, and Nietzschean adherent, D. H. Lawrence, who also identifies individuation as a process towards some ideal state: a movement away 'from admixture' towards 'utter individuality' (Lawrence 432). The barriers to a more perfect 'distinct being, who must act in his own particular way to fulfil his own individual nature' are, above all, those restrictions of the collective life, whereby 'the individual succumbs to what is in its shallowest, public opinion, in its deepest, the human impact by which we live together, to form a community' (Lawrence 439–40). That deepest impact, however, suggests a way back from an achieved distance to experience place less in an 'abstract way' – that is 'indirectly through the mind' – and more 'directly through the senses' (Tuan 152–53), a mode of apprehension more conducive to Lawrence's preference for feeling over intellect. Although this chapter addresses the larger geographical space of the industrial North-East, the region inspires through its cultural forms as much of an emotional commitment as any personal attachment to hearth and home. If modernism has appropriated the meanings of place by means of its hierarchical ordering or spatialisation, the industrial novels of the interwar years invite a closer affiliation with communal forms of social existence; so that the fulcrum of perception shifts away from the city and back to the region, from the amorphous community of intellect to that of the clearly defined lived experience of the local; it is in the return to community, suggested in Lawrence's later works, that the *miner* novelists of the 1930s, such as Heslop, begin to make significant interventions.

PRODUCING INDUSTRIAL SPACE

Heslop's local world was constructed out of his experience of 'northern' mining communities: New Hunwick, County Durham, where he was born in 1898; his first work underground, aged 13 years, in Boulby, North Yorkshire; and Harton Colliery, South Shields, where he worked as a miner until 1927 (Heslop, *Old Earth* 8, 184). At the same time, however, representations of the local are framed within Heslop's wider experience of travel, both within the political arena of the nation – as trade union activist and student at the Central Labour College, London (1924–26) – and beyond: as a British delegate to the Soviet Union's second Revolutionary Writers Conference (1928), and later working as agent for that government's Intourist travel organisation (Heslop, *Old Earth* 11–15, 195–242, 250–68). It is such a diversity that ostensibly locates him within the political arena of a 'popular front' cultural consensus and the assumption that social or socialist realism was the new more appropriate form, but Heslop's 'intermodernism' refuses any easy assimilation into either the Soviet or English models of the 'proletarian': spatial experience is represented in Heslop's work on multiple levels, both spatial and temporal, not on any single plane, consistent with certain forms of realism.[3] In Lefebvre's formulation, space in any society is not a given but is 'produced' or 'appropriated' according to the prevailing relations of production. Social space is to be understood in the dialectical relationship between three modes of spatial experience: everyday 'practice' or action governed by the way that an individual has a '*perception* of the outside world'; a '*conception*' of space in which the individual confronts the way space has been conceived by the engineers of the built environment; and thirdly the '*lived*' space of 'inhabitants' and 'users', which is 'dominated' by the perceived and the conceived, but which 'the imagination seeks to change' (Lefebvre 38–41).

In industrial society, then, *perceived* space is the ideological medium by which the relations of production are both produced and reproduced, since living in such a society requires certain kinds of spatial 'competence' and 'performance' (Lefebvre 33). In a mining village or town, certain routes and pathways to and from work and home are designated for use, certain ways of working within the underground space are 'overseen', and certain ways of inhabiting or using domestic space are established. *Conceived* space, by distinction, is visibly conveyed by the industrial environment's signs and symbols of the relations of production; it is through those 'representations of space' that the individual's place in the industrial world is communicated. In a mining village, the dominant symbol of the relationship of worker to industry is the pithead winding gear, often though not always on a rise, and the clustering around it, or radiating outwards from it, of the crowded dwellings built for mining families. The conceived spatial relation of mining is one of prescribed domination and subordination, materially reinforced for the male worker by the vertical spaces of the industry itself: the relations of over and underground, and the everyday spatial practice of going 'doon the pit'. The *lived* space of the industrial environment has its own vocabulary of signs and symbols, but as opposed to those of the conceived space, are not spatial 'representations' but 'representational' spaces (Lefebvre 33). Lefebvre's grammatical nuance suggests a more open, differently conceived set of meanings: not imposed from outside, but derived from communal custom and practice, or created as a result of local resistance. Lived or representational space is that which is defined by the user or the inhabitant in a way that resists the established or dominant modes of spatial being, working to shift, alter or revolutionise the relations of power. In a mining village such a space is defined by the outward signs of autonomous practice: the chapel, the public house, the Miners' Lodge or Institute, public spaces for meetings such as the park or parts of the street. In regional terms, spaces are often re-appropriated by different forms of conception or practice; for example, by the construction in regional centres, such as Newcastle or Durham, of the Miners' Federation headquarters and institutions, and the occupation of the streets for 'gala' celebrations.

ORDER AND DISORDER: REPRESENTING PUBLIC SPACE

Considering Lefebvre's idea of the dialectical relationship between the categories of 'perceived, conceived and lived' space, and since, according to him, space is produced by means of symbolic or signifying systems and practices, there is a close homology between his conception and the design of Heslop's novels, the titles of which are signifiers of their spatially symbolic organisation: *Goaf* (1926),[4] *The Gate of a Strange Field* (1929), *Journey Beyond* (1930), *Last Cage Down* (1935), *The Earth Beneath* (1946). They are thus indicators of a form of 'intermodernist' response, one which appropriates the established spatial vocabulary of modernist writing with its metropolitan metaphors of distance and separation, yet is also one in which the diverse spaces and places of the region – most often referred to as 'the North' – become the site of conflict over representation itself. The symbolic strategies of the writing, although ostensibly grounded in an allegiance to place, reveal in their subtle shifts of tone an identifiable critical distance, a modernist detachment which, while surprising in a writer of Heslop's political convictions, is an inevitable consequence of the diffusion of modernist currents of thought and influence. The opening chapters of *Goaf* take the reader to the public spaces of the Darlstone coalfield,[5] beginning with the day of the annual Darlstone Gala, which is

> . . . rich in the colour of the North, full of the significance of the North, brimming with the endeavour of the North. It is made of the people who warm the earth – that breed of men who taught the world how to mine treasures from the earth. It is made of the earth dwellers. (*Goaf* 10)

As the mining communities 'clutter about their banners and follow their brass bands' the carnivalesque yet orderly occupation of the city streets is a reminder to its inhabitants of who produces their wealth: those that toil and live in its *underground* spaces. Yet the metaphor of planes or strata of social being is reinforced by the visual representation of Darlstone's space: the towering and 'overshadow[ing]' cathedral which, 'beautiful in its dignity, dignified beyond expression', represents a 'medievalism blackened by a century of coal-dust, a gem seared and scarred by men who know no better' (*Goaf* 9).

The spatial and historical hierarchy here conveys the economic realities of capitalist production, but it also reduces the region's working class to a primitive, unknowing passivity. Such a spatialisation is reinforced by the assumption of an outsider's narrative position, in which 'the North' is defamiliarised as an exotic place and its communities seen as determined or limited by its spatial horizons. Bill Watson, the ex-miner and Labour Party MP, has 'gone the way of all mining flesh – into the mines; and like all trade-union flesh – out of them', but any honour that he might have gained, the constituents of Shielding have 'either flatly rejected or refused to sanction', out of a habitual hatred of 'its sons who do things in the outer world'. His oratory at the gala, moreover, addresses the passively receptive assembly 'not as free men, but as slaves to that throat of the earth, its ropes, its clanging bells, its hideous eternal yawn' (7, 10). Although Tom Drury, the young 'Left' activist and would-be lodge secretary, is himself an 'earth-dweller', defined by a line of earth-dwellers 'reaching far back into the past', he nevertheless has 'to learn the lesson that the mass is incapable of being led for any length of time. After being led, it must be driven' (16, 71). When his lodge rival seizes the opportunity to exploit the men's anger, the narrative abandons the *lived* world of worker self-determination in the lodge meeting, and follows through the streets the *perceived* trajectory of chaos and riot; the spatial representations are then dominated by the symbolic *conception* of a 'Pandemonium' in which '[t]he huge crowd became possessed of all the devils that rage can muster' (69).

In Heslop's texts, just as the miners' occupation of the streets is at once disciplined and riotous, so the built environment can be both stable and disorderly. The greater urban district of Shielding is an extended space for working-class leisure: planned or sanctioned, unofficial or accidental. Its Marine Park in *The Gate of a Strange Field* extends inland the leisure spaces of 'the great rugged pier' and long stretches of sand to include lawns, flower beds and a bandstand. Here in the designated space and time (conventionally Sunday evening) for official working-class culture 'the proletariat is always glorious and interesting', its people 'gay in their Sunday clothes', but the narrative voice is somewhat equivocal. There is a suggestion that municipal amenities, because they are provided – grass not to be walked upon, flowers only to be gazed upon, music that is not understood – are uninspiring (*Gate* 52–53).

The potential for autonomous expression, by contrast, is to be discovered further inland along the river. Here, the industrial region, as it appears in *The Gate of a Strange Field*, is, like Darlstone, archaeologically structured by a historical layering of urban use. The names of places, thoroughfares and organisations still commemorate the life of the local saint – the Venerable Bede – but the ancient remnants, such as St Bede's Church in Yarra, have been occluded by the unplanned disorder of urban housing and the extensive industrialisation along the banks of the region's main river. Tyme Dock's slum area is 'loathsome, hideous, smelling all the smells of the earth', but the possibility of its transformation exists where 'the bones of the great departed are intermingled with the cement of modern days' (*Gate* 128, 127). In Bede Street, 'modern in the midst of such desolation' stands the 'proud' Hunton Miners' Hall. Here the spatial hierarchy in which fleeting modernity is subordinated to ancient stability is overturned by a textual endorsement of organised labour's self-determined political future; the miners' hall is a place of 'love and esteem and hate and scorn' but to a young worker it represents 'the other side of the shield' of trade-union membership: the intellectual endeavour of miners, which defines a 'life ever so rich and expressive' (127, 134).

Such a richness is endorsed, self-referentially, by Heslop's own linguistic style. In *Goaf*, the centre of Shielding itself is dominated not by Bede, but by St Hilda, whose name is given both to the colliery, with its 'towering monstrosity of pit-head gearing' and the church which forms the fourth side of the market square. The 'grey, bald, closely shaven St. Hilda's Church . . . stretches a withered arm over the time-worn gravestones about the forgotten dead'; while on the other three sides 'stand public houses cheek-by-jowl, or leaning against each other over shops displaying rubber goods' (*Goaf* 14–15). The description reveals a spatial division between the imposed conceived spaces of work and religious practice, and those that are defined by popular use. The lugubrious *memento mori* of both pit-head and church are tempered by the cheerful personification, in which a fading bourgeois Sunday respectability is being mocked by Saturday night inebriation, and covert sexuality.[6]

In *Gate*, the spatial practice of a 'town in search of a bargain', is variously represented by the relatively innocuous 'delights' of the market itself, the 'wonderful sight' of Shielding's 'provincial and proletarian' Empire Theatre, or the darker spaces of 'oyster bars, public houses and prostitutes' (*Gate* 20–21). From the narrative perspective of the detached spectator, or of the native returned, much of what is observed is, in retrospect or at distance, deplored: it is a 'world of depravity'; but also it is a 'Saturday night . . . of amazing adventure' (*Gate* 16) through which the young miner moves, as does the user or 'practitioner' of the modern city, defying the '"geometrical" or geographical space of visual, panoptic, or theoretical constructions' of conceived space and creating a '"metaphorical" or mobile' urban world. The practice of 'walking' the urban streets produces surprising or informal ways of experiencing that space, creating holes or fissures in the 'accepted framework, the imposed order' (de Certeau 93, 107). Shielding also offers the excitement of the forbidden: of being 'lost . . . among the crowds', the fairground territory of predatory males in search of expectant females, and the enjoyment of the sight of 'strange men . . . who brought with them the mystery of ships and strange lands' (*Gate* 17, 18).

The symbolic spatial divisions between the proscribed and the unsanctioned areas of the public domain are paralleled in the representations of private space. Here, what is lived has to be established in the face of what is spatially provided. The privations of poverty, of a family crowded in a home that is 'uncomfortable, loveless, crude' (*Gate* 17) are counteracted by the symbolic centre of the miner's cottage: the built-in fireplace or range. As an object that locks the miner into the system of commodity exchange, it is 'a huge steel affair, built for the purpose of consuming coal', but every newly established home carries the memory of the *hearth*; the promise of a future which 'seemed to be outlined in its rosy heart' (*Gate* 101). Moreover, the central hearth is for Heslop typically 'northern', a local expression of endurance or resistance in the face of chronic hardship. Although continually burning both summer and winter – 'the most wasteful thing in the world' – the effect of the 'northern fireplace' is to engender a symbolic and sustaining warmth; the energy source of both fresh bread and the essential hot water. For Jim Cameron in *Last Cage*, it is a 'glorious thing to wash away the smell and filth of the mine, to become noble once more', while 'the warmth from the fire kindled fresh lights in his body'. Forgetting 'the tearing of men at toil and the gentle sobbing of the overworked ponies . . . [t]he fire lit new peace within him and he became a Hercules loving his frame'. Just as the hearth warms and rejuvenates, so too does its keeper, the miner's wife or mother. The ritual of carrying, filling and emptying the huge bath is emblematic of the totality of Elsa Cameron's life of 'struggle': since '[s]he was of the mines, born and bred deep down in the vales beneath the tombs[; h]ers was the tenacity of the dark places' (*Last Cage* 18–19, 89).

The 'Goaf': The Lived Underground Space

The link between an everyday surface existence and the underground space upon which it depends reveals a dialectical potential of darkness – the process of production at once oppressive and a source of powerful resistance – which is further realised in Heslop's deployment of the 'northern' word 'goaf'. It is through its symbolic resonance that the novels more fundamentally assert the lived or representational ground of mining experience. Its dialectical nature is evident from the first novel, in the way that it forms the core metaphor of a form which, beneath its ostensible realism, discloses a 'strange otherworld of dark anxiety and existential terror' (Holderness 27).[7] Because of the danger of imminent collapse, the goaf is like 'the gaping jaws of some immense hell' an 'awe-inspiring . . . fearful' presence, 'the home of a tremendous darkness . . . soundless as the uttermost depths of the sea'. Yet the word is used almost affectionately since there is also 'a superb dignity of danger about the goaf' (*Goaf* 124, 25), consistent with the paradoxical pleasure that miners experience in the 'gleaming seam of silver coal', the love of a 'darkness [that] is so intimate, so much part of their lives' (*Goaf* 113).

The image of the goaf works as a spatial metaphor on other dialectically related levels. As a symbol of the mine's dangers – it also means 'the part of [a] mine forbidden entry' (Griffiths 66) – it signifies to both worker and management alike the prohibited areas of everyday spatial practice, but in both the first novel, in which its symbolic potential is being worked out, and in the later *Last Cage Down*, the goaf becomes the site of struggle; over the extent to which the conceptions and practices of industrial organisation are subject to dispute by the lived experience of working underground. In *Last Cage Down*, Cameron, a skilled miner and the local 'lodge secretary', is also haunted by the goaf; a collapse of which during his working boyhood had 'drench[ed] his coming manhood with a sick fear of the mines' unknown' (*Last Cage* 9). Yet his fears are now exacerbated by managerial proposals to resume, by the use of new machinery, the mining of an abandoned and 'uneconomic' coal 'seam', which is surmounted by dangerously unstable rock. Here the goaf underpins the incursion of the miner's delegation into the territorial space of the colliery office, disclosing the yawning historical gap between working practices and managerial conceptions, between the unknown consequences of 'rationalisation' – what the manager Tate refers to as 'all over the earth, a cleansing process at work' – and the local knowledge of everyday accidents and full-scale mining disasters. For Cameron, this is the seam that killed his father; its reworking must be prevented by all the power of trade-union resistance, invoked by his defiant prophetic question to Tate, 'Shall you slay us men? . . . Shall you slay my people?' (*Last Cage* 32, 35).

The prophetic irony of the utterance is of course clear from the novel's title, but 'goaf' also signifies by the degree to which it is traversed or overcome. In the first novel, Tom Drury survives his entombment under a coal face fall by scrambling through into the forbidden space of the goaf, and is rescued by his political rival, Bill Watson, who also, expressly 'against the wishes of the colliery management', ventures after him (*Goaf* 215). A similar solidarity among political adversaries is achieved by another underground convergence in the closing chapters of *Last Cage Down*, in which Cameron descends to rescue the communist, Joe Frost (*Last Cage Down* 337). The symbolic union of the miners underground is achieved as a result of a shared knowledge of the lived space of the mine; a rational overcoming of an irrational spatial practice and a triumph over the *spaceless* darkness.

REGION INTO NATION: THE WIDENING ARENA

If the defiant entry into the 'goaf' and the surmounting of its terrors signify Heslop's novels' endorsement or reaffirmation of local knowledge and practice, then the more extended spatial metaphors of his writing critically assess the local within a wider national and international context. Joe Tarrant's earliest experiences of domestic squalor produce in him a desire to escape 'the shackles of industry' and to achieve 'a freer and better existence' (*Gate* 14, 35). For the solitary adolescent, such a desire is romantically inspired by Shielding's location as a sea-port and resort (*Gate* 35, 95); yet the romance of the sea soon gives way to an imaginative curiosity of a different order: that which is satisfied by an involvement with the broader networks of trade-union and political organisation. However, what might be a consistent homologous relation between spatial movement and historical progress is denied by a continuing dialectic of region.

The Gate of a Strange Field, in particular, addresses the relationship between region and nation, and is the novel which, most among Heslop's writing, follows closely the actual events of industrial struggle in the coalfields. After the postwar 'decontrolling' of the mines, there was during the 1920s a constant determination by the owners to increase working hours and decrease wages (Garside 175–76). It was the resulting acrimonious relationship between the miners and the capitalist owners that led to the bitter Lock-Out of 1921 and the General Strike of 1926 and dominated the years of economic depression and unemployment during the 1930s. The industrial struggles of the years from 1920 to 1926 form the basis of Heslop's narrative argument about the comparative merits of regional as opposed to national responses and forms of organisation. Miners' trade unionism in Darlstone County is focused almost entirely on local action through the 'lodges' and on representation at the regional headquarters;

Joe Tarrant's political 'awakening' begins with the realisation that the miner 'has too much at home', and is over-concerned with 'argu[ing] the "local position"' (*Gate* 118). The narrative trajectory is subsequently constituted by Joe's progress from assistant lodge secretary, to local executive committee member and national delegate. However, at the same time, there is a growing sense in the narrative of a failure of the rank and file by its representatives at the national level; firstly by the withdrawal of supporting action of its fellow unions in the Triple Industrial Alliance;[8] and secondly by what Heslop calls settlement of the 1921 strike by a 'trick', a reference to the National Executive's 'taking power as a Committee to negotiate a wages settlement' without insisting on a national wages structure (*Gate* 121–23, 27; Arnot, *Years* 330). Nevertheless, Joe is increasingly dissatisfied with the 'political wilderness of Shielding' (*Gate* 158) and dismayed by the narrowness of working-class culture: 'beer and fierce joy so long as the money lasts' (*Gate* 145).

The widening of Joe's political horizons is, moreover, reinforced by his affair with the educated miner's daughter, Emily Rutter, who, in opposition to Joe's 'materialistic,. . . political philosophy', is guided by an evangelistic idealism to achieve 'a *peaceful* . . . transition to heaven on earth' through the Labour Party. Although Joe is uncomfortable with such reformism, his sexual and political liaison – for which he deserts his wife, Molly, and young child – coincides with a new sense of mobility, and enables him to eschew the morally proscribed 'parochial wilderness of the North' (*Gate* 143, 177). Such a symbolic narrative forms a parallel to Joe's outward journey from regional to national action, as a member of the Executive Committee during the National Strike, but it is also characterised, as are the events of 1925–26, by a movement towards crisis. If the North is a wilderness, then it is equalled by Joe's wild sojourn through the 'wastes of Westminster' paralleling the political events from July 1925, through the National Strike of May 1926, and the long 'lock-out' of the miners over the subsequent seven months, at the end of which Durham was the last coalfield to capitulate (*Gate* 189; Arnot, *Years* 506). The section called 'Strife' constitutes a significant development of *Gate*'s realist or *Bildungsroman* narrative, and the completion of Joe's political education when, moving back and forth between centre and region, he comes to realise the limitations of the then present trade-union structure and its inability to effect any radical political change. In an often vituperative tone, the narrative voice describes Joe's discovery in the place of 'a fighting organization . . . a nauseating, clique-manufacturing hideousness'; an 'inner temple' of officials who, 'kept . . . in the lap of luxury . . . buried the dead that lay out on the plains of industrialism' (*Gate* 185). The suggestion is of an unwitting collusion of miners in their own demise; the lack of any local wisdom about 'strikes on a grand scale' is paradoxically equalled by a naive regional faith in the renewed national alliance of trade unions in support of the miners' struggle. It is with particular bitterness that a 'saddened'

Joe observes that locally 'the men did not understand the strike': 'they could not . . . see the coming and going of leaders desirous of escaping from the situation; they could not appreciate treachery' (*Gate* 232–33).

Joe's experience confirms other accounts of the capitulation of the trade union General Council; a group of men who arbitrarily called off the strike under the mistaken impression 'that an honourable understanding had been reached' with the prime minister. What they assumed to be 'assurances that a settlement of the mining situation can be secured' proved to be illusory (Arnot, *Years* 453, 450; Branson and Heinemann 101). Such a devastating betrayal of the rank and file at the national level is not offset in the novel by any regained faith in local or regional resistance; as a result of the strike Shielding is a dispirited place, like a mine 'polluted by blackdamp' (*Gate* 232). Yet a kind of redemption of the North is nonetheless discovered in Heslop's symbolic deployment of the romance plot. The narrative trajectory is built not only on the crisis of trade unionism, but also on that of Joe's romantic relationship with Emily. Her longing for 'industrial peace' symbolically parallels the treachery of the leadership, and Joe relinquishes her intellectual companionship in favour of Molly who, after their mutual reconciliation, becomes the idealised figure of both class and sexuality (243, 285). Despite her relative simplicity, and her desire not to return to a hated Shielding, Joe rejoices in their shared denial 'that everything in this country can be got gradually, without struggling for it' (226). The narrative is resolved in a final reductionism, a pairing down to essentials – structured on feeling rather than thought – in which for Joe, trapped after a fall in the mine, 'the futile ideals' of Emily are displaced by a vision of Molly, who represents a more tangible and enduring northern essence, an *embodiment* of the greater priority of struggle (283–85).

NORTH AND SOUTH: REGION AND GENDER

Although the iconography of identity, in which woman represents some social or collective ideal, must be critically qualified,[9] Heslop's gendering of region, to a degree, addresses the ideology of patriarchy in both *Journey Beyond* (1930) and his one excursion into the formal territory of the detective tale, *The Crime of Peter Ropner* (1934). Significantly, the original title of the former was *Martha Darke*, the eponymous protagonist, who makes the metaphorical journey from the place of 'darkness' to the more enlightened space of the South (Heslop, *Old Earth* 20). The historical consequences of the 1920s 'years of struggle' are then explored in a narrative of unemployment; a representational undermining of the conceived spatial paradigm in which London, rather than the industrial North, becomes a nightmare world of poverty and privation. On Martha's journey towards her new life in domestic service, the narrative establishes, again, the dialectic of region, in which cherished memories of the North – the sea prospect from Shielding, 'the pier and all its sweet memories'

(*Journey* 10) – are juxtaposed with those that acknowledge the poverty of its environment: the 'grimy backstreets', the 'airless home', the childhood 'blotch of drab colour thrown onto the vivid canvas of life' (*Journey* 12). London offers Martha the opportunity to 'get away from Shielding into a newer, a less stultified atmosphere, where the outlook was less barren' (41), but there are continually, throughout her new life, those moments of crisis when she longs for 'the playing fields of her childhood', or of ecstasy, when her 'soul had escaped and flown back to Shielding' (51, 68).

What begins as a narrative of mobility towards a new petit-bourgeois social existence – in which Martha marries a relatively prosperous shop-worker – subsequently, due to her husband, Russell's, unemployment, shifts to one of social decline and degradation, effectively resulting in his proletarianisation. The parochial intimacy of Shielding and the North is contrasted with the vastness of London's spaces that have to be traversed in search of work: the former's 'simple philosophy of . . . do as best you might . . . that comes to the miner from the strata, thousands of feet below the bones of the dead' forms the bedrock of Martha's 'tenacity' against Russell's discouragement and increasing dependency (204). The northern metaphor of vertical space compares favourably with London's historical layering, whereby Southwark, political and cultural birthplace of '[t]remendous historical processes', is now the place where they are 'returning to dust', where 'the modern world was dying' (*Journey* 188–89). Most devastating of all, however, in terms of the novel's spatial hierarchy is when Martha is imprisoned for theft, and, as a result, is disowned by her family. Despite both the corrupting influence of London and the smug moral censure of the North from which she now feels 'exiled' (230), Martha's source of moral strength remains essentially regional, an enduring northern resilience she shares with her only London friend and supporter, Patty. It is she who eventually offers Martha the practical solution of prostitution. What they have in common is an exceptional predisposition to altruism in a world in which 'we're all for ourselves' (252–53).

That same combination of regional virtues is also embodied in Jane Tillott, the miner's daughter in *The Crime of Peter Ropner*, but in this text Heslop emphasises class. After the General Strike of 1926, the Communist Party, which was gaining influence in the coalfields, advocated a policy of 'class against class', which had been adopted by the Sixth World Congress in 1928, discouraging any association with gradualist or social democratic movements in working-class politics (Branson and Heinemann 103; Myant 32). The influence of 'left' political tendencies within British trade unions is discernible in Heslop's detective novel, set in pre-war Britain, but written as a direct result of his involvement in the Minority Movement – an unofficial grouping of militant trade-unionists – which itself reaffirmed the political priority of class struggle (Heslop, *Old Earth* 17, 18). The failed alliance between working-class and bourgeois forms of political organisation is represented by a symbolic union between the maid, Jane, and her employer, the timber importer, Peter Ropner. As with Martha Darke, there is the quality 'of the spirited old North' in Jane, but also she embodies the enduring moral worth of 'the peasant who knows nothing nobler than splendid toil' (*Ropner* 170, 132); a direct antithesis of the southern 'bourgeois society' of corruption and monetary interest in which she becomes embroiled. After Peter Ropner has killed his wife's lover and returns, a weakened figure, to the house, Jane determines 'to make him a man once more'. Her physical and sexual 'conquering' of him, while holding out the prospect of moral and class redemption, eventually proves futile (*Ropner* 172–73). Returning from prison, Ropner learns that his victim did not drown in the Thames to which he was violently consigned, and the perpetrator is again consumed by the same murderous impulses. Peter Ropner's crime, then, is his inability to see beyond his own narrow self-obsession, which is inextricable from the *self*-interest necessary for commercial success.

BEYOND THE NATION STATE

Whereas Ropner's experience is characteristic of bourgeois subjectivity, trapped within its own isolation (which prison merely exacerbates), that of Joe Frost in *Last Cage Down* is of the working-class intellectual politically expanded by the new Russia of the Soviet Union. Here the spatial conflict is defined less by regional and more by larger geographical differences. Jim Cameron, like Peter Ropner, is also motivated by personal animosity, and threatens to kill the mine manager should resumption of work at the dangerous Yard Seam prove fatal; but although he is a respected leader and skilled orator, his interests are 'local and nothing more'; unlike his older and wiser comrade, Joe Frost, he does not see the 'tremendous fiery beauty of the revolution, the storm and stress of endeavour, roaring about history' (*Last Cage* 68, 76). As Jim's position is made increasingly precarious by clamorous public declarations of his hatred, Joe tries to persuade him that Tate is not a personal but a 'class enemy' and meanwhile quietly discourses – at street corners, at after-work classes – on Soviet progress on a massive scale. Both 'lodge' anger at Franton colliery and Darlstone district's preference that disputes were 'settled amicably', are inconsequentially parochial compared to Joe's visions of 'building socialism' at the Dnieper dam: 'a host of men and women pouring out their toil upon a gigantic construction which, when completed, was going to change the entire nature of the Ukraine' (*Last Cage* 51, 80). The larger image of transformation informs the final representations of 'the North', when it is eventually given to Jim to express the truth of Joe's discourse. Industrial Britain requires 'shattering and uprooting, so that the whole world could release its pent-up energy . . . so that out of the great strength of [the workers and peasants] could flow the newer, the higher, the eternal organization of mankind' (*Last Cage* 312).

Yet the nature of such a future remains amorphous, indistinct; as Joe and Jim survey the deepening effects of economic crisis, each experiences a different landscape. Joe, travelling through the region, describes a panorama of dereliction, of waste; the inactive mines and shipyards constituting a 'graveyard of gigantic industry . . . a nameless horror of industrial mortification' (*Last Cage* 295). In contrast, Jim, after Franton colliery has closed, walks through green fields of a now 'silent earth', witnessing a quieter, more natural process whereby the 'monstrous pitheads . . . seemed to blend with the quiet earth because they were part of the industrial decay'. His observation that the colliery is now 'peaceful and dying, dying in a deathly peace' looks forward to a new kind of endeavour in which industrialisation itself enters a new less destructive phase (*Last Cage* 308, 312). This vision echoes a similar kind of longing in *The Crime of Peter Ropner*:

> It is in the nature of things that Darlstone must turn back to simpler things . . . The peasant will come back to his desecrated hearth, and with a technique enriched by the passing of the years he will level the ashes which have come from other fires. (*Ropner* 132)

The suggestion here is that industrialisation has not eroded the essential and enduring pre-industrial forms of social being, but neither are the new skills disparaged or considered redundant. Such a dialectic of industry, in which mining and agriculture constitute two contending ideals of labouring humanity, forms the basis of Heslop's final tribute to 'the North' in a mood of postwar hope: in the Labour government's new social programmes and in its extensive nationalisation of the key industries, including that of coal.[10]

SPACE AND TIME: THE RETURN TO REGION

The Earth Beneath (1946), a chronicle of the Akers family from the early to the late nineteenth century, is underpinned by its retrospective on another 'tremendous moment in the history of the earth' (*Earth Beneath* 35), when the 'peasant' farmer, forced off the land by an act of legal trickery, leaves the place where he had 'walked . . . with slow strides, and with great clods of clay upon the soles of his boots, binding him to the land'. When John Akers settles in the rural community of Higrole and with his own rudimentary tools cuts the first drift, there is that initial feeling of wonder when he and his 'marras' first pause, 'their eyes glittering with satisfaction' and then uncover the seam where the coal 'lay in all its pristine loveliness to receive their strength' (Heslop, *Earth Beneath* 37, 53).

The moment of the production of industrial space on the rural/industrial borderland never occludes the representational spaces of a peasant social existence, since there is a continual sense that the 'earth' of the novel's title represents both the recently disturbed underground strata and the chronically tilled land beneath the labourer's feet. The latter, as signifier of an older lapidary force, assumes a moral and judgemental function when the earth itself raises a 'levy' on those who 'ventured to intrude upon the peace of its aeons'. The mine's first victim is a child, and when it is brought to the surface the magnitude of the achievement diminishes: 'Behind them, the newly-riven coal glinted in the light of a candle which they had forgotten, a cold, unforgiving glitter in each of its thousand eyes' (*Earth Beneath* 55).

From the cradle of industrial Durham, the novel expands historically and geographically into the diverse places of the region – to the different spatial experiences of seaport, city, village and town – and recalls those previously established panoramic narratives of broad historical transition inaugurated by Lawrence's *The Rainbow* (1915).[11] Yet *The Earth Beneath* is also marked by a spatial organisation that is much more narrowly focused on place than Heslop's previous two novels. The events and social revolutions of the century are certainly registered – references to the Chartists, the growth of trade unionism, the wider world of political change, even Marx – but these take second place in a narrative whose main preoccupation is always with the enduring human qualities of those that work the earth in a particular location. Characteristic of its spatial priorities are the alternating perspectives of distance and proximity. Imagining the social and physical transformations that coal will effect, the narrative voice sees from a distance 'Durham's lovely cathedral' casting a 'wistful stare over the conspiracy of artless men as they swarm in the fields of its forgotten ages', yet the image of industrial sprawl yields at closer quarters, in the underground spaces, to an aesthetic of mining, the work of which is 'the prerogative of gigantic men' whose movements 'were the very art creations of majestic strength and subtle craft' (*Earth Beneath* 65, 178).

However, the narrowing of focus onto the lived spaces of labour suggests that those whose world is so enclosed do not have the benefit of the wider vision. The paradox of guileful simplicity here reveals, again, an unknowing collusion of miners in a process of destruction. The summation of John Akers's achievement compares his skill to that of the cathedral's builders: while the latter 'had lifted beauty to the heavens', the builder of Roughing Gap colliery 'had sunk ugliness into the earth. In the eyes of John Akers the ugliness passed for beauty, a beauty which always culled [sic] from him a sigh of contentment' (181). Despite the artisanal pride that defines the labouring generations of the North-East, John's virtues are contained within narrow horizons, having 'asked no more of life than the satisfaction of labour completed honourably and well' (303).

The dialectic of space is finally emblematic of Heslop's intermodernist struggles with form and spatial representation. The 'mining way' is the consistent thread that runs through the entirety of Harold Heslop's novels; it is what defines the region's difference, its qualities of endurance, but it is also a limited *way* of life. If the production of industrial space brings ugliness then beauty prevails elsewhere in the *reproduction* of rural space on the region's industrial borderlands; an 'essence of Durham' glimpsed only when treading the time-worn paths through 'quiet fields' and 'ground, thickly wooded' (*Earth Beneath* 107). If there is a final hint of discontent, it is in John's regret that he did not return to the dales as he had originally planned. At heart, he had always remained 'a peasant' and is 'distressed' that whereas he had 'fathered a new race of men . . . [h]is sons had not known the land' (277). Bones and earth are the final symbolic components of a historically and spatially extended oeuvre, which, having explored the stranger fields of an industrialised region, returns to its moral and emotional centre: its labouring heartland. Significantly it is not the minister's casting of the earth that constitutes the final symbolic act of *The Earth Beneath* but that of the sexton, who covers 'the bones of John Akers with the brown clay of Higrole . . . slowly, almost tenderly, as if the task was one that honoured him' (324). The supervention of the customary benediction by the labourer's tribute is emblematic of Heslop's textual class struggle: to find its own intermodern way in the interim years of cultural uncertainty.

Notes

1. 'Proletarian literature' is here defined as that which is produced by working-class writers, and does not include works *about* working-class life by outsiders: as for example Henry Green's *Living* (1936).
2. For the debate, see Margolis (23–24), a condensation of 'The Writer's International Controversy' in *Left Review*.
3. As for instance in texts that construct a reader who identifies with just 'one set of discourses and practices' (Belsey 91)
4. Goaf: a north-east dialectic term which Heslop defines as 'the space between the floor of the mine and the roof when all the coal has been extracted' (Heslop, *Last Cage* 8). *Goaf* is the title of the first British publication in 1934, but the novel was initially published in the Soviet Union in 1926, translated into Russian as *Pod Vlastu Uglya* (Heslop, *Old Earth* 12).
5. Heslop substitutes fictional for local names as follows: Darlstone (Durham); Shielding (South Shields); Yarra (Jarrow); Tyme (Tyne).
6. The phrase 'rubber goods' is a euphemism for condom.
7. The reference is to the work of the miner novelist Walter Brierley, but the method is characteristic of the genre.
8. An alliance, created in 1915 between the MFGB, the National Union of Railwaymen, and the National Transport Workers Federation. See Arnot, *Years* 173–81.
9. See, for instance, Smith 207–08.
10. Nationalised in 1946; see Arnot, *One Union* 188.
11. For other antecedents, compare Lewis Grassic Gibbon's trilogy *A Scots Quair* (1932–34); James Barke's *The Land of the Leal* (1938).

Works Cited

Arnot, Robin Page. *The Miners: One Union, One Industry*. London: George, Allen and Unwin, 1979.

—. *The Miners: Years of Struggle: A History of the Miners' Federation of Great Britain (from 1910 onwards)*. London: George Allen and Unwin, 1953.

Belsey, Catherine. *Critical Practice*. London: Methuen, 1980.

Branson, Noreen and Margot Heinemann. *Britain in the Nineteen Thirties*. London: Panther, 1973.

de Certeau, Michel. *The Practice of Everyday Life*. Trans. Steven Rendall. Berkeley: University of California Press, 1984.

Garside, W. R. *The Durham Miners, 1919–1960*. London: George Allen and Unwin, 1971.

Griffiths, Bill. *A Dictionary of North East Dialect*. Newcastle: Northumbria University Press, 2004.

Heslop, Harold. *The Crime of Peter Ropner*. London: The Fortune Press, 1934.

—. *The Earth Beneath*. London: T. V. Boardman, 1946.

—. *The Gate of a Strange Field*. New York: D. Appleton, 1929.

—. *Goaf*. 1926. London: The Fortune Press, 1934.

—. *Journey Beyond*. London: Harold Shaylor, 1930.

—. *Last Cage Down*. 1935. London: Lawrence and Wishart, 1984.

—. *Out of the Old Earth*. Ed. Andy Croft and Graeme Rigby. Newcastle: Bloodaxe Books, 1994.

—. 'The Working Class and the Novel'. *The Labour Monthly* 12 (1930): 689–92.

Holderness, Graham. 'Miners and the Novel'. *The British Working-Class Novel in the Twentieth Century*. Ed. Jeremy Hawthorne. London: Arnold, 1984.

Jameson, Fredric. *Postmodernism or the Cultural Logic of Late Capitalism*. London: Verso, 1991.

Lawrence, D. H. 'Study of Thomas Hardy'. 1936. *Phoenix*. London: Heinemann, 1970.

Lefebvre, Henri. *The Production of Space*. Trans. Donald Nicholson-Smith. Oxford: Blackwell, 1991.

Margolis, David, ed. *Writing the Revolution: Cultural Criticism from 'Left Review'*. London: Pluto Press, 1998.

Myant, Martin. '1935 – The Turning Point'. *Britain, Fascism and the Popular Front*. Ed. Jim Fyrth. London: Lawrence and Wishart, 1985.

Nietzsche, Friedrich. *Human, All Too Human*. 1886. Trans. Marion Faber and Stephen Lehmann. Harmondsworth: Penguin, 1994.

Smith, Anthony D. *Modernism and Nationalism*. London: Routledge, 1998.

Tuan, Yi-Fu. 'Place: An Experiential Perspective'. *The Geographical Review* 65 (1975): 151–65.

Williams, Raymond. *The Politics of Modernism: Against the New Conformists*. Ed. Tony Pinkney. London and New York: Verso, 1989.

PART II
COMMUNITY

4

STELLA GIBBONS, EX-CENTRICITY AND THE SUBURB

Faye Hammill

Outside the window, rows of little houses and gardens went past, with occasionally one of those little ruins that may be seen all up and down the railway lines of Greater London since the autumn of 1940, and in the blue sky the balloon barrage was anchored low above the roofs and gleamed pure silver in the evening light. The train was just leaving the suburbs and the barrage and entering the unprotected country. Shame, thought Alicia, who, like many other people, was rather fond of the balloons.

(Gibbons, *The Bachelor* 28)

In *The Intellectuals and the Masses* (1992), John Carey writes: 'The rejection by intellectuals of the clerks and the suburbs meant that writers intent on finding an eccentric voice could do so by colonizing this abandoned territory. The two writers who did so were John Betjeman and Stevie Smith' (66). Whilst Carey's insight forms a useful starting point for this discussion, his restriction of the suburban literary terrain to just two writers must be disputed. Many other names should be added to the list, and one of the most important is Stella Gibbons, who wrote in – and about – the north London suburbs throughout her career. Her novels resist the easy assumption that suburban culture is unchallenging, intelligible, homogeneous and highly conventional. Gibbons's fictional suburbs are socially and architecturally diverse, and her characters – who range from experimental writers to shopkeepers – read and interpret suburban styles and values in varying and incompatible ways. At times, she explores the traditional English ways of life which wealthy suburb dwellers long for and seek to recreate; at other times, she identifies the suburb with the future, with technology, innovation and evolving social structures.

In Gibbons's best-known book, *Cold Comfort Farm* (1932), there are no suburbs, only the two extremes of central London and deepest Sussex. Nevertheless, as Raymond Williams notes in *The Country and the City* (1973), there is a 'suburban uneasiness, a tension of attraction and repulsion' in *Cold Comfort Farm*'s attitude towards the countryside and toward the literature which celebrates it (253). The novel's complex response to both rural England, on the one hand, and the ultra-modernity of interwar London, on the other, is what makes it – in effect – a suburban text.[1] Yet, like Gibbons's other books, *Cold Comfort Farm* refuses to endorse any singular or stable suburban view-point; the tendency of her oeuvre is to construct the suburb as a place which expands the range of possible points of view on British modernity.

During the 1930s and 1940s, Gibbons wrote several novels focusing more explicitly on suburban environments: *Enbury Heath* (1935), *Miss Linsey and Pa* (1936), *My American* (1939), *The Bachelor* (1944) and *Bassett* (1946).[2] These fictions pay detailed attention to the forms of domestic and professional work that sustain suburban existence, as well as to the impact of war on this lifestyle, and they combine affectionate celebration of the pleasures of the North London environment with a certain dismay at the ecological effects of the expanding city. For Gibbons, the suburb offered an ideal vantage point for exploring both urban modernity and countryside traditionalism, and for observing both literary modernism and the vestigial Romanticism of popular rural fiction. Her suburban location also correlates with her ex-centric positioning in relation to metropolitan literary culture and her resistance to processes of canon-making and consecration.

This essay will explore the pre-war and wartime suburban geographies mapped out in three novels, *Miss Linsey and Pa*, *My American* and *The Bachelor*, a selection which reveals the range of Gibbons's perspectives on London and its environs. The discussion will examine the alternative modernities that are constructed in these novels as well as their continued investment in pastoral visions of England, arguing that the negotiation between these two impulses marks the narratives as intermodern. Gibbons's fiction upsets dualities between intellectual and bourgeois; urban and rural; modern and traditional; modernist and middlebrow; and it also challenges the gendered discourses that have reinforced these dualities. In this sense, she reinvents the suburb as a crucial site for the development of an intermodern aesthetic.

Intermodernism and the Suburb

The suburban fiction of the early decades of the twentieth century was positioned between two influential literary paradigms: metropolitan modernism and regional writing. Stella Gibbons's novels share in regionalists' nostalgia for a disappearing rural England, but simultaneously participate in the modernist engagement with the new, whether in terms of social organisation, architecture or patterns of consumption. Gibbons's relation to the modern is best understood in the framework of the more expansive definitions of modernity developed by recent research on early- and mid-twentieth-century culture. In her 2004 book *The Parlour and the Suburb: Domestic Identities, Class, Femininity and Modernity*, Judy Giles argues that: 'the paradigmatic public space of modernity has been the city . . . with the result that the private sphere has frequently been understood as a refuge from the modern, a repository of traditional values' (4). Countering this assumption, Giles takes as her starting point the contention that 'responses to "the modern" are to be found not only in narratives of the public city but also in stories of, for example, the home, consumer relations, married sexuality, domestic service' (4). Lynne Hapgood adopts a similar approach in *Margins of Desire: The Suburbs in Fiction and Culture, 1880–1925* (2005), suggesting that if we accept that modernism was an urban phenomenon, then 'the shifting of literary locations to the suburbs can also represent the desire to forge a different kind of modernity, an alternative to High Modernism, through more co-operative and popular literary forms' (10). She argues, further: 'The way in which the horizontal expansion of the suburbs challenged vertical social hierarchies is mirrored in the challenge an expanding suburban culture posed to established literary values' (5). In their suburban texts, intermodern writers such as Stevie Smith, John Betjeman, Elizabeth Bowen, E. M. Delafield and of course Stella Gibbons pose exactly such a challenge, both to the aesthetic of metropolitan modernism and to the nationalist ideology of the rural idyll. By the 1930s, modernism – the radical avant-garde of two decades earlier – had been transmuted into the dominant prestige artistic form; that is, it had become identified with 'established literary values'. Regional fiction was also, for nationalistic reasons, accorded a special prestige during the interwar years.[3] It was possible, therefore, for intermodernists to move the frontier, to discover in the suburban terrain the best possibilities for the regeneration of cultural values.

As part of their resistance to dominant literary paradigms, intermodern authors countered the tendency to associate suburbs with damage. Many influential Edwardian and interwar writers from across the range of political commitments and literary styles deplored the destruction of the countryside by housing estates and expanding transport networks. Preoccupied by their perception that a supposedly authentic English culture (strongly identified at this time with the rural) was being obliterated, these writers failed to acknowledge the suburb's potential to embody progress by improving the health and quality of life of the lower and middle classes. In *Howards End*, E. M. Forster's narrator says of a station a short distance from London: 'The station, like the scenery, struck an indeterminate note. Into which country would it lead – England or suburbia?' (29–30). The passage in Evelyn Waugh's *Vile Bodies* (1930) describing Nina's nausea on looking down from an aeroplane at a view of 'straggling red suburb; arterial road dotted with little cars; . . . some distant hills sown with bungalows; wireless masts and overhead power cables' (171) is a frequently cited expression of disgust at the homogeneity and ugliness of the suburbs. A less well known – and, in the context of the novel as a whole, more ambivalent – example comes from Rosamond Lehmann's *The Weather in the Streets*: 'Every time I come along this road there's a fresh outbreak of bunga- lows', the heroine Olivia laments, adding: 'England gets squalider and squal- ider. So disgraced, so ignoble, so smug and pretentious' (24–25). This hostility to the suburb, which the novel explores rather than endorses, is founded partly on an assumption that the monotonous repeating designs which structured suburban developments corresponded to the habits of mind of the people who lived there.

Such judgements are strongly inflected by class; that is, by a contempt for salaried workers, who constituted a large proportion of the suburban popula- tion, and a fear of their increased visibility and influence. But the class identity of the suburb was, in fact, neither stable nor clearly defined. In their construc- tion, land was redistributed into small units, offering each family on a street a property which was at once individually theirs and yet exactly the same as everyone else's. Hapgood comments: 'This process of individuation became a formidable barrier to the vertical strategies of class hierarchy, social engineering and political grouping' (4). The attempt to define suburb dwellers in class terms is further complicated by the broad reach of the term 'suburb', which embraced residential areas from the leafy and spacious to the congested and jerry-built. In the different boroughs of interwar London, the standard and style of living varied enormously. John Carey's comment on Betjeman is useful here:

> What makes Betjeman distinctive . . . is the emotional intensity with which he invests the suburbs. This takes the form of love or hatred, according to the age of the suburb concerned. The older suburbs, and the even older countryside they replaced, shimmer in a nostalgic haze. . . . Modern suburbs, on the other hand, are monstrous . . . harbouring the mixed bag of atrocities with which Betjeman associates progress – radios, cars, advertisements, labour-saving homes, peroxide blondes, crooked busi- nessmen, litter, painted toenails and people who wear public-school ties to which they are not entitled. (66)

In Gibbons's suburban novels, no such clear chronological distinctions are maintained. Her narratives certainly delineate the pleasures of affluent and spacious suburbs and contrast these with conditions in the more cramped, deprived areas of London. But her scenes of ugliness are generally set in decaying Victorian terraces rather than in new commuter developments, and – unlike Betjeman – she rarely deplores the vulgarity of suburban tastes. Labour-saving devices, radios and cinema are in general endorsed, because they increase the amount and quality of leisure available to the lower and middle classes. Gibbons's fictional suburbs are populated by a mix of characters with divergent educational and class backgrounds, and indeed, much of the interest of her narratives derives from her subtle distinctions among various suburban architectures and lifestyles.

MISS LINSEY AND PA (1936)

The narrative energy of *Miss Linsey and Pa* derives largely from its geo-graphical movements through London and its environs. At the beginning, the middle-aged Miss Linsey and her elderly father are forced to leave their home in Pitt's Lane, an imaginary village on the north-western edge of London, due to the diminishing profits of their greengrocer's shop. They move to a squalid boarding house in the fictional Radford Street, which is located in Holloway, near the Caledonian Market. Here, their cousin Len and his father keep a shop. Miss Linsey takes a job housekeeping for two literary women living in Bloomsbury (Dorothy Hoad and Edna Valentine Lassiter), and subsequently a position as childminder to an educated, socially progressive family in St John's Wood (Giles and Perdita James). The Radford Street boarding house, however, proves to be the death of 'Pa', who is pushed out of a window by a mentally unsound fellow resident. Finally, Miss Linsey is rescued by her brother Sam, who takes her back to Pitt's Lane.

In the first chapter, Len remarks that Miss Linsey has to 'come to live in London and get a job' (10). To some extent, the novel sustains Len's distinction between Pitt's Lane (country) and Holloway (city), but it also traces the social and infrastructural changes which were gradually collapsing this distinction. A convention established in the early twentieth century was that anywhere within reach of the Underground system, but outside of zone 1, could be classed as a suburb, so that Holloway might arguably count as one of the innermost suburbs while Pitt's Lane, where a new tube station has just been opened as the novel begins, is indisputably transforming into an outer-edge suburb. *Miss Linsey and Pa* offers no stable perspective on urban modernity and the expand-ing suburbs, but rather a series of incompatible, subjective visions of a rapidly altering metropolis. The different characters hold varying views, with Miss Linsey's being the most complex, while the narrator's discourse is often ironic and sometimes difficult to decode. The reader is left to decide for herself which accounts of London are being affirmed and which satirised.

The primary interest of the story depends on the drama and colour of sub-urban streets, and Gibbons reveals what Carey, referring to the work of Stevie Smith, describes as 'a taste for suburban sensations' (Carey 67). At the same time, the narrative – especially in its earlier phases – evinces a distaste for sub-urban sprawl which almost aligns it with the horrified, conservative responses of Waugh or Forster:

> Pitt's Lane was only three miles from the tramlines and shops of Finchley, but until 1933 it was still a village. Then the owner of Pitt's Lane House sold the mansion and its grounds to the builders, the villas on the Pitt's Lane Estate grew like mushrooms (but were less to be desired), a branch of the Underground ran out there – and London had a new suburb.
>
> There were, of course, minor results of this event. Some charming meadows and old trees were destroyed; but we are used to that in England and we do not mind because we have plenty more. Dealers in antiques bought the wrought-iron gates of the house and the mantel-pieces carved by Sovani in 1740 with Cupids and myrtle; and Mr Harry Linsey was driven out of business by the Wholesale and Retail Fruiterers Association, Ltd. (25)

Despite these changes, Pitt's Lane remains a semi-rural location, with birds, trees and access to the open countryside. By contrast, Holloway is in general represented as a most depressing place, where 'the horizon was hidden by dull roofs, square or twisted chimneys, blackened walls and dingy windows' (12). The Linseys' lodgings feature 'a broken gas mantle, a rusty gas-ring, sickly pink walls from which in several places the paper hung damply, and scuttling beetles' (22). They have very little privacy, and are continually vulnerable to the intrusions and demands of their landlady and her other lodgers. Gibbons's unappealing representation of the boarding house constitutes an implicit affirmation of the modern suburban lifestyle to which the Linseys aspire. The early twentieth-century suburban ideal was one of comfort, modernness and above all privacy: the new garden cities and housing estates mainly consisted of semi-detached houses with the latest conveniences and individual gardens, each designed to house a nuclear family with no servants.

In *Miss Linsey and Pa*, then, the conventional duality between country and city becomes a duality between inner and outer London. A third element is added with the scenes set in bohemian households in Bloomsbury and St John's Wood, but these set-ups are invariably ridiculed. Perdita James, under pressure from her social set, feels obliged to attempt free love and peculiar new methods of childrearing, and the accounts of her attempts to raise her daughter as if she were a primitive child are ludicrous and almost surreal. She is eventually persuaded to embrace a more traditional mode of marriage and motherhood. Similarly, the novelist Edna Valentine Lassiter apparently subscribes to the idea that 'no story could end happily; every intelligent novelist knew that' (112). Eventually, though, she acknowledges a longing to make her heroine 'have a healthy baby without any details, and to write a long description . . .

of same having its bath' (112). Her repressed instinct, in fact, is to write a book very much like *Miss Linsey and Pa* itself, which has a happy ending and contains several descriptions of an appealing baby. Instead, Edna Valentine decides to enact this plot herself, and she leaves her companion Dorothy, gets married and gives up writing

Perdita and Edna Valentine are both redeemed from their forced and painful 'modernness' through the sane, practical interventions of Miss Linsey. The posturing, highbrow Dorothy Hoad, however, is beyond rescue. She considers that 'most women were cows' (61), wears jewellery of 'fiercely modernist design' (55), and dresses in men's clothes. Dorothy Hoad repeatedly interrupts conventional romance plots and disrupts family structures: she forces Edna Valentine to continue writing gloomy, shapeless stories, seeks to involve her in a lesbian partnership, and tries to prevent her engagement. Interestingly, Dorothy is also identified with the serious modernist's contempt for the masses. Accidentally passing through Radford Street, she decides that it 'was not a place where a sensitive and intelligent person would be from choice'. Buying cigarettes from Len's shop, she observes:

> how mechanically he got out the packet, without interest, lifelessly. Like an automaton. But that was what their lives made of these victims of the economic system. They became automata: wireless-educated, cinema-thrilled, fed on tinned food, having no deep contact with Beauty, without which Life was only existence. (54–55)

Len, Miss Linsey and Pa are indeed obliged to eat tinned food and entertain themselves at the cinema; this is all they can afford. But they are not in the least like automata; indeed, they all appear far more sensitive to beauty than is Dorothy Hoad. They, too, are pained by the ugliness of Radford Street, but each finds a private vision of loveliness there: Pa is enchanted by the birds kept by the owner of the boarding house, Len likes to look from his window at the tower of the Caledonian Market, 'soaring with curved eaves like a Chinese building against the turquoise sky of April' (12), and Miss Linsey thinks 'how pretty the lit shop windows looked', and admires 'the new leaves trembl[ing] in the rings of lamplight at dusk' (75). The novel – like many other intermodern narratives – awards considerable dignity and agency to respectable lower-class characters such as Miss Linsey, Len and Sam, and thus Gibbons resists the modernist insistence that suburban living and popular culture turn the lower classes into an unindividuated mass.

Certain manifestations of the modern, then, are emphatically rejected in *Miss Linsey and Pa*. They include unconventional sexual relationships, educational experiments, bohemianism and aspects of the modernist aesthetic (particularly the rejection of closure and happy endings). Suburban modernity, on the other hand, is represented ambivalently. The text reveals anxiety about the obliteration of the countryside surrounding London, and also about the ugliness and squalor which are generated in the inner suburbs as wealthier Londoners move further outwards. On the other hand, the new pleasures of suburban life are evoked in Miss Linsey's blissful resettling in Pitt's Lane with Sam and his little boy Freddie. They are pleased by the arrival of a cinema there, and also by the planned construction of a 'gargantuan' block of flats whose inhabitants will be potential customers for Sam's wireless shop (342). Sam, the narrator remarks, 'believed in progress' (342). There is an edge of irony here: Sam's point of view is set against the equally legitimate alarm of other Pitt's Lane residents at the destruction of their peaceful village. Nevertheless, Sam's version of progress is affirmed more strongly than that espoused by the supposedly radical characters such as Perdita James and Dorothy Hoad.

In the context of the debates of the era, this juxtaposition of different concepts of 'progress' takes on a politicised meaning. Judy Giles asks:

> Why, given that many of the ideas that underwrote twentieth-century town planning originated with radical or socialist thinkers and provided improved living conditions and a better quality of material life for so many in the first sixty years of the twentieth century, has suburbia been so consistently denigrated by those who espouse democratic, socialist, Marxist and broadly left-wing sympathies? (32)

Her suggested answer is that the condemnation is related to 'class divisions and anxieties at a specific historical moment as well as to gendered ideas about time and space', which have led to a perception of the suburb as a feminised space of 'mediocrity, passivity and homogeneity' (33). Stella Gibbons's novels counter this perception, presenting the suburb as a place of enterprise, variety and dynamism, and identifying the suburb dweller with the future. The Linseys' newfound prosperity results directly from their ability to adapt to the requirements of modern lifestyles: at the start of the story, the traditional family business collapsed because of competition from the larger retailers attracted by the new housing estates, but by the end, the Linseys are successfully appealing to the spending power of the newly arrived homeowners. The novel's final scene traces Miss Linsey's contentment to the combination of natural beauty, modern amenities and domestic warmth which define her home in the outer suburbs: 'It was just half-past seven on a clear, sighing moonlit night through which the leaves came rocking down; and the green and red lights of the railway, a mile off, looked very near and bright when Miss Linsey and Freddie had peeped out of the window at them while she was putting him to bed' (342). This contentment is a little precarious – will there always be space for trees in Pitt's Lane, and will the tall new buildings eventually shut out the view of the moon? There is an element of anxiety here about the liberal narrative of progress; nevertheless, if there is to be progress, the novel suggests, it cannot simply be driven from the wealthy metropolitan centre. Rather, it will necessarily depend on the dynamism and adaptability of the suburb.

MY AMERICAN (1939)

The integration of a solitary woman of precarious gentility into a prosperous, loving home also forms the basic plot of *My American*, though the protagonist, Amy Lee, is a very different kind of heroine from Miss Linsey. At the start of the novel, Amy is a child living with her intelligent yet unsuccessful father on a meagre income in Highbury Fields, North London. By the end, she is a famous author of bestselling novels, sharing a large New England house with her American husband, Bob Vorst, whom she first met at the age of twelve, when he was visiting London. The intervening chapters alternately unfold Amy's and Bob's lives. Bob is from a well-to-do, socially elite family, but a car accident leads him to become involved with a criminal gang. As for Amy, on the death of her father she is adopted into the already large family of a neighbour, and subsequently earns a living as a clerk in the office of a boys' paper, *The Prize*. She also continues to write the thrilling, Gothic stories which have always absorbed her, and once she begins to publish them, she rapidly attains wealth and popularity. A lecture tour of the US introduces her to the adult Bob, and they fall in love. A series of dramatic events connected with drugs and kidnapping intervene before they can marry.

Kristin Bluemel argues that the writers she classes as intermodern are 'importantly eccentric and radical . . . because they consistently resist inhibiting, often oppressive assumptions about art and ideology – about standard relations between literary form and sex, gender, race, class, and empire' (7–8). This argument would certainly apply to many of Gibbons's novels. Her depiction in *My American* of the success of a working-class, female author is unusual in itself; Amy's early exclusion from the literary establishment is emphasised by the contrast between her status and that of her employer at *The Prize*, Lord Welwoodham, whose private income enables him to act as arbiter of literary taste. In order to publish her work in *The Prize*, Amy must disguise her gender: she signs her first submission 'A. Lowndes', and the editor simply assumes that the story is by a man. By the end of the novel, however, the literary scene has changed, and Amy buys the ailing *Prize*. She broadens its appeal so that girls too will enjoy it, reducing the number of adventure stories and including domestic realist fiction.

The *Prize*'s shift in literary mode parallels the shift in Amy's own attitude to life. As a girl, her solitariness arose from her preoccupation with her imagined worlds:

> Day by day she cared less for people and more for imaginary pictures so strong that they were more like feelings or dreams than ideas inside her

head. . . . If she was lonely, she did not know it. The dream-images in her mind absorbed her interests and affections with dangerous ease, as anyone who has ever lived with such phantoms will immediately recall their power to do. *Empty, vast and cold were the halls of the Snow Queen. They were all lighted up by the vivid lights of the aurora.* . . . (131)

This account addresses a reader who can empathise with the protagonist, but the passage also clearly suggests the perils of such detachment from ordinary life. Amy's fantasy life feeds directly into her bestselling novels. Gibbons's critique of Amy's (and her readers') dangerous absorption in the sensationalised narratives of popular culture might at first sight seem to be connected to the strictures of intellectuals such as the Leavises and the Frankfurt group, who argued in different ways that popular fiction and the mass media degraded emotional responses and produced a false consciousness and passive acceptance of the existing conditions of life.[4] But in fact, Gibbons turns out to be concerned more with straightforward moral values and also with literary form. She has some of her American characters accuse Amy of 'glorifying criminals' (378) and making 'bad men and bad ways fascinating to our boys and girls' (297). Also Bob, drawing on his own sordid experience of gangs and criminals, tells her that her stories simply aren't convincing because she has no personal knowledge of the underworld she describes.

Once she experiences real danger and fear in her own life (when Bob is nearly murdered), Amy can no longer create fiction out of these things, and encounters writer's block. But as she settles into marriage and motherhood, she turns to 'stories of family life', which reveal 'the variety and interest of every day' (436). Gibbons points out the economic implications of this choice: 'she could no longer be called a rich woman . . . ; her new kind of book did not immediately prove so popular as her former kind' (430). Eventually, though, she wins a large audience, explicitly identified as female, and presumably also suburban. Her stories charm readers because of their authenticity: they 'communicated (because she herself felt it) to the passing of an examination or the breaking of a betrothal the excitement she had once given to escapes from death and last-minute rescues' (436).

Amy's 'second manner' is not wholly concerned with American home life (436); she also draws on her memories of London and English domesticity. Indeed, she always viewed London with the eyes of an artist, even if – as a young writer – she did not understand its potential as material for fiction. The early chapters of *My American* include detailed, evocative descriptions of the North London streets as they appear to Amy:

She took in the golden windows of the shops, the cold winter smell of the celery piled outside a greengrocer's, the lovely face of Dolores Costello gazing out dreamily from a cinema hoarding. Amy loved walking in

London; yet hardly knew that she loved it. Unnoticed as a leaf, . . . she moved lightly along, in a dream, but a dream in which she noticed a thousand funny or frightening or pretty things and people. (10)

Amy turns her gaze on the suburb, investing it with sensuality and vibrancy, and this mode of vision marks her out as an artist.[5] Her vision of London breaks through conventional ways of seeing, discovering excitement in the material suburb and the dramas which unfold there:

Amy was leaning out of the Highbury sitting-room window to get a breath of fresh air, staring at the glittering lights sweeping upwards on the hills of Hampstead and Highgate and the roofs glistening with frost under the small violet moon [and] . . . feeling how exciting was the scene spread before her.

Suddenly the side door of the house slammed and she looked down. Dora Beeding ran down the street with no hat on towards the public telephone box on the corner. Amy could hear the quick sound of her high heels on the pavement as she ran and once she slipped on the frost and only just saved herself from falling. (54–55)

Dora's mother is shortly afterwards taken away in a taxi to give birth, and the following chapters explore the daily life of the working-class Beeding family, in which Amy assumes a share. Their meals, living space, household routines and childcare practices are all detailed, as well as the operation of the bakery they own. This preoccupation with the daily lives of working people clearly marks out Gibbons as an intermodern writer, and the closing pages of the novel suggest that Amy too will begin to address such subjects in her books.

The relationship between Amy's writing and Stella Gibbons's is complex. In the early part of her career, Amy's literary aesthetic is not inspired by her local surroundings, and her approach is implicitly contrasted with Gibbons's own. The domestic material and suburban landscapes which form so much of the matter of My American differ markedly from the romantic, highly-coloured and terrifying adventures recounted in Amy's stories. But in order to prove that the best fictions are set in worlds with which the authors are familiar, Gibbons ends up in a contradictory position. Her own novel includes extended sequences set in America (a country she had not visited), and one of its plot-lines concerns crime, violence and illicit sex. To reject such subject matter, she has first to represent it, and indeed, the narrative momentum of the episodes about Bob's involvement with the gang only underlines the appeal of thriller plots. And yet, the scenes set in London and its outskirts are certainly the most memorable and effective parts of My American, so that while the novel engages with other narrative modes, it finally affirms both realism and the suburban imaginary.

THE BACHELOR (1944)

The Bachelor centres on a recently built seven-bedroom family house called Sunglades, in a village four miles from 'St Alberics' (clearly St Albans) in Hertfordshire. The name 'Sunglades' has pastoral overtones, but also an unmistakably suburban ring, as befits a house of the 'pseudo-Tudor' type (79). 'Mock-Tudor' houses were modelled on the architecture of a pre-urban England, while the larger structures of suburbs and garden cities were inspired by the ideal of *rus in urbe*, that is, the recreation of a rural lifestyle within a city by means of small private gardens and tree-lined streets. The people who live in Sunglades – a middle-aged brother and sister, Kenneth and Constance Fielding, and their cousin Frances Burton – attempt to construct a rural idyll in a location only twenty miles from London. They enjoy walking in the woods, and Constance maintains flowerbeds while Kenneth spends his evenings tending the fruit and vegetables. Their adoption of rurality as style is part of their aspiration to the traditional lifestyle of the leisure class, emblematised in the walled kitchen garden, which formerly belonged to a now-demolished country house, Treme Hall.

The narrator draws attention to the social changes which have led to the proliferation of houses like Sunglades:

> Because St Alberics was only twenty miles from London, none of the villages within five miles of it had a traditional, full village life. Improved communications, death duties, and the decline in agricultural industries, together with the building of many large handsome houses by wealthy people who had no interest in their nearest village, had reduced Treme, Cowater, Blentley and the rest to shells of villages; not deserted or decaying, but flourishing (especially since the war) with a mock-suburban life. (43)

The phrase 'mock-suburban' suggests the colonisation of rural England by suburban styles; an interesting reversal of the traditional perception of the imitative quality of the suburban aesthetic. But Gibbons points out that as London gradually connects itself to the small communities surrounding it, these villages become imitation suburbs, rather than other way around.

In exploring the economic and social relations which underlie the leisure and comfort enjoyed by the Fielding family, Gibbons also invokes the larger contexts of war and empire:

> Kenneth Fielding and his two sisters, children of a solicitor owning an old-established firm in St Alberics, had inherited in 1920 a comfortable fortune, left to them by three very wealthy old aunts. It was invested in sound undertakings in the western parts of the British Empire, and since the war, despite the crushing income tax, the Fieldings had not found themselves noticeably less comfortable. Kenneth continued to attend the

offices and nominally direct the firm that his grandfather had founded but as the years went on he tended more and more to lead the life of a retired soldier of independent means, and to leave the active management of Fielding, Fielding and Gaunt to Mr Gaunt. (23)

The relative luxuriousness of life at Sunglades astonishes the eastern European refugee, Vartouhi, who arrives to live there and provide domestic help. Her industrious labour in the house (which is minutely detailed) contrasts markedly with the idleness of Constance and Frances, whose reluctance to do their own housework emphasises their embattled sense of class identity. They also refuse to engage in the democratic and socially-levelling activity of war work. Constance, a pacifist, convinces herself that in employing Vartouhi she is furthering international understanding, though in fact her action represents a self-interested solution to the wartime shortage of domestic servants.

The unavailability of servants forced a re-evaluation of middle-class femininity, which could no longer be understood in terms of a leisured lifestyle supported by the labour of working-class women. Vartouhi's inclusion in *The Bachelor* emphasises that the privileges enjoyed in the Home Counties and the more prosperous margins of London are based, as Judy Giles puts it, on 'class inequalities that were reproduced daily . . . at the very heart of private (and feminised) life – the middle-class home' (86). The figure of Vartouhi gestures, in addition, towards a further set of inequalities based on race or ethnicity. Chiara Briganti and Kathy Mezei point out that it represents an exception to the general tendency of 1930s and 1940s domestic novels, which rarely 'incorporate issues of migration and foreign domestic spaces into their surprisingly insular portraits of home' (29). (*Miss Linsey and Pa* is another exception, since one of the Radford Street lodgers is a black man, who helps Miss Linsey on the night her father dies.) In *The Bachelor*, questions of national identity and international relations repeatedly invade the domestic sphere. They are addressed directly in the conversation of Richard, a young friend of the Fielding family, who is committed to communism and gives away most of his money to support prisoners from the Spanish Civil War. A different set of political opinions is explored in Constance Fielding's discussions with her Swiss friend Doctor Stocke, author of didactic plays about European reconstruction. He makes an extended stay at Sunglades, despite the resistance of Kenneth, who dislikes 'Foreigners all over the place', and particularly objects to a 'neutral' being accommodated in his home (263). Constance, on the other hand, finds foreigners more congenial than lower-class British people, and takes Vartouhi in on purpose to fill up one of her spare bedrooms so that she need not house any more evacuees from London. Constance's pacifism forms a stark contrast to Vartouhi's vehement opinions on the enemy nations responsible for the invasion of her country: 'I go to the Fedora Pictures to see some Germans and some

Italians and some Japanese all blown up. Is a varry good thing' (226). *The Bachelor*, then, dramatises a range of perspectives on war, without entirely endorsing any, and its larger purpose is to explore the impact of international conflict on domestic relations.

Foreign spaces are briefly represented in the novel, in the opening and closing sections set in the imaginary country of Bairamia, Vartouhi's homeland. These scenes are not really integral to the narrative, though, and the true role of Bairamia in the text is to enable the celebration of an idealised rural England. For Richard, in love with Vartouhi, Bairamia briefly provides a vision of romance. She tells him that she misses the 'little red flowers and white flowers in the mountains in my country', and the hot sun and blue sea (148), and he is enthralled. But he soon begins to reflect:

> if an Englishwoman told a Bairamian that she lived in a country where there were green meadows with rivers where blue and yellow flowers grew, and stone churches a thousand years old whose bells rang above black trees, that would seem as romantic to him as Bairamia does to me. (149)

This idyllic description is lent added poignancy by the awareness that the English landscape is under continual threat from bombs and potential invasion.

The scenes in Bairamia are not the only ones that move outside the domestic setting. The characters frequently travel to London or to St Albans, which was already in effect a suburb of London. Gibbons's representations of the sub/urban landscapes of the war years recognise their tendency to ugliness whilst also acknowledging unexpected beauties. 'St Alberics' is

> softly coloured and cheerful and pleasing to the eye, although there was not a single completely beautiful object in sight except the evening sky. The pale old houses were marred by huge advertisements sprawling across them, shouting at the people to Dig for Victory and Save Fuel, and the newer shop-fronts were either in the Diluted Gothic style of the early nineteen-hundreds or copies of brick Regency fronts that looked flat and mean; yet the ancient shapes of the streets were charming. They were like the beds of old streams: the weeds on the bank vary in thickness or type and trees are cut down or new ones grow, but the path of the water remains much the same. . . . Every now and again there were alleys leading into paved courtyards where geraniums and pansies and beans grew in window boxes outside ancient little houses, or a flight of worn steps led down to a smooth lawn. . . . It is nice to get out of London, [Betty] thought, even though it is such a little way out. (39)

Nostalgia for a picturesque but vanishing England is clearly legible here, especially in the references to imitation Gothic and Regency buildings. They are implicitly contrasted with the supposedly more authentic, traditional English style embodied in the little old cottages with their steps worn by generations of feet treading the same path.

The organic community suggested in the comparison between streets and stream beds is being obliterated by the commercial and political pressures which are brought together in the enormous advertising posters. Ironically, though, the posters demand that the people of England should return to the practices of an earlier agrarian age, becoming self-sufficient by growing their own food, and walking rather than driving. These new behaviours temporarily recreate an old-fashioned atmosphere:

> This evening the High Street was crowded, but crowded with people, instead of the lengthy procession of cars coming out from London that would have been passing through it at this time three years ago. Women were wheeling perambulators down the middle of the road and there were many horse-drawn vehicles. (38)

It is interesting that this nostalgic scene is suddenly rendered strikingly modern by the appearance of 'a graceful dog-cart driven by a girl in a sweater and trousers' (38). The whole passage describing St Alberics is ambivalently positioned between an embracing of the modern and a wistful consciousness of the past, and this is also true of the representation of suburban landscapes elsewhere in Gibbons's 1940s writing. The self-consciousness and sophistication of her fictional evocations of wartime nostalgia mark her out as an intermodern writer, who is concerned to explore the 'different kind of modernity' located beyond the limits of the inner city in a way that challenges familiar dualities of urban and rural, modern and traditional, elite and ordinary, international and domestic (Hapgood 10).

CODA

For her first novel, *Cold Comfort Farm*, Stella Gibbons won the prestigious Femina Vie Heureuse prize.[6] Her response to the award reveals how little she had sought or experienced public notice. In her correspondence with the honorary secretary of the committee, Winifred Whale, Gibbons warmly expresses her surprise and gratitude, but misapprehends the nature of the presentation ceremony, asking if it is a private meeting and whether she might bring her husband. It was in fact a large invitation-only event, which was widely reported in the London papers, and winners could submit a list of personal guests. Gibbons invited twelve (mainly her relatives), and expressed concern that this might be too many, whereas another winner, Charles Morgan, had no compunction at inviting 170 acquaintances and minor celebrities.[7] Gibbons's subsequent letters to Whale reveal her alarm at the prospect of the acceptance speech, and she asks for suggestions as to what she should talk about,[8] indicating her total inexperience in public appearances. Following her award, Gibbons was invited to become a member of the prize committee, but declined on grounds that she was too busy;[9] the real reason may have been her tendency to resist the institutions of canon-making, which of course include literary prizes. Also, Gibbons's identification with her suburban home seems consonant with her choice to remain on the fringes of metropolitan literary culture, and to critique it sceptically in her novels.

Many modernist writers contemptuously associated the suburban with the mediocre and the feminised. I would argue, by contrast, that the suburb can be productively associated with the intermodern, and both can be viewed as sites of subtle yet far-reaching subversion and challenge to dominant codes of cultural value. The work of writers such as Gibbons, Stevie Smith, Betty Miller or Rosamond Lehmann resists critical attempts to read suburban writing as the lesser half of either urban high modernism or romantic nationalist ruralism. Their intermodern perspective disrupts accepted critical paradigms, since they locate themselves in a literary no-man's land between urban high modernism and pure pastoral, between the experimental and the realist. For these writers, the suburbs offered a special point of view from which to observe both the conventional and the eccentric, both high and popular culture, and also to reflect on the spaces between them. As Giles points out: 'Suburbia, as much as the city against which it is often defined, is . . . both a product of modernity and a space in which the dilemmas and contradictions of modernity can be articulated' (33). It is, therefore, an ideal space for the intermodern writer.

NOTES

1. I have discussed this aspect of *Cold Comfort Farm* in detail elsewhere. See Hammill, '*Cold Comfort Farm*'; Hammill, *Women, Celebrity and Literary Culture* (167–73). In *Women and Celebrity*, I align Gibbons's work with the middlebrow as well as invoking the newly developed term 'intermodernism'. It is beyond the scope of this essay to define the differences between middlebrow and intermodernism, since middlebrow is a highly complex and perhaps overdetermined field. It embraces an enormous range of cultural production and extends beyond intermodernism in both geographical and chronological terms. But it is problematic because it has frequently been used in a derogatory sense. Whilst I would not wish to detach Gibbons from the broad and extremely relevant context of middlebrow culture, the more restricted category of 'intermodern' is especially helpful in interpreting the novels I discuss here.
2. Several of Gibbons's later novels are also set in the North London suburbs: *Here Be Dragons* (1956), *A Pink Front Door* (1959), *The Charmers* (1965), *Starlight* (1967) and *The Woods in Winter* (1970). Whilst these retain many of the preoccupations of her 1930s and 1940s work, certain shifts in emphasis can also be detected, correlating with the altering social structures of the post-World War II decades.
3. Anthea Trodd writes: 'The classic status enjoyed by rural writing in this period derived from the insistently diffused belief that the real England was rural England . . . in which continuity with the past was still clearly visible' (103). A common

love of the countryside, as articulated in rural writing, was constructed in political discourse as one basis for national unity.

4. F. R. Leavis propounded his campaign against newspapers mainly in *Scrutiny*, but see also Leavis and Thompson. Q. D. Leavis presented popular fiction as the enemy of serious reading and intellectual engagement (see *Fiction and the Reading Public*). The Frankfurt theorists proposed that commercialised culture had seduced the masses, negating their revolutionary potential.

5. It also suggests an interesting connection with interwar advocates of modernist visual art, who pointed to its potential for disrupting habitual ways of seeing. Frank Pick, a high-ranking transport executive who hoped that the posters he commissioned from modernist artists for display on the London Underground would transform the aesthetic sensibilities of the metropolitan public, wrote in 1927: 'There is a conventional way of looking at things which it is hard to disturb. There is a protective habit in city dwellers of not looking at things at all which is fortunate otherwise they could hardly go on living in some cities. Posters come to disturb or destroy such habit or convention.' See Pick, 'Underground Posters', London Transport Museum archives, B6 Box 4, Copy A, p. 3. (qtd in Saler 100).

6. For more detail on the prize, and the selection of *Cold Comfort Farm* as winner, see Hammill, *Women, Celebrity, and Literary Culture* 173–78.

7. FVH Papers. Folder 5/5 Letters from Prize-Winners.

8. FVH Papers. Folder 5/5 Letters from Prize-Winners.

9. Noted in FVH Papers. Item 1/2/38. Minutes, 21 Oct. 1936.

Works Cited

Bluemel, Kristin. *George Orwell and the Radical Eccentrics: Intermodernism in Literary London*. Basingstoke: Palgrave Macmillan, 2004.

Briganti, Chiara and Kathy Mezei. *Domestic Modernism, the Interwar Novel and E. H. Young*. Aldershot: Ashgate, 2006.

Carey, John. *The Intellectuals and the Masses: Pride and Prejudice among the Literary Intelligentsia, 1880–1930*. London: Faber and Faber, 1992.

Dentith, Simon. 'Thirties Poetry and the Landscape of Suburbia'. *Rewriting the Thirties: After Modernism*. Ed. Keith Williams and Steven Matthews. Harlow: Longman, 1997. 108–23.

Femina Vie Heureuse Papers. Cambridge University Library. MS Add. 8900.

Forster, E. M. *Howards End*. Ed. Oliver Stallybrass. Harmondsworth: Penguin, 1975.

Gibbons, Stella. *The Bachelor*. London: Longmans, 1944.

—. *Cold Comfort Farm*. 1932. Intr. Lynne Truss. Harmondsworth: Penguin, 2006.

—. *Miss Linsey and Pa*. London: Longmans, 1936.

—. *My American*. London: Longmans, 1939.

Giles, Judy. *The Parlour and the Suburb: Domestic Identities, Class, Femininity and Modernity*. Basingstoke: Palgrave Macmillan, 2004.

Hammill, Faye. '*Cold Comfort Farm*, D. H. Lawrence, and English Literary Culture between the Wars'. *Modern Fiction Studies* 47.4 (2001): 831–54.

—. *Women, Celebrity and Literary Culture between the Wars*. Austin: University of Texas Press, 2007.

Hapgood, Lynne. *Margins of Desire: The Suburbs in Fiction and Culture, 1880–1925*. Manchester: Manchester University Press, 2005.

Humble, Nicola. *The Feminine Middlebrow Novel, 1920s to 1950s: Class, Domesticity and Bohemianism*. Oxford: Oxford University Press, 2001.

Leavis, F. R. and Denys Thompson. *Culture and Environment: The Training of Critical Awareness*. London: Chatto and Windus, 1933.

Leavis, Q. D. *Fiction and the Reading Public*. 1932. London: Chatto and Windus, 1968.

Lehmann, Rosamond. *The Weather in the Streets*. 1936. London: Collins, 1968.

Oliver, Reggie. *Out of the Woodshed: The Life of Stella Gibbons*. London: Bloomsbury, 1998.

Saler, Michael T. *The Avant-Garde in Interwar England: Medieval Modernism and the London Underground*. New York and Oxford: Oxford University Press, 1999.

Trodd, Anthea. *Women's Writing in English: Britain 1900–1945*. Harlow: Addison, 1998.

Waugh, Evelyn. *Vile Bodies*. 1930. Harmondsworth: Penguin, 1938.

Williams, Raymond. *The Country and the City*. 1973. London: Hogarth, 1985.

5

INTERMODERN TRAVEL: J. B. PRIESTLEY'S ENGLISH AND AMERICAN JOURNEYS

Lisa Colletta

J. B. Priestley is famous as 'a man of the people', the stolid BBC broadcaster who gathered the nation round its radios in hope and pride during the early war years. Despite the fact that Priestley became a well-known novelist, playwright and social critic in the 1920s and 1930s, his reputation as a cultural figure became firmly established with his radio *Postscripts*, which followed the Sunday evening news and made him 'in many ways the voice of the 1940s, second only to Churchill in the public's imagination' (Fagge 104). It is somewhat ironic that he received his greatest fame on the radio, though, because throughout his career he maintained a deeply felt – though thoughtful – distrust of the media of mass communication and the kind of celebrity it creates.[1] Radio turned Priestley into a celebrity, and his broadcast work 'brought him national and international fame' (Buitenhuis 445). It is probably for this reason, as well as the political disillusionment that followed his being taken off the air, that he describes his radio work as being 'ridiculously over-praised, so much that I dislike hearing it even mentioned' (*Margin* 218). Additionally, it was largely his popularity as a public figure that led the cultural elite to dismiss him as a 'middle-brow' writer,[2] and he suggests in his memoirs that his celebrity, created by the mass medium of the radio, was in part responsible for the way both he and his writing were later received:

> I found myself tied, like a man to a gigantic balloon, to one of those bogus reputations that only the mass media know how to inflate. I never

asked for it, didn't want it. This sudden tremendous popularity, which vanished in a few years and indeed was put into reverse by the same mass media, gave me no pleasure, merely made me feel a mountebank. (*Margin* 220–21)

Even before the war, Priestley had his misgivings about mass media and consumerist culture, but he balanced his unease with an awareness of the democratic and technological possibilities that it could foster (Fagge 108). After the war, he felt the opportunities presented by capitalism and technology were lost, as American-style consumerism and the culture of celebrity seemed poised to swamp the rest of the world.

Priestley's position against mass culture, which he believed turned people into undifferentiated consumers and destroyed local and authentic culture and identity, plays a large part in the literary and historical assessment of his 'conservatism', of his being seen as an insular 'little Englander' whose idea of Englishness promoted a nationalist mythology. Recent scholarship has effectively challenged this view of him, examining the nuance of his cultural critique and debunking his middlebrow status.[3] This essay is not so much concerned with examining Priestley through the lens of debates about middlebrow literature, canonical modernism or even 'Englishness' per se, but instead focuses on Priestley's deeply ambivalent examination of the changes occurring in British culture in the late 1930s.[4] This ambivalence is expressed in his admiration for the authenticity and vitality of the past, though at the same time he abhors the social and economic injustice of the class system that defined it; and in his concomitant hope for the future despite his disdain for modern mass culture that turns everyone into a consumer.

The conflicts between past and present, capitalism and democracy, technology and mass media are made concrete in his examinations of England and America, and they are given literary shape in two of Priestley's travel works of the thirties – *English Journey* (1934) and *Midnight on the Desert* (1937). However, Priestley is too subtle a thinker to reduce these conflicts to the simplicity of an England v. America opposition, and both works extend and complicate his views of the enormous changes in the relationship between audiences and mass media and his speculations about what the result of these changes might mean for the latter half of the twentieth century. He saw the locus of these changes in America, and even though *English Journey* purports to be a tour both around and into the whole of England, the influence of America can be seen in nearly every aspect of his travels – from the change in social relationships and class consciousness to the manufactured quaintness of the countryside and the crass but essentially egalitarian consumerism of Blackpool. *Midnight on the Desert* is subtitled 'Chapters of Autobiography', but it is actually a travel narrative jammed with social and political observations about

America which confirmed for Priestley that it will be nearly impossible for England – or any other country, for that matter – to withstand the conquest of American popular culture brought about by the seductive medium of the Hollywood movie. Though Hollywood had an obvious appeal to intermodern writers who were interested in the making of the new and had grown weary of the grim life in England between the wars, those who went there, such as Anthony Powell, Hugh Walpole, Aldous Huxley and Evelyn Waugh, were quick to see that movies, for good or ill, were clearly becoming the most powerful story-telling medium of the age, and that Hollywood's dominance of the film industry meant Hollywood's aesthetic, moral and intellectual dominance of cultural values around the world.

This is the anxiety Priestley expresses throughout his *English Journey* as he sets out to examine the physical, social and cultural landscape of England, looking for distinct local culture that might resist the mass consumerism of contemporary life and American pop culture values. Priestley's hope was in the English people, who might draw strength from the past but reject the class system and oppressive industrialisation of the nineteenth century. He saw the economic and political contraction of the thirties and forties as an opportunity for cultural change, but he was not motivated by a desire for a return to the long ago. His relationship to the landscape and the people in it is ambivalent and complicated, admiring of local culture but looking to an invigorated future in which cities and the countryside remain vital. He imagines this future belonging to all of England's people, not just as day-trippers and tourists, but as engaged citizens who keep their homes, and work the land and are part of a community (*English* 52).

In the 'To the Cotswolds' chapter of *English Journey*, Priestley expresses little patience for those who would romanticise England's past. Throughout the work, Priestley sees nostalgia as something that props up an unjust class system and his sympathies are with the 'modern'. Dining with a 'Cotswold enthusiast', who is also described as 'a thorough hater of everything modern', Priestley counters the man's argument against the inhumanity of our machine age with the contention that

> . . . comely objects in a museum or in a rich man's house gave one a very faulty notion of the actual life of the past, when most people had to do without nearly everything and were far less merrie than he appeared to suppose, that machines, rightly used, simply did away with a horrible dead weight of miserable toil and that anyhow a machine was not the bogey thing he seemed to think it but really an elaborate tool, and that our business now was not to sentimentalise the Middle Ages but to take the whole roaring machine-ridden world as it is and make a civilised job of it . . . (50)

Priestley rarely gives in to seeing just the rural beauty of the landscape, and for him the quaintness of the villages is always connected to the people who built them and lived in them. To him the Cotswolds are 'the most English and the least spoiled of our countrysides', but the appeal rests in the congruity between the landscape and the architecture, 'an exquisite harmony of line and colour' that are products of a definite tradition (41). What is important is that the tradition was a living thing, persisting over hundreds of years, passed from generation to generation: 'If you told a Cotswold man to build you a house, this is how he built it' (41). What is lamentable is that this working tradition in harmony with the landscape is being lost to mass production and a museum-like (or movie-like) thrall to Cotswold 'charm', and the little towns and villages are becoming show places and 'glorified tea establishments for tourists. . . . Ye Olde Chipping Campden nonsense' (41). Priestley argues that the beauty of the Cotswolds should be valued as an English national treasure, but he fears that the quaintness of that life will be commodified, frozen in an imagined history.

Priestley wants to retain what is, in his view, an authentic English country-side, but this desire is coupled with a renunciation of the privilege and class system that allowed it to flourish in the first place. His trip to a manor house in the area is described with bemused censure, and he sees the owner as a parody of the country squire, 'a very courteous and charming English gentleman of leisure'; Priestley is put off by the gentleman's clothes and demeanour, by the fact that 'the twentieth century was not in evidence' (147). Though there is a certain admiration for the squire's eccentricity and his whimsical collection of spinning wheels, costumes, model wagons, weapons and old musical instruments, the values associated with country house culture have no place in the modern, industrial world. Despite heartening idiosyncrasies in the face of bland and uniform modernity, his life is essentially history dressed up in the nostalgic forms associated with traditional English country life, precisely the Englishness promoted by Hollywood movies. After discussing his visit to the manor house, Priestley reasserts the social function of his travels:

> . . . I am here, in a time of stress, to look into the face of England, however blank or bleak that face may chance to appear, and to report truthfully what I see there. I know of deep distress in the country . . . and I know there is far, far more ahead of me. We need a rational economic system, not altogether removed from austerity. Without such a system, we shall soon perish. All hands must be on deck. My eccentric but charming friend of the fantastic manor house, who lives an antique dream of life supported by an unearned income, cannot possibly be counted as a hand on deck. (49)

English Journey focuses on rural England in the first two chapters; for the most part Priestley is in towns and cities, where his narrative of nation, work, values and the people is a more comfortable fit with his interests in politics and economic justice. What he finds in both the picturesque countryside and the urban, industrialised cities is hardly reassuring. Though written when there was a craze for travel literature, *English Journey* is not the kind of narrative that was popular between the wars. As John Baxendale points out, publishers were eager to provide a growing suburban, reading population with travel books that presented a vision of England that was 'cosily reassuring and easily accessible by motor-car' (91). Most of these works reinforced ideas of national unity and a mythic past, but Priestley's concerns were more aligned with Charles Madge and the Mass Observation Movement, which called for the 'anthropological study of our civilization' (Dodd 128). Priestley was engaged in examining the social and cultural landscape of the whole nation, not just those parts that suggest a green and pleasant rural England or a sentimental view of mill towns and the working classes. His *English Journey* partakes of some of the characteristics of travel narratives but remains radically distinct from most of those published during the decade because it emphasises social investigation and economic stress. Reflecting on a different landscape and nation, *Midnight on the Desert* displays the same emphases as, four years later, Priestley tries to reconcile the industry and energy of the American people with their complacency and materialism.

Both of these works have a complex and uneasy negotiation with the past and the present, with technology and media, and with the people themselves. Though in *English Journey* the past sometimes seems better than the present in that it was more 'authentic', idealising the past has created national institutions that are moribund and trapped in a decadent genteel dream world. In *English Journey* – before his trip to the United States – Priestley privileges the working-class city and culture of his native Bradford. Despite the catalogue of ugliness, dirt and poverty that had come to be associated with England's northern industrial towns, he also finds real, complicated life. Amid the slag-heaps, cindery waste, doss-houses, slums and mill chimneys, there are also town halls and mechanics' institutes, literary and philosophical societies, pier pavilions, fried-fish shops and chapels – 'things which speak of something more positive: a distinctive way of life, a culture' (Baxendale 98). These signs of democratic culture and community cannot disguise the effects of ravaging capitalism of England's Victorian and Edward captains of industry. What had also been 'a green and pleasant land' had become 'a wilderness of dirty bricks . . . blackened fields, poisoned rivers, and ravaged earth' (*English* 318). England's future, therefore, cannot lie in a return to the past, which seems rooted in either the bucolic Merrie England or the industrial excesses of the nineteenth century, and Priestley envisions a 'third England . . . a post-war England, belonging far more to the age itself than to this particular island[.] America, I supposed, was its real birthplace' (*English* 319). His third England balances his distrust of certain American values with the possibilities of class-less democracy.

Priestley's attitude toward America is alloyed, and after his visits to Hollywood he develops an even more complex response to America's influence on postwar England. At the end of *English Journey*, he is anxiously aware that America's celebrity culture and consumerist values are on the ascent, defining not only what England looks like but what it will value:

> This is the England of arterial and by-pass roads, of filling stations and factories that look like exhibition buildings, of giant cinemas and dance-halls and cafés, bungalows with tiny garages, cocktail bars, Woolworths, motor-coaches, wireless, hiking, factory girls looking like actresses, greyhound racing and dirt tracks, swimming pools, and everything given away for cigarette coupons. (*English* 319)

The indulgences in the new England are the cheap luxuries of American consumer culture sold by Hollywood films, and Priestley's wariness comes from his understanding of just how powerful this seduction is. As a result he is less sanguine about the future of English democracy after the war. He becomes cognisant throughout his English travels that people fall into apathy as long as they are comfortable and reasonably distracted with the trappings of the 'good life', and if they see themselves reflected in the glamorous mirror of celluloid or the mass media, then life and work become mere imitations of something that is fake to begin with.

Like many intermodern writers who came of literary age in the thirties, Priestley worked sporadically in radio, film and television, and tried his hand in nearly every genre of writing.[5] As Roger Fagge has claimed, though, Priestley was temperamentally suited to the written word and to theatre, and for the most part he felt that electronic media was responsible for turning 'the people' into 'the masses' (103). After a few visits to Hollywood, Priestley was quick to see that its films sell spectacle, mere appearances, to the masses, but very soon appearance becomes all there is, what Guy Dubord describes as 'a negation of life that has invented a visual form for itself', and that culture takes on the spectacular values of the movies (Dubord 8). This becomes true for every aspect of life, from the make-up counter at the Woolworth's to the landscape that once sustained a population, and even the cities become representations of themselves connected by a long line of cement that rushes travellers from one point to another without stopping where there is 'nothing' to see. Though aware of the dangers of consumer-driven mass culture, he also notes that there is hope in its democratising power. At the end of *English Journey* he contemplates the new 'Americanised' England as he arrives in London on a foggy, wet afternoon: 'If the fog had lifted I knew that I should have this England all around me at the northern entrance to London, where the smooth wide road passes between miles of semi-detached bungalows, all with their little garages, their wireless sets, their periodicals about film stars, their swimming costumes and tennis rackets and dancing shoes' (320). However, the fog does not lift, and he has to wait, unable to see or move forward, and to contemplate 'this newest England', considering it and evaluating it from the murky envelope of his memory and expectations:

> Care is necessary . . . for you can easily approve or disapprove of it too hastily. It is, of course, essentially democratic. After a social revolution there would, with any luck, be more and not less of it. You need money in this England, but you do not need much money. It is a large-scale, mass-production job, with cut prices. You could almost accept Woolworth's as its symbol. Its cheapness is both its strength and its weakness. It is its strength because being cheap it is accessible; it nearly achieves the famous equality of opportunity. In this England, for the first time in history, Jack and Jill are nearly as good as their master or mistress; they may have always been as good in their own way, but now they are nearly as good in the *same* way. Jack, like his master, is rapidly transported to some place of rather mechanical amusement. Jill beautifies herself exactly as her mistress does. It is an England, at last, without privilege. (320)

Setting aside the problematic gender politics here, Priestley suggests that the ability to consume equally makes people equal, which of course is the foundational ideology of American capitalism. He is alarmed by the proliferation of cheap goods and the voracious appetite for periodicals about film stars, but this is balanced by his concern with the ability of all citizens to acquire them without regard to social class and privilege. Priestley does question, though, what might become of a culture whose identity rests on appearances and consumption. In that society there is no room for those who are unable to establish themselves as consumers, and like Auden, he feared that 'people would soon be part of the trash' and to the scrap heap would go the old, the unattractive, the poor, 'no longer creators of wealth but an expensive nuisance' (Bernhard 23).

Clearly in the mid-1930s, in the England of 'the slump', economic equality was of primary importance – the rigid class system was still very much in place, and the upper classes were much less affected by the economic stresses of the time – but Priestley is just as clearly concerned about the future such equality will bring. He fears that what is uniquely English might be swamped by the allure of cheap luxury and the power of Hollywood talkies. He was a product of Edwardian England and resented the deeply entrenched values of social superiority that allowed only certain classes to have access to ease and comfort, while the working and lower classes were reduced to a drudgery that somehow seemed the correctly ordained order of things. So while he is made uneasy by the global forces that are producing this new England, he does acknowledge that it 'is as near to a classless society as we have got yet' (*English* 321).

In Priestley's puzzling out the contradictions in American culture, he begins to read England a bit differently, seeing in its history a culture that might possibly resist the empty consumerism of American popular culture. Priestley went to the United States in 1935, after he had written *English Journey*, to winter in Arizona because of his wife's ill health and to work on a novel. The memoir of his experiences, *Midnight on the Desert*, published in 1937, reveals a Priestley enamoured of the desert landscape because it is without history, or at least not marked by a history that was personally troubling for him. Like many English in the American desert Priestley responds powerfully to the 'emptiness' of the desert. Paul Fussell has claimed, when faced with the vast desert of the North American West, 'Anglo-Saxon writers go all to pieces', and often metaphors become strained in the effort to describe the enormity and the seeming emptiness of the desert (158). With a history that is unfamiliar to them, most writers project their own emotional or ideological bias onto it. For Priestley, the American desert is the exact opposite of the traditional, quaint, deeply signified landscape of rural southern England:

> In the silence, slowly picking my way, I thought about this Arizona country. The New World! . . . We called it new because it was not thick with history, not a museum and a guide-book place. Man had been here such a little time that his arrival had not yet been acknowledged. . . . There is no history here because history is too recent. (2–3)

There is a history, and it is for the most part a tragic one, but what is important for Priestley is that this is not his history, and his experience of America, like all good travel experiences, gives him a new way of seeing home from abroad, a way of unifying his responses to class, landscape, consumerism and national identity, upon his return to England. Of course, the comparison between 'home' and 'abroad' is the bedrock of all travel literature, but I would argue that engagement with America prompted Priestley, as well as other English writers, to examine English identity in the face of economic stress and imperial decline in a very specific way.

While the United States did offer values that Priestley found admirable, they were not to be found in the traditional places, like music or books. America, Priestley argues, should be admired for the 'boldest and most triumphant enterprises, those colossal feats of civil engineering and large-scale building that seem to be the foundations of a new civilisation' (*Midnight* 54). Europeans might sneer at the grandiosity, the bumptiousness of America's bigger and better mentality, but 'to sneer is to diminish yourself', writes Priestley, and

> we have been disappointed in America because we look in the wrong direction for its marks of noble achievement. We look for arts and philosophies when we should be looking at the new office building, the

new bridge or highway; and we look for a few great men in the old way, artists and philosophers and scholars, when we should be looking at the thousands of new common men who mixed the concrete and threw the rivets. (*Midnight* 54–55)

Priestley admires American workers, energy and industry, so he focuses on work, equality of opportunity, and a thoroughgoing embracing of the new. The emphasis on labour allows for the possibility of the kind of classless society that Priestley idealised, where interaction between people does not 'hint at any suspicions of inferiority or superiority'. This is what he finds in the American West, and 'to return to England, after a few months of this, is like dropping back into the Feudal System' (*Midnight* 101). However, America's lack of history has made it vulnerable to its own success, and the nation, according to Priestley, must understand the responsibility that comes with leading a revolution. America promises a modern, classless democracy for the rest of the world, but there needs to be planning in order to keep it from squandering its potential the way England did after the Industrial Revolution, which 'led the way to the slag heaps and dirty back alleys and poisoned air, to the greed and cynical indifference of competitive industrialism' (*Midnight* 89). Because Britain 'failed the world', it is now America's turn: 'America is in front', but it doesn't seem to know where it is going (*Midnight* 89).

Priestley's faith that the 'Time Spirit' of the age is working hardest in the United States, 'even harder than it is in Russia', rests on his hope in the enterprise and courage of 'the engineers and builders and even [its] wayside population', but this faith is dramatically dimmed after his 'work' in Hollywood (*Midnight* 89). In *Margin Released*, Priestley reveals that he picked up 'odds and ends of script work', driving to and from Hollywood so that he could work at the ranch in Arizona, 'taking the magic money away before it could turn into dead leaves', but he never worked under contract in Hollywood itself (*Margin* 215). What scriptwriting he did was only for hire, and he refused to have his name listed in the credits. He describes Hollywood as a place of boosters and boomers, fortune-tellers, bogus mystics and publicity men, all representative of an America that he 'neither understood nor enjoyed'; they and the sprawling city itself 'somehow suggest this new age of ours at its silliest' (*Midnight* 174). He shares with his compatriots an unsettling awareness of the inauthenticity of everything in Hollywood, even the landscape:

The orchards and gardens had been cunningly devised by an art director for Metro-Goldwyn Mayer. The mountains beyond were by United Artists. The villages had come from Universal City. The boulevards were running through Paramount sets. Even the sunlight, which was pleasant but not quite the real thing, had probably been turned on by Warner

Brothers. . . . The fruit so lusciously decorating the roadside was film fruit, meant to be photographed, not tasted. (*Midnight* 175)

Priestley's description echoes those of other British novelists who went to Hollywood between the wars. All describe a city that seemed like an enormous film set, entirely without history or connection to the landscape itself, vast and alienating, created – erected – without a thought to the people who lived in it. Evelyn Waugh describes the Petronian luxury of the mansions, and Anthony Powell remarks on the fantastic buildings and the ornate cinemas, which furthered the spectacular and unreal values that the films themselves privileged and had no connection to past, present or geography (54). Huxley compares the sun to a giant klieg light, illuminating the movie set of the city (5). And Christopher Isherwood describes Hollywood as 'a great sprawling, dazzling new place – like a World's Fair', echoing Priestley's observation that Los Angeles has an air of the 'fancy fair and bazaar' (*Kathleen and Christopher* 136; *Midnight* 175).

The fancy fair aura of southern California extends to its inhabitants, who see themselves as characters in a film, a role that imparts glamour even as it reduces individuals to type, robbing them of their individuality. At one point Priestley refers to all Hollywood actors and actresses generically as 'Cutie the Blonde' and 'Tough Guy', and he wryly observes that 'movie stars were people born to achieve reality in a photograph' (179). However, he also notices that 'even the ordinary people . . . appear to have developed an odd theatrical quality, as if they were all playing character parts' (*Midnight* 175). He notes that no matter where he went in the United States, he received more questions about Hollywood than about any other topic, and those – even from intelligent people – were usually about movie stars. The mass medium of film made their appeal universal and their individuality ephemeral, for their only true reality existed on celluloid, a moving photograph onto which audiences could project their own desires:

> With ordinary persons, a photograph is a mere blurred hint of their true personality. But a film star dwindles and fades in the flesh. This is why the fuss that is made about film stars when they emerge as persons, descending upon the outer world, is so absurd and well-spiced with irony. It is the photograph that should be waited for and cheered, not the actual Person . . . who can never in person be anything but ghosts of their screen appearances, though these in turn are only shadows. . . . With them the substance must always be less than the shadow. (*Midnight* 179–80)

The transient reality of the celebrity is composed of the tricks and gestures of their performance of self, gestures which are, as Leo Braudy claims, 'easily detachable from whatever substance they once signified', and their personalities,

mediated through films and photographs, become collages, 'made from fragments of themselves – polished, denatured, simplified' (4–5). Hollywood culture
is celebrity culture, because the mass medium of film requires celebrity, an aesthetic based on easily identifiable signs and not on individuality.[6] The power of
movie images – their ability to freeze a performance for posterity and reproduce
it for millions – made actors into celebrities, not necessarily for their work, the
thing that mattered so much to Priestley, but for *what* they represented and the
way they were represented to the public. The perfect and infinitely replicated
movie star creates the effect of divinity, what Braudy refers to as 'the feverish
effect of repeated impacts of a face upon our eyes' (6). Unlike the theatre, where
each performance is a unique achievement, film makes a performance and the
performer reproducible; it doesn't so much suggest uniqueness and individuality but the *appearance* of uniqueness and individuality. Mass media create and
require easily recognisable types, virtually eliminating the authenticity of the
unique individual – the very foundation of Western art and culture. Braudy
notes that in a celebrity culture 'the fame of others, their distinguishing marks,
becomes a common coin of human exchange', a code of meaning more forceful
than words and easier to express than the codes associated with other categories of identification, such as religion, nationality, political belief or family (4).
Celebrity makes identity visible, marked by the surface performance of a lifestyle, and the Hollywood lifestyle is one where the performance of reality and
identity is as fluid and exchangeable as a movie role.

The ability of appearance – over unique achievement – to construct and perpetuate value is at the heart of Priestley's eventual condemnation of Hollywood
and by extension much of American culture as it falls under the spell of the
make believe: 'I feel there is something disturbing about this corner of America,
a sinister suggestion of transience. There is a quality hostile to men in the very
earth and air here' (*Midnight* 175). Hollywood's transience and impermanence
disallow the building of community and identity that is necessary for a nation
to be politically active and alert, and Priestley senses very early on that the
way Hollywood manufactures identity and sells it back to audiences will result
in the standardisation of a people without building a real sense of identity or
creating a real political agency based on communal experiences and shared
values. 'It is all as impermanent and brittle as a reel of film', and he suggests
that no one feels quite at ease or at home in Hollywood, regardless of their
success, because the only reality is that of the films (*Midnight* 176). The effect
on both those who work in Hollywood and those who gobble up Hollywood
gossip and follow the lives of films stars is the same; you have to become part
of an imaged community that eviscerates real value and political action:

> You will have to say good-bye to most of the great realities of our com-
> munal life. Very soon the strife of nations and the fluctuations of universal

trade will dwindle into dim little topics, only fit for a few hundred feet of newsreel. The real roaring world will disappear. . . . The head of Metro-Goldwyn-Mayer will soon seem a much more important figure than the President of the United States himself. The great questions will suddenly change their form if not their urgency. Will Chaplin finish his new picture? Has Garbo retired to Sweden? What is the new schedule for colour at Paramount? Why did the director walk off the lot? Is So-and-so still feeling 'that way' about Such-and-such?. . . [You] are in a new world, where the sun is switched on and off in the studios, and the stars are so many handsome young men and women. It exists, this world, to make films. And that other, outside world exists in order to buy those films, and to provide material for still more films. Is there a threat of war, then what about another war picture? Are there Communists in China, Fascists in Spain, then what about sending a few camera-men out for some good 'back projection'? That, in brief, is the Hollywood point of view. (*Midnight* 176–77)

The seeming triviality of Hollywood, movies and the culture of celebrity and entertainment is therefore deeply serious and troubling.

Even before his trip to the American West, Priestley was aware that the cultural change effected by American films represented a shift as remarkable as any world war, but his reaction to this cultural sea change is nuanced. This he argues is an alluring, new way of living – fast, crude, vivid – that may materially improve the lives of people around the globe but undermines real democracy and the political agency of the people by a visual sleight of hand that substitutes consuming for genuine action. At the end of *English Journey* he conjectures that 'a liberal supply of cheap luxuries might . . . create a set of people entirely without ambition or any real desire to think and act for themselves, the perfect subjects for an iron autocracy' (*English* 322). America sells the world 'a new civilisation, perhaps another barbaric age', and the signs of it are everywhere in the energy and shiny newness of Hollywood, 'trivial enough in themselves, but pointing to the most profound changes, to huge bloodless revolutions' (*Midnight* 88). The attenuation of individual and communal identity in favour of a mass-marketed appearance of identity and value is Hollywood's threat, both to America's own democratic values and to those of the rest of the world. Priestley describes Sunset Boulevard, and he notes the fast pace, 'the pretty frivolity', the promise of anything you want whenever you want it: 'Very soon there would be something like this road all over the world, penetrating Africa, glittering across Asia. *Gas, Eats, Hot and Cold Drinks*: something like this would be spelt out, in paint by day, in neon lights after dark, all the way from Shanghai to Capetown' (*Midnight* 86, 88).

The homogenising power of Hollywood subverts the very notion of national and individual identity, and Priestley feared – as early as 1934 – that celebrity culture would undermine English identity. He wryly notes near the end of *English Journey*, 'What pleases Hollywood has to please South Lincolnshire', registering the effects of Hollywood on the younger generation in England (*English* 299). He observes that in the new England – 'though the young people will not play chorus in an opera in which their social superiors are the principles' – things are a bit too cheap, that 'too much of it is a trumpery imitation of something not very good even in the original' (*English* 321). More and more, Priestley felt that England was enacting a Hollywood version of itself, perpetuating country-house nostalgia and creating a new kind of class system based on wealth and appearance. He reminded anglophile Americans during the war that the struggle against Hitler would not be won by 'the England the films are so fond of showing us: the old Hall, the hunt breakfast, the hunt ball, the villagers touching their caps, all the old bag of tricks' (*Bright* 135). And in *English Journey*, Priestley asserts that England is not a landscape but a social system, and that the lingering aristocratic tradition impedes progress and undermines the real values of the nation; it only serves to construct and maintain a tourist-attraction Englishness that results in staleness and depression (Baxendale 95).

Of course, as the thirties ended and Europe was engulfed in yet another world war, Priestley rallied the British against fascism and Hitler and appealed to precisely the qualities he feared they were losing. In his Sunday evening *Postscripts*, his populist, collective notion of England, which subsumed the rest of Britain into England, seemed to be shared by the entire country, and his entreaty to stereotypical English characteristics as courage in adversity, humour and resoluteness of purpose unified the nation. As the 'the voice of Britain', he drew on a nostalgia that he might not have tapped in his pre-war writing. Broadcasting on 7 July 1940, he asks his audience to 'cry at once with Shakespeare . . . "God for Harry, England and Saint George"' (*All England* 42).

The BBC broadcasts not only unified the nation but forged, through the traumatic experience of war, a collective identity that Priestley thought might be able to resist the globalising influence of American consumerist culture. In the pamphlet that developed from his work at the BBC, *Out of the People* (1941), Priestley outlines an almost utopian plan for postwar reconstruction based on the highest ideals of democracy. It appeared at a time when the British people hoped that the expectations nourished during the war might then be fulfilled. For Priestley, the 'people' are the best way to resist mass consumer culture. The collective heroism that the British showed during the war could and should be harnessed to move towards a 'larger redemption', and the behaviour of the common people proved that 'our society can be redeemed from apathy, cynicism and materialism' (*Out of the People* 8). To the question 'What is Britain?', which echoes his question at the end of *English Journey* about whether some of the industrial towns in the North are still even part of England, abandoned as they were by the rest of the country, he answers, 'Britain is the home of the British people' (45). He claims that the 'ordinary English' still have 'a deep-seated morality' and a belief in 'the central human dignity of the individual' and that in Britain more than elsewhere 'individuality and character are more important than function' (*Out of the People* 71).

Out of the People makes claims for collective political engagement and socialist reforms. It is an idiosyncratic work, born of his experiences throughout the thirties, the violence of war and the communal spirit engendered by his BBC broadcasts. Given his distrust of mass movements and of cheap consumerist values, his focus was on the people themselves, and he understood this to be a struggle between a populist but unique identity rooted in national life and tradition and 'Admass', a collectivity based on mass publicity and commercialism. In one of his early broadcasts, Priestley described the war as being between opposing views of civilisation, and 'a war between hope and despair' (qtd in Fagge 104). Of course, he very literally meant the fight against Hitler and totalitarianism, but as time went on he also meant that the fight was about the future of democracy, which had to involve the full participation of the people and responsible democratic practice – 'there could be no going back to the past' (Fagge 104).

With uncanny foresight, Priestley outlines the obstacles that stand in the way of true democracy in the modern world: the loss of dignity and respect for the individual, authoritarian governments and industries and mass media that are both manipulated by those in power and in turn manipulate the people. Priestley describes an increasingly mechanised workforce that leads a 'robot-like existence', for whom 'Hollywood and the cheap press do not provide antidotes but only change the flavouring of the poison . . . their very dreams come from another mass production factory' (*Out of the People* 59–60). Priestley was not alone in his hope that the values of unique national culture might be a way of resisting the colonising power of Hollywood. Only those English who for personal and complicated reasons were desirous of cutting themselves off from their country – like Isherwood and Huxley – were able to embrace fully the radical ahistoricty and transience of Hollywood. Priestley turned back to England to search for what might be redeemed, because, as Baxendale very rightly claims, 'he did want to be English' (108).

By the end of the 1940s, 'Priestley's optimism was increasingly overtaken by his disillusionment' (Fagge 107). Eventually, he was even accused of being out of touch with the people, who increasingly liked Hollywood films, mass media and cheap luxury goods. Despite his nuanced observations about culture and media, Priestley's dichotomy of 'culture' or 'admass' was perhaps too rigid, and what emerged in the decades after the war was 'a complex and contradictory combination of the two' that was difficult for him to reconcile (Baxendale 108). However, as the voice of the people during a moment of huge historical change, he was thoughtful and prescient about American popular culture's global influence, which was only just beginning to be understood. His writing of the time reveals the anxiety inherent in the loss of a once-vital current in national life and the siphoning of political energy into the distractions of consumer culture.

Notes

1. Siân Nicholas, '"Sly Demagogues"', discusses how the BBC attempted to harness the power of the radio personality for propaganda purposes during the war, claiming that 'Priestley was, above all, the first example in Britain of a particular kind of radio personality: the first non-politician to whom listeners regularly tuned to hear his personal political and philosophical views. This kind of broadcaster was not uncommon on American radio at the time but on British radio such personalities had always been actively discouraged' (248). Also, see Peter Buitenhuis.
2. Virginia Woolf famously referred to Priestley as a 'trademan of letters' (qtd. in Brome 133), and Nicholas writes that most at the MOI (Ministry of Information) and BBC thought that Priestley would be fairly manageable as a radio personality. When proved wrong, Minister of Information Duff Gordon, who was responsible for taking Priestley off the air, referred to him as 'a second rate novelist who had got conceited by his broadcasting success' (Nicholas 260). Baxendale quotes Q. D. Leavis, who dismisses Priestley for his 'complacent, hardy knowingness' (109).
3. For challenges to the middlebrow status of Priestley and his oeuvre see Baxendale, Fagge and Henthorne. There is a growing body of criticism that engages middlebrow writers and issues of culture and class in the thirties and forties. See Kristin Bluemel, *George Orwell and the Radical Eccentrics*; Bernard Bergonzi, *Reading the Thirties*; Rosa Maria Bracco, *Merchants of Hope*; John Carey, *The Intellectuals and the Masses*; Andy Croft *Red Letter Days*; Stella Deen, ed., *Challenging Modernism*; Alison Light, *Forever England*; and Keith Williams and Steven Matthews, eds., *Rewriting the Thirties*.
4. There is an enormous bibliography of scholarship on Englishness and on national identity, most examining the 'imaginary' nature of the construct even as it creates and reinforces deeply held values and identifications.
5. Many intermodern writers were attracted to the media of broadcasting and film, both because they were eager to experiment with new ways of representing experience and because they hoped to earn a lot of money. They wrote in a variety of genres for 'new' media, even if they saw themselves as primarily novelists or playwrights. This is true for Waugh, Powell, Wodehouse, Huxley, Isherwood, Auden, Dodie Smith, Hugh Walpole, Graham Greene and George Orwell, to name just a few. For studies of British novelists who worked in film, both in the UK and in Hollywood, see Peter Conrad, *Imagining America*; David Fine, *Los Angeles in Fiction*; H. Mark Glancy, *When Hollywood Loved Britain*; Sheridan Morley, *Tales from the Hollywood Raj*; Paddy Scannell and David Cardiff, *A Social History of British Broadcasting*; and John Russell Taylor, *Strangers in Paradise*.
6. Leo Braudy's *The Frenzy of Renown* is a classic work on the theory of celebrity. See also James L. Baughman, *The Republic of Mass Culture*; Gary Cross, *An All-Consuming Century*; Faye Hammill, *Women, Celebrity, and Literary Culture between the Wars*; Aaron Jaffe, *Modernism and the Culture of Celebrity*; Joshua Gamson, *Claims to Fame*; and Clive James, *The Meaning of Recognition*.

WORKS CITED

Baughman, James L. *The Republic of Mass Culture: Journalism, Filmmaking, and Broadcasting in America since 1941*. Baltimore: Johns Hopkins University Press, 1997.

Baxendale, John. '"I Had Seen a Lot of Englands": J. B. Priestley, Englishness and the People'. *History Workshop Journal* 39 (1995): 87–111.

Bergonzi, Bernard. *Reading the Thirties: Texts and Contexts*. Pittsburgh: University of Pittsburgh Press, 1978.

Bernhard, Brendan. 'Coming to America: Isherwood and Auden in the New World'. *The L.A. Weekly* 21 February 1997: 16–24.

Bluemel, Kristin. *George Orwell and the Radical Eccentrics: Intermodernism in Literary London*. New York: Palgrave Macmillan, 2004.

Bracco, Rosa Maria. *Merchants of Hope: British Middlebrow Writers and the First World War*. Oxford: Berg, 1995.

Braudy, Leo. *The Frenzy of Renown: Fame and its History*. New York: Vintage, 1986.

Brome, Vincent. *J. B. Priestley*. London: Hamish Hamilton, 1988.

Buitenhuis, Peter. 'J. B. Priestley: The BBC's Star Propagandist in World War II'. *English Studies in Canada*. 26.4 (2000): 445–72.

Carey, John. *The Intellectuals and the Masses: Pride and Prejudice amongst the Intelligentsia, 1880–1939*. London: Faber, 1992.

Calder, Angus. *The People's War: Britain, 1939–1945*. New York: Pantheon, 1969.

Conrad, Peter. *Imagining America*. New York: Oxford University Press, 1980.

Cook, Judith. *Priestley*. London: Bloomsbury, 1997.

Croft, Andy. *Red Letter Days: British Fiction in the 1930s*. London: Lawrence and Wishart, 1990.

Cross, Gary. *An All-Consuming Century: Why Commercialism Won in Modern America*. New York: Columbia University Press, 2000.

Deen, Stella, ed. *Challenging Modernism: New Readings in Literature and Culture, 1914–1945*. Burlington: Ashgate, 2002.

Dodd, Philip. 'Views of Travellers: Travel Writing in the 1930s'. *Prose Studies* 5.1 (1982): 127–38.

Dubord, Guy. *The Society of the Spectacle*. Trans. Donald Nicholson-Smith. New York: Zone Books, 1995.

Fagge, Roger. 'From *The Postscripts* to Admass: J. B. Priestley and the Cold War World'. *Media History* 12.2 (2006): 103–15.

Fine, David. *Los Angeles in Fiction*. Albuquerque: University of New Mexico Press, 1984.

Fussell, Paul. *Abroad: British Literary Traveling between the Wars*. New York and Oxford: Oxford University Press, 1980.

Gamson, Joshua. *Claims to Fame: Celebrity in Contemporary America.* Berkeley: University of California Press, 1994.

Glancy, H. Mark. *When Hollywood Loved Britain: The Hollywood 'British' Film.* Manchester: Manchester University Press, 1999.

Hammill, Faye. *Women, Celebrity, and Literary Culture between the Wars.* Austin: University of Texas Press, 2007.

Henthorne, Tom. 'Priestley's War: Social Change and the British Novel, 1939–1945'. *The Midwest Quarterly* 45.2 (2004): 155–70.

Huxley, Aldous. *After Many a Summer Dies the Swan.* New York: Harper and Row, 1939.

Isherwood, Christopher. *Kathleen and Christopher: Christopher Isherwood's Letters to his Mother.* Ed. Lisa Colletta. Minneapolis: University of Minnesota Press, 2005.

Isherwood, Christopher. 'Los Angeles'. *Horizon* 93–4 (1947): 1142–47.

Jaffe, Aaron. *Modernism and the Culture of Celebrity.* Cambridge: Cambridge University Press, 2005.

James, Clive. *The Meaning of Recognition: New Essays 2001–2005.* London: Picador, 2005.

Klein, Holger. 'Home is Utopia: Priestley's Vision of and Ideal Society'. *War and Literature* 11.1 (2005): 50–73.

Light, Alison. *Forever England: Femininity, Literature and Conservatism between the Wars.* London: Routledge, 1991.

Morley, Sheridan. *Tales from the Hollywood Raj: The British, the Movies, and Tinseltown.* New York: Viking Press, 1983.

Nicholas, Siân. '"Sly Demagogues" and Wartime Radio: J. B. Priestley and the BBC'. *Twentieth Century British History* 6.3 (1995): 247–66.

Priestley, J. B. *All England Listened: The Wartime Broadcasts of J. B. Priestley.* New York: Chilmark Press, 1967.

—. *Bright Day.* London: Heinemann, 1946.

—. *English Journey.* New York and London: Harper Collins, 1934.

—. *Margin Released: A Writer's Reminiscences and Reflections.* New York: Harper and Row, 1962.

—. *Midnight on the Desert.* 1937. London: Readers' Union Limited and Heinemann, 1940.

—. *Out of the People.* London: Heinemann, 1941.

—. *Rain upon Godshill: A Further Chapter of Autobiography.* London: Heinemann, 1939.

Powell, Anthony. *Messengers of the Day.* London: Heinemann, 1978.

Scannell, Paddy and David Cardiff. *A Social History of British Broadcasting.* Cambridge: Blackwell, 1991.

Taylor, John Russell. *Strangers in Paradise: The Hollywood Emigres, 1933–1950.* New York: Holt, 1983.

Waugh, Evelyn. *The Diaries of Evelyn Waugh*. Ed Michael Davie. Boston: Little Brown, 1976.

Williams, Keith and Steven Matthews, eds. *Rewriting the Thirties: Modernism and After*. London: Longman, 1997.

PART III
WAR

6

UNDER SUSPICION: THE PLOTTING OF BRITAIN IN WORLD WAR II DETECTIVE SPY FICTION

Phyllis Lassner

England, June 1939. As Helen MacInnes's 1941 novel *Above Suspicion* begins, Frances and Richard Myles, artist and intellectual respectively, are lured away from Oxford's dreaming spires to become activists against the encroaching threat of Nazism and the dangers of isolationism. Recruited by MI6 to find a British agent lost in Germany, they must shed their innocent personae to discover Nazism's most lethal designs.[1] Like the British spy's work in MacInnes's 1942 novel, *Assignment in Brittany*, the pair's mission dramatises the recognition that Britain's future must be tested on European ground, and to do so, the two Myles must assume the roles of detective decoys and spies.

England 1940. As Margery Allingham's 1941 novel *Traitor's Purse* begins, Albert Campion, private detective and wayward scion of little England, struggles to lift the amnesiac fog that has enveloped his personal and political consciousness. The detective is catapulted into the disorientations and denials of Britain under siege from enemies within and without. As in Allingham's two other novels of the 1940s, *Black Plumes* (1940) and *Coroner's Pidgin* (1945), the detective's mandate in *Traitor's Purse* will be to unearth Britain's home-grown enemy and to do so, he must assume the roles of both detective and spy.

The World War II detective spy novels of Helen MacInnes and Margery Allingham invite literary historical analysis that links the cultural ideologies of Britain's war against Nazism to the literary value of detective and spy fiction. Combining complex weaves of narrative forms with political and cultural concerns, these novels provide new criteria that challenge any doubts about the legitimacy of these literary genres. Coupled with the marginal position of their authors, these wartime fictional experiments support the concept of inter-modernism. One narrative experiment in particular illustrates the intermodern historical nexus of these novels. The dual roles assumed by Allingham's and MacInnes's World War II detective spies combine elements derived from both genres at a time that demands multiple forms of intelligence gathering to unmask the disguised enemy. Although deeply concerned with disturbances in the domestic social order, these novels underscore the terror of total conquest, ranging from suspicions of collaboration and betrayal to the destruction of British culture and identity. [2] If the conclusions of these fictions inscribe hopes for victory, they also warn that the spy's acquired intelligence is only partial and inconclusive and that the enemy remains adamantine. Ultimately, instead of reassuring their contemporaneous readers with formulaic solutions, these novels register a political plea. They demonstrate that despite Britain's forti-tude in standing alone against invasion, the island nation could not continue to do so without American intervention. Widely read in the United States, these novels seek American recognition and identification with Britain's desperate straits. In *Above Suspicion* and *Assignment in Brittany*, the MacInnes novels I will examine, two American journalists convey this appeal. [3] In Margery Allingham's 1940 novel, *Black Plumes*, it takes an American artist to shed light on Britain's internal dangers.

In their representations of World War II's fears and demands, both writers alter the face of detective and spy fiction. If, as Gill Plain observes, crime and detection fiction is 'about confronting and taming the monstrous', Allingham's and MacInnes's hybrid detective spy fiction translates the generic 'unspeak-able' into the historically particular threat of Nazism (*Twentieth Century* 3). [4] In literary historical terms, Michael Denning observes aesthetic shifts in the spy thriller between 1929 and 1940 which reveal 'dissatisfaction with earlier thrillers with a faith in the form's possibilities' (61). Between 1940 and 1945, Allingham and MacInnes create possibilities by working with such spy fiction conventions as meanings of codes, 'hermeneusis', and the 'guilt' embedded within 'statecraft and diplomacy' (Hepburn 25–26). From detective fiction, they take conventions of clues, 'exegesis', and 'guilt within the context of a home or family' (Hepburn 25–26). Allingham and MacInnes fuse these fea-tures to question relationships between the ethics of detecting and spying and the urgency of saving Britain in a necessary war. With the hope of victory, they contemplate what may be essential changes to the traditional social and cultural order they depict. In effect, these 1940s fictions achieve a form of nar-rative experiment that will not end with high modernism in 1940 or global victory over the Axis powers in 1945 but will leave a legacy of questions about classifying genres and the prestige hierarchies in modern fiction. This legacy provides support for intermodernism as a category of analysing modern fiction that slips between modernism, realism and speculative fiction to ground its narrative experiments in historical and political analysis.

That both detective and spy thrillers are considered genre fiction keeps them in their marginalised place as a mere step up from pulp fiction. While millions of readers, including highbrow modernists, have indulged their penchant for safe thrills by plunging into the steady stream of crime and spy fictions, few repay the pleasure by granting them even middlebrow status. Middlebrow fiction at least aspires to serious purpose even if it fails the literary elites' test of formal innovation. In recent years, however, this genre fiction has yielded evidence of a surprising seriousness. From the 1920s through the Golden Age of Agatha Christie, Dorothy Sayers and Allingham, and beyond to John Le Carré's Cold War, critics now find innovative aesthetics with more than enough political, cultural and social critique to go around.

While the literary reputation of Margery Allingham (1904–66) resides in the pantheon of the Golden Age, with two biographies and a proliferating body of criticism, Helen MacInnes (1907–85) has yet to make the cut. [5] Despite her Scottish birth, patriotism, production of more than twenty novels and winning the Columbia Prize for literature in 1966, she appears in none of the recent encyclopaedias of modern British women writers. Nor is there a full biography or much literary criticism to illuminate her writing career. Yet as Mary K. Boyd notes, MacInnes's popularity has remained constant. She infused her spy thrillers with questions about identity politics, with sophisticated literary allusions and 'changing standards of social behavior [and] changing fashions in literary style' (68, 66). Unlike modernists' rebellious depictions of modernity's dislocations, MacInnes has no such pretensions. And yet, as I will argue, she creates narrative disjunctions that raise disquieting questions about the romance of Britain's righteous war and the spy thriller.

Assumptions that formulaic plots and outcomes render detective and spy fiction conservative also plague judgements about their authors' politics. [6] Despite Alison Light's pathbreaking rescue of Agatha Christie and other conservative women writers, MacInnes and Allingham are all too often branded politically and culturally conservative and then dismissed. They are read as choreographing nostalgic rear guard actions to save Britain's traditional social and ethical order. The culprits in these fictions, however, are usually those who have enough power to exploit Britain's wartime uncertainties for their own political and economic conquest. As Allingham's and MacInnes's 1940s novels show, both writers are deeply ambivalent about restoring a mythic rural order representing national and cultural stability and security. A prime example is Allingham's 1945 *Coroner's Pidgin*. The novel's usual complement of murders belies its central concern about national art treasures that were hijacked on their way to safekeeping in 1940 and are still missing at the end of the war. As the plot turns, the treasures have been sheltered in the basement of a Victorian

Gothic house whose owner is named Miss Pork and whose reception rooms are notable for their 'baroquerie' (*Pidgin* 165). If such satire reeks of snooty self-righteousness, it is also self-critical. For in its Home County setting, with its overstuffed decor and cache of purloined objects d'art, the house supplies a pungent critique of British cultural hegemony at its most endangered modern moment. As the redoubtable Superintendent Oakes remarks, the significance of looting Britain's national treasures is of greater import than murder.

The import of this comment for Allingham's place in modern literature is its linkages between the nation's cultural integrity and identity. The very nature and legitimacy of British cultural identity are at stake in this theft. For instead of British provenance, these national treasures are mostly European and Asian. That cultural production and transmission have from time immemorial been multicultural there is no doubt. Furthermore, from ancient times, a hallmark of imperialism has been the seizure and display of art to celebrate the right-eousness of conquest. The victor endows the expropriated art with cultural value by protecting it from contamination by the inferior culture of origin. In the light of Britain's history of cultural imperialism, with its ingathering of Elgin marbles and gates of the Assyrian Empire, Allingham's satire suggests poetic justice. The critical perspective here belongs to Miss Pork. A national treasure in her own right, Miss Pork assesses the artifacts in her protection as 'a lot of stolen property' (*Pidgin* 178). In this case, the cultural rationalisations of a home-grown enemy collude with the Nazis' plan to claim eminent domain over all national cultures.

Allingham's satire of British cultural imperialism suggests an intermodern intervention. Most considerations of high modernism call it quits at 1940, skipping over writing of World War II to establish a late modernism. Whereas many modernists had embedded their politics of the 1930s in narrative experi-mentation, and by the 1940s many critics preferred to separate modernist aesthetics and politics, there were others during the 1930s and 1940s who pro-duced imaginatively polemical anti-fascist novels. By the time Germany was invading Britain, the realities of death and destruction imposed a new narrative challenge about political representation. Whereas Allingham narrates stories about Britain's dangers to itself, MacInnes dramatises Britain's responsibilities and inevitable links to Nazi occupied Europe. For MacInnes, the battlegrounds are European home fronts where the political ethos of Britain is tested against cultural and sexual relations with resistors or collaborators.

Plotting tensions between traditional social hierarchies and Britain's political and cultural imperatives, each of Allingham's three wartime novels explores the nation's survival in relation to its national myth of cultural superiority. Her 1940 novel *Black Plumes* begins conventionally, with a murder. Reading the title thematically, however, reveals the anxieties accompanying the passing away of a traditional order. The first sign of anxiety is the victim's identity, a parvenu son-in-law, who in life and death destabilises the social and cultural grounds of a venerable cultural site: an art gallery owned by the aptly named Ivory family of impeccably imperial social standing. 'At first blush 39 Sallet Square, where one could negotiate anything from a castleful of Rembrandts to a humble modern woodcut, was a cool and lovely private house' (*Plumes* 5). The sly troping of 'castleful' and Ivory resonates with feudal and imperial pillage and plunder. In its modernity, however, the 'cool and lovely private house' is invaded by the new conqueror – global capitalism. How times have changed since the dowager, Gabrielle Ivory, could afford to sustain her inherited wealth.[7] Art and culture no longer represent the birthright of 'golden age' gentry, but are now commodities sold to the highest bidder in the déclassé marketplace (*Plumes* 2). Linden Peach attributes the modernity of crime fiction to the 'expansion of urban environments, centralising of capital and socio-economic power, control of the metropolis over aesthetic conventions' (4). In *Black Plumes*, culture may be centred in a socially expanding London, but its value has become international political capital. When an important contemporary painting is slashed, the family's reaction betrays fears that modern commerce has made violent incursions into 'a history of wealth and prestige ... unequalled in Europe' (*Plumes* 2). In a metafictional turn, Allingham's novels of the 1940s detect and spy on the global spoils of culture and its artifacts.

A spy in plain sight, Allingham's Albert Campion will interrogate the political economy of Britain's cultural identity. Although the facts remain murky, it is clear from his first appearance that Campion's ambiguous relationship with his aristocratic family launches him into a differently advantageous position – a form of self exile. Rather than subscribe to the social codes that constitute and defend the time honoured confines of Belgravia and the Home Counties, Campion performs them in order to decipher and deconstruct them. In effect, he thwarts the plots of those who oppose the social and political changes instigated by the war. In Allingham's 1945 *Coroner's Pidgin*, when Campion is reminded that a 'Duke' is still 'privileged beyond all the normal bounds of civilized behavior', the narrator informs us (129):

> At the age of four and a quarter, Mr. Campion had taken a poor view of the excuse and did so now, with the added advantage of knowing that ninety-nine per cent of the world agreed with him. All the same, he found it interesting to note that the remaining one percent still existed, and was at large. (130)[8]

Regardless of the nature of the crime or its site, Campion is always a British double agent working within and against the social order. He is an intelligence agent who has been briefed from birth about the traditional social hierarchies that created prevailing myths of Britain's heroic past and that bear on its present and future. His position is socially, culturally and politically liminal;

he resides in a space between past and present, between the old aristocracy and becoming a self-made man – he is an intermodern detective spy. Not only is he self-made in his detective spy role, but in his amnesiac state in the 1940 *Traitor's Purse*, he must learn how to spy on himself in order to detect the crime that threatens the nation from within. Deliberately ambiguous, the title refers to the treachery of which Campion hasn't a clue. When he awakes in a hospital and intuitively runs from unspecified danger, despite the signs of murder, the real crime is so daring and global it defies detection: a traitor's plot to sabotage Britain's economy. Nowhere is this elusiveness more apparent then when the mysterious number fifteen crops up everywhere. Does it represent a date, an address or an encoded plan? Campion can't even tell if it's a clue or a code.[9] He is in epistemological limbo, where he must choose whether to model himself after the past or present, neither of which he can understand. He can reconstitute himself, that is, reconstruct the past to recreate who he was, to become and perform as a self-made clone. In short, he can perform himself as a traditionally realistic artifact. He can also allow his identity to become modern, to develop into a more fluctuating, uncertain being, to broaden the base of his liminality and fractured consciousness, all at the moment his amnesia threatens to erase it altogether.

Campion's persona, probably modelled on Dorothy Sayers's Lord Peter Wimsey's upper class superciliousness and kindly diffidence, assumes critical import if we view it as a performance. Expressing his liminal social position, this performance both clashes with and finds comfort in the *louche* position of his Bottle St flat adjacent to an abandoned police station. This position reconceives the meaning of surveillance – a bemused, semi-detached perspective on the privileged squares of Mayfair and Belgravia. From this perch, he sees through the 'stoic gallantry' of privilege and the aggression of the *demi monde* to their crimes and collaborations (*Pidgin* 6). In turn, Campion's hallmark vacant stare, focused somewhere between his ambiguous social position and his clients' guilt and innocence, exposes the social or political anarchy that underlies more obviously venal motives.[10] In *Coroner's Pidgin*, when a Mayfair doyenne, Lady Carados, lodges an inconvenient corpse on Campion's bed, she demonstrates upper-class confidence in its '*sans reproche*' and staying power, both of which will be challenged by his detective and counterspy work (*Pidgin* 129). In 1945, Campion may feel a modicum of sympathy for Lady Carados, but the violence of modern warfare and spying echoes in her fading social power. It also echoes in a jolt to the stability of Campion's self-construction. Here in *Coroner's Pidgin*, the very moment the nation celebrates victory over Nazism is interrupted by an intertextual reminder from the 1940 *Traitor's Purse* that Campion's earlier bout of amnesia 'did [him] a permanent injury' (*Pidgin* 37). I maintain that this 'permanent injury' extends to the destabilisation of the traditional social order. In *Coroner's Pidgin*'s 1945 setting, a space between victory over Nazism and the meaning of peace to the social fabric of the nation, Campion's war weariness clouds the value and values of 'the golden age before the wars' represented by Lady Carados (6). [11] At this postwar moment, 'The brilliant picture of the past faded into the dust and rubble of the present, and Mr Campion blinked' (9). Most often interpreted as a sign of Campion's tried and true diffidence, this blink marks an intermodern critique. In that instant, he must absorb, decipher and respond to the relationship he detects between the performance of social and political stability and instability and their implications for the upheavals he foresees.

In *Traitor's Purse*, Campion's studied vacant stare and blink are destabilised by threats of war and yield to amnesia. This trauma clouds the relationship between past and present when Campion finds himself in a hospital emergency ward, a metaphoric stand-in for the urgent opening moments of World War II. At a time of tumultuous geo-politics, when European fascism is the muse of Oswald Mosley, his aristocratic wife Diana and his Blackshirts, this novel investigates the dangers within the nation's deeply entrenched privileged 'one per cent'. [12] Campion's performances in this novel as detective and spy are designed to discover connections between his liminal social role, his political mission and between Britain's past, present and future. Just as Campion's amnesia in *Traitor's Purse* obscures the nature and boundaries of his personal and professional worlds, so its implications expand. Amnesia begs the question, what is being forgotten? And by whom, especially since the amnesiac doesn't know who he is? Though nominally, Campion is the victim, and as the novel extends its field of enquiry, it leads us to infer that at the moment of German invasion, amnesia refers to the British nation as a whole. Britain may very well be in danger of forgetting its survival instincts. If the nation is to save itself, it must overcome the isolationism that memorialises the losses of the Great War.

> He belonged to a post-war generation, that particular generation which was too young for one war and almost prematurely too old for the next. It was the generation which had picked up the pieces after the holocaust indulged in by its elders, only to see its brave new world wearily smashed again by younger brothers. (*Purse* 99)

Amnesia compels Campion to navigate through an unknown personal, classed and political topography that conceals collaboration with the enemy. Most disorienting are the vexed definitions of loyalty. What defines a Briton when the enemy turns out to be totally committed to a British ideal based on the nation's triumphalist imperial history?

Allingham's decision to suspend the characters of Campion and the nation in an amnesiac state provides an intermodern space in which she meditates on the political and cultural import of her narrative experiment. Amnesia works metonymically to revise the plot outlines that shape the conventional character of the British gentleman detective. In an about face figurative turn, Campion's amnesia erases the social and cultural codes against which he had partially rebelled and which still compel his loyalty as he detects its miscreants. Ironically, his mental fog clarifies his social and political identity by unveiling the political extremism infecting his class. Just as the Nazis are planning to invade Britain, Campion discovers a homegrown enemy comprised of upper-class avowed patriots who constitute an underground British government openly known as the Masters of Bridge: 'that remarkable and ancient institution which, from being a provincial curiosity, part charity and part museum, for a hundred and fifty years, had blossomed forth in the early part of the century into one of the most valuable centres in the country' (*Purse* 120). With hereditary offices, with total economic, judicial and cultural control over the old English town of Bridge, the Masters consider themselves 'the best of' the nation (140).[13] They will save Britain from sinking into 'the Dark Ages again' (142).

Though it represents tradition, the Masters' seat of power appropriates change. A 'genuine period piece', the principal's house 'had been considerably improved by modern austerity and modern money' (24). Money in this place and time becomes even more modern in the Bridge plot to put 'the British Empire on a company footing, with a personal invitation to every tax-payer to invest his all in it' (141). The Masters would then flood the country with counterfeit pounds sterling, creating a financial and political crisis that could only be solved by a coup leading the venerable Bridge to fascist power. The assumption that social hierarchies represent an essential British cultural tradition is sustained here by the modern mechanism of money laundering which joins hands with the industrialised but retrogressive politics of Nazism.

Campion's struggling detection transforms his social mask into his reality in order to disarm the enemy whose loyalty to his privileged class masks betrayal of his country. Although Campion is recognised as part of exclusive clubby old England, welcomed in Bridge by the Masters, he sees himself more ambivalently. The fable of the town's flood and resurrection may thrill him with 'superstitious fear', but his emotional journey incites his suspicions about his reaction (53). Like the nation's decision to enter the war, he translates nostalgia for a mythical time into political analysis of clear and present danger. Only when his and the nation's amnesia lifts, does he uncover and thwart the Masters' plot and the nation begin its self-defence. The homegrown enemy, Lee Aubrey, a man of pedigree, privilege, personal charm and good looks, is like a rancid fairy-tale hero; he will transform his plan for national victory into a fascistic opportunity. Aubrey's fascist politics make him an obvious villain, but his character recalls the historical reality of Oswald Mosley's imprisonment in 1940, when this novel was written. In their similarities, both Aubrey and Mosley represent the moment when belief in the old social order is radicalised by political treachery.

The urgency one feels in reading *Traitor's Purse* recalls the self-deceived collusion of Oswald Mosley's followers across the social and economic spectrum. The Masters of Bridge represent those in the upper classes who were convinced that their privilege would be respected and maintained by the Nazis. That such treachery inspires fear in 1940 is not surprising, but even in 1945, Allingham's fiction conveys lingering suspicions of those who assume aristocratic privilege. My case rests with reading her 1945 *Coroner's Pidgin* intertextually, alongside her 1940 *Traitor's Purse*. Although the solution to *Coroner's Pidgin* absolves RAF hero Lord Johnny Carados of the crime for which he is increasingly suspected, just before the novel ends, Campion is beset with a doubt that aligns him with Hepburn's insight: 'Spies are emblems of doubt insofar as they live at a distance from conviction and keep testing allegiances' (5–6). Recalling *Traitor's Purse*, we find a disquieting resemblance between the casual but privileged charm of Johnny Carados and Lee Aubrey. Such resemblance suggests that the threats of 1940 are still unsettling; they disfigure the victorious pastoral ending of *Coroner's Pidgin* by threatening the restoration of the social order.

The disjunctions here between peace and doubt resemble modernist critiques of a coherent national identity and sense of purpose, critiques that fulfilled the modernists' self-styled identity as upholders of minority culture. Yet a defining mark of modernism was also a yearning for wholeness, which in the face of two devastating world wars, many artists expressed as conjoining mythic and fragmented narrative forms. Allingham's intermodernism registers suspicions of mythic and fragmented forms as well as of a marginal identity. Her 1940s novels would view a self-styled marginal identity as abstracting political and historical realities into an aesthetic of wishful thinking. Looking back from 1940 to the political and cultural treacheries of the 1930s and from 1945 to the origins of an unwanted but necessary war, Allingham's World War II novels assess the political risks of modernism's mythic desires, self-fashioned elitism and the function of narrative experiment. By 1940, her intermodern geo-political perspective exposes the drive for mythic wholeness as evading the era's lacerating political dangers.

Reading Allingham's wartime detective novels as critical responses to modernism's political risks reveals how her interpretation of the word 'fragmentation' creates an intermodern narrative experiment. These novels represent the fragmented individual and collective experiences of waging a defensive war on the home front. As Campion's amnesia and the novel's treacherous landscape demonstrate, this representation is allegorically dystopian rather than conventionally realistic or formulaic.[14] Carved within a gargantuan but natural rock formation, the Masters' villainous cavern of 'financial dynamite' calls critical attention to mythic comforts – fascist aesthetics and those White Cliffs of Dover that symbolised Britain's naturally defensive wall (*Purse* 171). Allingham's diorama of a nativist fifth column exposes the internal dangers of

Britain's social and economic fissures at the very moment the nation relies on myths of unified national valour, security and stability. *Traitor's Purse, Black Plumes* and *Coroner's Pidgin* expose the duplicity of mythic wholeness by identifying and analysing Britain's wartime national identity as deeply divided and in need of questioning. With a narrative method we can call speculative political realism, *Traitor's Purse* dramatises the political reality of a nation endangered by the economic and social tyranny of an entrenched old order. Buoyed by mythic belief in their primordial powers of leadership, the Masters of Bridge conspire to exploit Britain's economic and class division. The Masters' plan would appeal to the unifying war effort of the labouring classes and 'various social service schemes functioning in the poorer districts of the industrial towns' (*Purses* 174). Albert Campion's amnesia, which leaves him with a fractured sense of self and relation to the nation that he serves, reflects not only his dual positions as insider/outsider and as detective spy, but also how the nation must not lose sight of its social and economic dualities as it hopes for a new Britain after victory.[15]

Echoing Allingham's concerns, MacInnes's 1942 novel, *Assignment in Brittany*, features a British intelligence agent, Martin Hearne, who discovers discontinuities between his identity, life and work and the social and cultural codes that have shaped his loyalty to the nation for which he risks his life. Unlike Allingham's characterisation of Campion, MacInnes obscures Hearne's social origins. He appears as a seasoned agent whose social position can be inferred from his knowledge of languages, history and political sense of purpose, but whose assignments both solidify and revise his cultural attitudes. Like Campion, Hearne must lead a double life to be a successful spy and detective. His mission in France in the summer of 1940 is based on adopting the identity of Bertrand Corlay, a Frenchman rescued from Dunkirk whom Hearne uncannily resembles. Unlike stock thrillers, this doubling questions the political and ethical ambiguity in the relationship between the spy's double identity and double indemnity. Hearne's discovery that his double is not just an odious personality, but an insidiously well defended and disguised collaborator, reflects the ethical and emotional tightrope the British spy must walk. Hearne must be a convincing impersonator while constantly adapting to the surprises his double presents. He must integrate himself into Corlay's family, the Frenchman's village community and its fifth column while deciphering and juggling his double's emotional entanglements to figure out his own. Like Campion's liminal position, Hearne's identity is both mysterious and recognisable, an empty and overdetermined signifier. Submerging his identity into Corlay's requires that 'Hearne' disappear. The result of the merger, however, is restorative. It grafts Britain's defensive war onto French ambivalence and rescues French political and cultural integrity in Hearne's instrumental role as a British spy.

Hearne's discoveries about relations between being a secret and double agent complicate his personal and political realities. In turn, these realities are obscured by the very codes designed to facilitate his mission. Like Campion in *Traitor's Purse*, Hearne must spy on himself to uncover the hidden meanings of his mission. His assignment consists of transmitting coded messages to the British regarding German fortifications along the coast of Brittany from which Britain could be attacked. [16] But Hearne is also compelled to revise his mission when he makes several unforeseen discoveries: Corlay's collaborationist codebooks, his attraction to Anne, Corlay's estranged fiancée and the sexual exploitation of Corlay by his collaborator lover, Elise. The disjunctions between Hearne's political and strategic codes and Corlay's also connect them. Although their political positions conflict, as Hearne digs deeper into Corlay's codebooks, the act of deciphering sheds light on his own conflict between personal desire and political commitment. The political distance between the two men remains absolute but Hearne's discovery of his own priorities while deciphering the enemy's codebooks creates a critical connection. Uncovering everything he does not want to be creates questions about individual responsibility in a spy world that mandates duplicitous ethical decisions as it fragments knowledge and individuality. MacInnes's intermodern depiction of the spy's search for subjectivity and moral agency insists that the contingencies of World War II create necessary psychological dissonances but ethical coherence. This relationship contrasts sharply with modernist narrative ruptures which lament but thrive creatively by rebelling against the ethical and cultural smash-ups of those who perpetrated World War I. With no lament, MacInnes's intermodernism launches a counteroffensive against Nazi cultural supremacism and its annihilation of creative critique.

In order to accomplish his extended mission, to detect and pretend to join the French collaborators and their encoded plans, Hearne must find double meanings in his experiences and discoveries within the Corlay household and their village, Saint-Déodat. He must read both with and against the grain of his official spy sourcebook. Reading with the grain enables him to decipher the Nazis' plans; reading against enables him to decipher French collaborationist plans by understanding Saint-Déodat's ambiguous history. He learns that its people still adhere to its feudal motto, '*Nothing changes*', even beyond the 1789 revolution that destroyed the village, but since its efforts to rebuild, the motto's meaning had translated into 'avoid[ing] trouble by strictly minding their own business' (*Assignment* 29, 30; author's italics). Juggling both readings questions the complicated relationship between French and British historical memory and the meaning of war for Britain and the Continent. Hearne's momentary vision of the rural French order is all too similar to that of little England: 'Time seemed suspended in the silence of these fields. . . . Living here, one could . . . believe the delusion that peace was self-perpetuating'

(*Assignment* 45). Combined with the village's desire to 'avoid trouble', the novel asserts that in its isolationism, the deluded pastoral vision is collusive with the Nazis. Like the Mosleyites' vision of British-German reciprocity, the collaborators of Saint-Déodat have convinced themselves that Nazi Germany will ensure a 'separate Brittany, friendly to Germany, . . . secure and happy' (*Assignment* 127). Working with the desire of Breton nationalists for self-rule, MacInnes highlights the dangers of misreading Germany's political rhetoric. Even with a Nazi victory, the collaborators ensure their own undoing.

Political fantasy and immediate danger coalesce in a timeless and monumental image. Mont Saint-Michel rises

> like a mystic mountain of medieval fantasy and delicacy, from the strength of the granite rocks which held it secure in the surrounding miles of golden quicksand. Now the tide was out, and the long narrow causeway, which was the only connecting link between the continent of Europe and this island of tiered turrets and pinnacles, looked forlorn and purposeless. (*Assignment* 202)

This marvellously lyrical, alliterative and paradoxical image conveys the dangers of Nazi culture and of German military occupation of Mont Saint-Michel. It also represents the dangers of French cultural confidence. Because France fails to recognise its self-deceptions, it distrusts the Briton's mission and weakens its own resistance. The image of Mont Saint-Michel also reminds us that Nazi ideology draws upon mystical medieval and pastoral romantic mythologies while asserting its supremacism with the granite hard power of its military machine. But if the quicksand threatens the invader's secure base, it also symbolises the disabling effects of collaboration. The once mighty monument to religious power is displaced by Nazi occupation. The causeway that linked the island to Europe is replaced by a line of German bunkers. Reconnecting French national culture to Europe and to Britain is the plot that gives meaning to Mont Saint-Michel in this World War II novel. The British spy will navigate the quicksand with the help of a French child and rescue Anne, the Frenchwoman he loves. He will take her from a besieged island icon of French spirit back to his own threatened island nation. In so doing, he rescues the continuity of French culture by forging reconciliation between the rival allies.

Allingham's and MacInnes's 1940s thrillers are driven by a sustained textual energy that is fuelled by the hyper-tense drive to defeat and remain distinct from the enemy. In order to assert ideological distinctions, Allingham's and MacInnes's fictions also reveal similarly problematic national myths. Detecting the Masters' plot in *Traitor's Purse* exposes the dangers of Britain's myth of national unity. Plotting Polish resistance in MacInnes's 1944 novel *While Still We Live* debunks myths of Nazi eugenics, racial superiority and Slavic slave mentality. Allingham's and MacInnes's textual energies also question the distinctiveness of British political culture as it engages the European nations Britain would save from collaboration and defeat. The infiltration of British spies throughout Allied and occupied Europe creates spheres of influence that will be challenged by the end of the war and the British Empire. Britain's shrinking global power is evident in these novels as Campion returns to solve national crises. MacInnes's spies return to Britain's open-ended future.

The metafictional thrust of Allingham's and MacInnes's 1940s novels calls for revising the criteria governing literary hierarchies that privilege modernism and devalue detective spy fiction. In narrative experiments of their own, Allingham and MacInnes adapt their plotting to the urgency of the historical moment and in effect, defy precepts of both modernism and genre fiction. They reject the psychologically inflected terror 'that lies beyond language' or the roller coaster ride of thrills and chills that 'forfeits ratiocination for intuition' (Hepburn 28, 26). Instead, the tensions of pursuit and flight prod their heroes and heroines to reflect on the epistemological and ethical intricacies of coding and clues as well as the ethical compromises and cultural tensions they must encounter on their way to defeating the enemy. Nowhere is this reflection more evident than in MacInnes's chase scenes, which seem to move in slow contemplative motion – Hearne's tremulous escape over Mont Saint-Michel's quicksand and the Myleses' stumbling foray over a Tyrolean mountain. For the contemporaneous British or American reader, the thrill is superseded by the uncertainty of an ongoing war against a formidable enemy. Even as the British spies live to get away and/or the Nazi or collaborationist cabal is foiled, suspense of historical and global proportions remains – how is the defeat of Nazism plotted and what would this mean for the character and nature of the allied nation?

To combat Nazism, French collaboration, Austrian acquiescence and to support Polish resistance, MacInnes's detective spies conclude that the meaning of defence and victory lies in empathetic espionage and detection. *Above Suspicion* depicts this interpretation of intelligence gathering in the discovery that the ethos of British antipathy to Nazism consists of cultural myopia. Frances Myles's disguise in a dirndl fails because it is simply a deluded gesture of passing. Even more than a masquerade, her performance highlights a form of condescension that assumes the locals' blindness about their own cultural authenticity and political self-deception. In the novel's opening, the Myleses conform to the spy thriller's 'innocent abroad' who is 'not the sort of enthusiastic and willing amateur' but rather 'incompetent and inexperienced amateur in a world of professionals' (Denning 67). The British couple do not, however, remain unenthusiastic and incompetent for long. The novel charts their growing awareness of the necessity of using their artistic and intellectual talents to recognise and decipher unanticipated implications of their mission.

These include relationships between protecting their own agents and the victims who are falling in between them and the Nazis.

One scene in *Above Suspicion*, though narrated only from its margins, implants itself in the Myleses' memories unlike any other and alters their cultural and political consciousness. In Nuremberg, 'From the quiet blackness of the little alley to the left of them came a bitter cry, the high, self-strangling cry of fear or pain, or both' (*Suspicion* 107). When Richard Myles and the American journalist, Van Cortlandt, try to investigate, they are stopped by a Nazi brown shirt whose perspective glosses the assigned meaning of the British rescue mission: 'It is only a Jews' Alley' (*Suspicion* 107). Out of sight of the Myleses, the American and of readers, never to appear as a character in his own right, the Jew is caught in a limbo bounded by Nazi persecution and British recognition of an unfolding tragedy. In the service of their mission, the British and the American cannot help. Nonetheless, the Jew's place in a no-man's land of statelessness reminds the Allied characters, even as they become more vulnerable with every move, of their own privileged positions. The Jew's condition also inspires a vision of a British mission that extends far beyond the rescue of their own agent and agency. With a polemical thrust, the narrator's voice merges with Frances's caustic recognition:

> If only the methods of hate and force had been resisted at the very beginning: not by other countries (for *that* would have been called the unwarranted interference of those who wanted to keep Germany weak), but by the people of Germany, themselves. But of course, it had been more comfortable to turn a deaf ear to the cries from the concentration camps, to harden their hearts to the despair of the exiles, to soothe their conscience with praise of the Fatherland. And now, it had come to the stage where other peoples would have to do the dying, on barricades of shattered cities, to stop what should have been stopped seven years ago. (*Suspicion* 111; emphasis in original)

Inserting a polemical lamentation invites us to view the detective spies' position and the Jew's historical bind as a critical intermodern relationship. By implication, this literary and historical relationship extends analogically to enquiries about the characterisations of victim and agent in fiction of the 1940s.

In Allingham's wartime novels, regardless of the victim's individual identity, it is the British people and the nation that are threatened. As a British agent, Campion must become politically engaged, not only on his international secret mission, but on the home front where the appearance of locally motivated crimes must be deciphered for their geo-political meanings. MacInnes's *Above Suspicion* plots the question of what can be deciphered, learned and transmitted in wartime fiction through the absent presence of the Jewish victim. He is the encoded clue for which no encryption manuals or spy missions exist. The

Jew in 1939, the novel's setting, and in 1941, the time of its publication, is positioned outside the insider plots of double crosses and betrayals that characterise victims in spy fictions of other periods. For the narrator and detective spies, as well as for readers then and now, the Jew represents difficult, by which I mean painful and untranslatable, wilfully and circumstantially disregarded and belated intelligence, knowledge and understanding. In 1939 and 1941, what is available for representation is the bitterly empathetic recognition of a spy fiction that is yet to be written.

After publishing *Assignment in Brittany*, her fictive battle with Nazi collaboration, MacInnes waited until 1944 and 1945 to publish two novels that respond to the narrator's plea in *Above Suspicion*. These later novels stage the British commitment to 'fight on the barricades' and to help Poles and Austrian Tyrolese 'stop what should have been stopped seven years ago'. In her 1944 novel *While Still We Live*, as Germany bombards Poland, Sheila Matthews, a young Englishwoman, commits her empathy for the victimised nation to its resistance. She joins a band of roving Polish partisans, but like MacInnes's other World War II novels, adventure is tempered by a polemic that in its historical citation, resists any universal message. In response to Sheila's empathy with German humanity and suffering, a Polish doctor provides the lesson of bitter critical irony:

> Why, the poor dear Germans have never done anything at all! Their land has been the cockpit of Europe where other more powerful nations came to fight and rape and steal. . . . Surely it must be clear to you. That's why they have no industries, no factories, no well-equipped laboratories. . . . And all those German firms and salesmen you find throughout the world. . . . Why they aren't Germans at all! It's all a capitalist lie, a stab in the back by Jews and Communists. (*While* 306)

Read as a mutually reinforcing intertext, the 1939 settings of *While Still We Live* and *Above Suspicion* provide literary historical explanations for the repeated figure of the Jew. We now know why the Jew is being beaten in the Nuremberg alley. As a critical response to the sentimental impulses that Sheila Matthews represents, the twinned images of the Jew expose the dehumanising rationalisations that underwrote Nazi persecutions. In turn, the explanation humanises the absent, silent presence of Nazism's victims. Although the Nazis' victims have no story of their own in MacInnes's fiction, they remain a haunting presence in the altered political consciousness of her spies and in the plots that did not rescue them. Haunted by history is an intermodern story.

NOTES

1. I want to thank Elizabeth Maslen and Kristin Bluemel for their learned and wise comments on this essay. Allan Hepburn notes that with their arcane knowledge, Oxford

and Cambridge 'spy-catchers' are experts at 'solving puzzles that seem to have no solutions. They infer information from the smallest scraps of evidence' (57).

2. Michael Denning's claim that the political subjects of spy thrillers are 'only a pretext' for 'adventure formulas', excludes Allingham's and MacInnes's 1940s novels (2).

3. Although MGM's 1940 film of Phyllis Bottome's novel *The Mortal Storm* travestied her feminist critique and her characters' Jewish identity, she felt its plea to Americans was worth it.

4. Gill Plain discusses how World War II changes Allingham's 'gender agenda [. . .] from the "problem" of femininity to a crisis of masculinity' ('"Cry"' 61). While Plain emphasises 'the search for stability' over that for 'social change', I see Allingham questioning the value of stability ('"Cry"'67).

5. Allingham's 1940s novels defy descriptions of Golden Age crime fiction as 'socially enclosed' (Knight 78) or crime fiction that is 'feminized' in its 'domestic scale of action, the politeness of the language, the effeteness of many of the detective protagonists' (Horsley 38–39).

6. Wesley Britton notes that before Hitler's onslaught, spy fiction conformed to the 'romance' of 'protecting national interests' and did not 'reflect cultural and ideological fears beyond the racism and anti-Semitism that dominated the period' (19). Horsley finds that the 'liberal ethos' of crime fiction privileges 'a conservative mythologizing of individualism', but for Allingham and MacInnes, World War II produces a collective approach (18–19).

7. In a 1944 book review Allingham reveals her strong criticism of 'feudalism', while her wartime memoir, *The Oaken Heart*, celebrates 'neighbourliness and the worth of country (as opposed to 'County') folk', showing her wartime 'intense personal, social, and literary reassessment' (Jones 13–14).

8. Campion's critique accords with the 1942 Beveridge Report which led to Britain's health and education reforms. The implementation of the report was both a reward for the people's valour and politically wise.

9. Allan Hepburn defines a code as referring 'to something not itself, whereas a clue, like a hair left at a crime scene, synecdochically relates to the crime' (61).

10. In her 2001 book, Susan Rowland argues that Campion's 'foolish' look 'exhibits weakness' (19). More persuasive is her 2004 discussion of his 'gothic identity' as 'far more dangerously ambivalent than his fictional contemporaries', Peter Wimsey and Hercule Poirot, suggestive of a 'dark savior of England' (29). Victoria Stewart sees Campion's amnesia related to establishing 'who might be on which side' (65).

11. Richard Martin links *Coroner's Pidgin* to 'serious questions' about the nature of postwar British society and effects on 'those whose success was a direct product of the carefree conditions of their world in the 1930s' (146).

12. The Blackshirts became non-operational well before the war. John Atkins explains the lack of aristocratic Nazi sympathisers in spy novels from the 1930s through the 1950s as related to a middle-class readership 'not anxious to reveal the less pleasant face of the Establishment' (223).

13. Allingham's upper-crust villains disprove the claim that in her novels the nation's heritage 'must remain in the keeping of those who have had the ancient privilege of caring for it' (Horsley 58). As the very professional Campion demonstrates, she does not, moreover, utilise 'notions of amateurism' in order to 'naturaliz[e] the ruling elite' (Denning 34).

14. The rise of fascism and Nazi occupation of Europe were fertile grounds for British women's dystopian writing. Katherine Burdekin's 1937 *Swastika Night* predicts a catastrophic future controlled by a German–Japanese axis, Storm Jameson's 1936

In the Second Year and Naomi Mitchison's 1935 *And We Were Warned* depict fascist takeovers in Britain. Jameson's 1942 folkloric dystopia *Then We Shall Hear Singing* portrays the Nazi occupation of Czechoslovakia. For discussion of these dystopias and other anti-fascist women writers, see my *British Women Writers of World War II.*

15. Rowland's view of Campion 'as an other within "England"' who detects 'what is "English" and what is "other", the alien invader', accords with my own (*Agatha* 67).

16. In actuality, British spies in Europe did not work alone, but with rival British departments and networks that included French and Polish resisters. Couriers and transmitters worked under 'extraordinary handicaps' and were often compromised and caught, with many casualties (West 43).

Works Cited

Allingham, Margery. *Black Plumes.* 1940. New York: Bantam, 1983.

—. *Coroner's Pidgin.* 1945. London: Vintage, 2006.

—. *Traitor's Purse.* 1941. New York: Bantam, 1983.

Atkins, John. *The British Spy Novel.* London: John Calder, 1984.

Boyd, Mary K. 'The Enduring Appeal of the Spy Thrillers of Helen MacInnes'. *Clues* 4 (1983): 66–75.

Britton, Wesley. *Beyond Bond: Spies in Fiction and Film.* Westport: Praeger, 2005.

Denning, Michael. *Cover Stories: Narrative and Ideology in the British Spy Thriller.* London: Routledge and Kegan Paul, 1987.

Hepburn, Allan. *Intrigue: Espionage and Culture.* New Haven: Yale University Press, 2005.

Horsley, Lee. *Twentieth-Century Crime Fiction.* Oxford: Oxford University Press, 2005.

Jones, Julia. '"A Fine, Sturdy Piece of Work": Margery Allingham's Book Reviews for *Time & Tide* 1938–1944'. *Clues* 23.1 (2004): 9–17.

Knight, Stephen. 'The Golden Age'. *The Cambridge Companion to Crime Fiction.* Ed. Martin Priestman. Cambridge: Cambridge University Press, 2003. 77–94.

Lassner, Phyllis. *British Women Writers of World War Two: Battlegrounds of Their Own.* Basingstoke: Palgrave Macmillan, 1998.

Light, Alison. *Forever England: Femininity, Literature and Conservatism between the Wars.* New York: Routledge, 1991.

MacInnes, Helen. *Above Suspicion.* 1941. Boston: Little, Brown, 1942.

—. *Assignment in Brittany.* Boston: Little, Brown, 1942.

—. *While Still We Live.* 1944. New York: Crest/Fawcett Publications, 1964.

Martin, Richard. *Ink in her Blood: The Life and Crime Fiction of Margery Allingham.* Ann Arbor: UMI Research, 1988.

Peach, Linden. *Masquerade, Crime and Fiction.* Basingstoke: Palgrave, 2006.

Plain, Gill. '"A Good Cry or a Nice Rape": Margery Allingham's Gender Agenda'. *Critical Survey* 15.2 (2003): 61–75.

—. *Twentieth-Century Crime Fiction: Gender, Sexuality and the Body*. Edinburgh: Edinburgh University Press, 2001.

Priestman, Martin. *The Cambridge Companion to Crime Fiction*. Cambridge: Cambridge University Press, 2003.

Rowland, Susan. *From Agatha Christie to Ruth Rendell: British Women Writers in Detective and Crime Fiction*. Basingstoke: Palgrave, 2001.

—. 'Margery Allingham's Gothic: Genre as Cultural Criticism'. *Clues* 23.1 (2004): 27–39.

Stewart, Victoria. *Narratives of Memory: British Writing of the 1940s*. Basingstoke: Palgrave, 2006.

West, Nigel. *Secret War: The Story of SOE, Britain's Wartime Sabotage Organization*. London: Hodder and Stoughton, 1992.

7

TRIALS AND ERRORS: *THE HEAT OF THE DAY* AND POSTWAR CULPABILITY

Allan Hepburn

The adjudication of good and evil preoccupied tribunals and writers in the years around World War II. From the Moscow show trials of the late 1930s through the postwar trials of Nazi criminals and collaborators, legal proceedings did not guarantee the impartial administration of justice. The trial as a judicial event, with all its attendant ambiguities, was adapted by intermodern writers as a paradigm for journalistic and novelistic narrative. As a narrative structure, the trial creates opportunities for confession, alibi and verdict. In every instance the trial arbitrates guilt and innocence. Elizabeth Bowen responds to the pervasive atmosphere of postwar culpability in fictional form in *The Heat of the Day* (1949). In this novel, culpability has national and international ramifications that touch specifically on the future of Europe. Unaddressed guilt caused by wartime activities grows into a terrible legacy for Europeans. War trials arbitrate guilt but cannot assuage a guilty conscience or eliminate guilt from national consciousness. Bowen thought a great deal about criminal offences and guilt. A member of the Royal Commission on Capital Punishment, which was struck in 1949 and tabled its recommendations in 1953, she weighed the advantages and disadvantages of capital punishment, specifically in relation to convicted murderers in Britain. More locally, in *The Heat of the Day*, an inquest into the death of a traitor proves inconclusive. The narrative mode of interrogation, however, presupposes his lover's culpability. As Bowen came to realise during and after the war, all trials have their errors, whether of personal judgement or the cultural imperative to judge.

In various genres, Bowen thought over the narrative possibilities of trials. In 'The Unromantic Princess', a short story for children published in 1935, she uses the trial comically, in the manner of Lewis Carroll's *Alice in Wonderland*, to criticise arbitrary power. A young man who does not throw a ball back to a princess is arrested and tried for the preposterous crime of wounding the princess's feelings. The king tells the culprit, 'By the law of the land you are threatened with a very serious punishment. People have been beheaded for treason, you know' (*Bazaar* 105). The boy apologises and all ends well. Nevertheless, the story makes a pitch for commonsense application of the law rather than arbitrary death sentences. The princess and the boy, who ultimately marry, propose to modernise the entire state. As against this fairy tale, the issue of punishment looked quite different to Bowen after the war. In a review of Whittaker Chambers's *Witness*, she evokes the 'climate and import' of the postwar era, which she diagnoses for its effect 'of moral no less than political dissolution' ('Informer' 9). In the same review, Bowen associates the dramatic unmasking of a communist spy – what she calls 'the confrontation of accuser by accused'('Informer' 9) – with Alistair Cook's journalistic account of the Hiss case, published in book form as *A Generation on Trial*. The dissolution of politics into murkiness after the war ran parallel to, and was not necessarily clarified by, the administration of justice through trials, including those of Alger Hiss and the Nazi criminals at Nuremberg.

The sombre mood after the war is partly attributable to the possibility of being denounced for a variety of actual or thought crimes. Indeed, the trial has a specific literary lineage from the 1930s through to the 1960s. Two international successes, Arthur Koestler's *Darkness at Noon* (1940) and George Orwell's *Animal Farm* (1945), represent culpability brought about by unjust hearings and verdicts. Rebecca West documented in a journalistic mode the first Nuremberg Trial in *A Train of Powder* (1955); the trial established limits to emerging international law. West also covered the trials of Lord Haw-Haw and John Amery in *The Meaning of Treason* (1949), which she expanded with further examples of duplicity in *The New Meaning of Treason* (1964). Hannah Arendt probed the political consequences of emerging international law in *Eichmann in Jerusalem* (1963). The existential consequences of culpability migrate into accusations of treachery in John Le Carré's espionage thriller, *The Spy Who Came in from the Cold* (1963), in which a British mole, Alec Leamas, pretends to defect to East Germany. Arrested and beaten, Leamas is arraigned before a tribunal consisting mostly of police, wardens and spectators who belong to the Communist Party. The president of the tribunal emphasises the administrative rather than juridical nature of Leamas's trial: '"The proceedings are secret, remember that. This is a Tribunal convened expressly by the Praesidium. It is to the Praesidium alone that we are responsible. We shall hear evidence as we think fit"' (Le Carré 163). To hear only evidence deemed 'fit' is to decide a priori on the admissibility of certain information and points of view. As Le Carré's bestselling novel indicates, literary representations respond to the understanding of the trial itself as an instrument of punishment, not justice, in which ideological stances and perceived treacheries are judged. In such instances, innocence or guilt is beside the point.

CULPABILITY IN *THE HEAT OF THE DAY*

Like other intermodern writers, Bowen adopts the trial as a narrative event to expose the shades of culpability and the effects of judgement on national subjects. In *The Heat of the Day*, Stella Rodney, who works for the Ministry of Information, is having a love affair with Robert Kelway, denounced as a Nazi spy by a counter-espionage agent named Robert Harrison. After Kelway's death, either by suicide or misadventure, the coroner interrogates Stella to determine her moral character and her involvement in the death. The inquest, as a mild version of legal arbitration, indirectly tests Stella's national allegiances and culpability. When asked about the identity of the man who had tailed Kelway, Stella evasively answers, 'I cannot tell you whom Captain Kelway may have had in mind: I have no idea' (*HD* 340).[1] She knows perfectly well that Harrison suspected Kelway and that Harrison had been loitering in the street on the night of Kelway's death. By dissembling, Stella protects Robert's reputation and her own. By not disclosing the full truth, she inadvertently draws attention to her possible culpability.

In a promotional summary that she wrote about the novel, Bowen describes Stella's position in a sequence of questions that obviate guilt: 'How far dare we know each other; how far is the heightened vision of love compatible with a willing blindness; how far might not an enormity be one form of honour?' ('Heat' HRC 5.5). In this synopsis, the first two clauses refer to Stella, who, having fallen in love with Kelway at the height of the Blitz, refuses to endorse Harrison's accusations that Kelway is a spy. The 'enormity' in the third clause has application to several people and situations in the novel. The enormities of betrayal compound the enormities of war. If Stella perpetrates an enormity, it is surely to ignore Kelway's culpability because she loves him (Hepburn 140, 148–52). Yet the 'enormity' of Kelway's betrayal of Britain might be a form of honour insofar as the complacency and insularity of the British middle class, from which Kelway issues, foster treachery; his exposure of the banality of such treachery could be construed as a point of honour. In the same promotional note, Bowen further insists that the implications of *The Heat of the Day* exceed its wartime setting. She points out that the violence of warfare, while felt as an external pressure, does not enter representation. The novel concerns the meaning of history as it extends into personal lives and into the future: 'The possibility of there being no present, nothing more than a grinding-together of past and future, enters, at a point in the story, a woman's thought. Against that, there is the actuality of moments, and the power of a moment to protract itself and contain the world. All through *The Heat of the Day*, what might be drama runs into little pockets: this is a domestic novel. Within view of the reader there is no violent act. Persons hesitate or calculate; and at the same time are inseparable from history' ('Heat' HRC 5.5). The domestic novel registers the impact of war on a human, not epochal, scale. It works out the effects of history on characters during the war and, in an enlarged perspective, during the postwar as well.

In this regard, *The Heat of the Day* exists in a double time-frame: 1942 to 1944, the span of the plot, overlaps with 1945 to 1949, when Bowen, thinking about the implications of European history, drafted the novel. In an assessment of 'English Fiction at Mid-Century' published in 1954, she claims that the 'wholesale destruction' of war forces 'moral drama' into the forefront of novelistic representation (211). Against the ubiquitous atmosphere of devastation and executions, Bowen speculates on history in its moral dimensions. Individual choices, she concludes, have historical consequences. Faced with devastation, Europeans invent new laws, or laws that are provisional, not permanent. Moral dramas arise when no clear law covers human behaviour. The war also divides people from their previous political commitments or class allegiances: communists who believe in international solidarity in the 1930s turn into patriots during the war; fascists during the war renounce their allegiances and disclaim responsibility for their actions as soon as the war ends. *The Heat of the Day* thus confirms the intermodern preoccupation with the consequences of political commitment prior to and during the war. Legal culpability is one aspect of the intermodern, insofar as guilt can be demonstrated by trial or inquest.

The Heat of the Day specifically addresses the uncertain future of Europe as an extension of its troubled and bloody recent history. As Bowen saw the emerging political situation, moral commitment was, in part, invested in nationality. As Marina MacKay argues, World War II forced writers in Britain to scrutinise their 'political and moral claims of insular nationality at a time when allegiance was demanded as rarely before, the national culture at risk as it had not been in centuries' (2). Bowen pondered the legacies of pre-war, nationalistic Europe in the ruined, reconstructing postwar world. In *The Heat of the Day*, the trope of inheritance is applied to the destiny and potential of Ireland specifically and Europe generally. Roderick Rodney, Stella's son, inherits an Irish country house called Mount Morris from a distant relative. Roderick, an unmarried soldier stationed in England, thinks of his inherited property as an assurance of survival: 'The place was his future, which was something to have' (*HD* 216). Placement of the pronominal clause suggests that the *future* rather than the *place* is 'something to have'. In the same vein of wishful thinking, Stella pictures Roderick and his wife at Mount Morris in the indefinite future (218). Never having been to the house, Roderick can only conjecture what obligations his inheritance entails. When he visits his unhinged Cousin Nettie at a nursing home, Roderick avoids talking about ancestors and the past. 'No, what I want to talk about is the future' (228), he insists. The novel mediates Roderick's possible 'historic future' (52) after the war and Stella and Robert's love affair in the 'futureless day-to-day' during the war (109).

When Rosamond Lehmann read *The Heat of the Day* in February 1949, she wrote an impassioned letter to Bowen calling the book a 'masterpiece', while anxiously wondering whether 'Roderick is at Mount Morris now' (HRC 11.6). Lehmann wants to eliminate doubt about whether Roderick survives the war and takes up his inheritance. Bowen leaves the question of what is about to come unresolved by not narrating information about Roderick's survival and inheritance. While visiting his Irish property, he thinks about the lineage of owners which might end with him: 'who would, indeed, aspire to be the final man?' (*HD* 352). The phrase resonates with George Orwell's working title for *Nineteen Eighty-Four*: 'The Last Man in Europe'. The 'last man' or the 'final man' sums up the tradition that produced him, but that tradition, that specifically European tradition, possibly ends with an heirless heir. Roderick conjectures that he will not survive combat while storming the 'Fortress of Europe' (*HD* 352). If he leaves Mount Morris to his mother, his only relative, he reverses the customary transmission of ownership. *The Heat of the Day* thus implicitly asks what duties children owe their elders.

In her writings of the 1940s, Bowen pictures various children as the emblem of the future. *The Heat of the Day* closes not with Roderick's fate, but with the destiny of Louie Louis's child. Although Louie calls her baby 'Tom' after her husband, Tom has been away fighting and cannot possibly have fathered the child. Late in the narrative, a telegram announces Tom's death abroad. Illegitimate and unfathered, the infant shows an 'intention to survive' (371). The survival of the child heralds the postwar, for the novel ends in September 1944 when the 'last of the enemy' has been cleared 'out of the Channel ports' (371). In narrative terms, the baby's intention to survive offsets uncertainty about Roderick's fate. Offspring of a confused mother and an unknown father, the baby inherits the future, if anyone does. In general terms, the war entails 'disrupted lineage and lost proprietary continuity' (MacKay 102). The future of Britain, as Bowen suggests, does not conform to a straightforward geneal-ogy of legitimacy and inheritance. Moreover, British inheritance is implicated in the future of the West. *The Heat of the Day* concludes with emphasis on the word 'West': Louie Louis, pushing little Tom in a pram, looks up to see three swans in straight flight 'disappearing in the direction of the West' (372). In a broad political perspective, the West was guarantor of the reconstruction of Europe. From the West – Western Europe, the US – came the moral and financial resources to reconstruct war-ravaged Central and Eastern Europe. From the West also came resistance to Russian occupation of Central and Eastern European countries and the emergence of the Soviet bloc.

As Bowen knew, the future of the West was not all that clear in the late 1940s. In three newspaper articles that she filed on the Paris Peace Conference in 1946, she evokes the future through the trope of the child. In the original draft of these articles, Bowen links the destiny of children playing in the Luxembourg Gardens with the decisions taken by delegates inside the Luxembourg Palace thrashing out the details of reparations and frontiers: 'In my consciousness, I feel a connecting thread between the men, in there, sitting round the green tables, and the children, out there, playing among the green lawns' (HRC 8.7). Bowen concludes this draft with a return to the child, stand-in for the average European confronted with the escalating tensions of the Cold War:

> It could but be obvious to a child, to a savage, that Poles, Czechs, Ukrainians, Yugoslavs are attached to the U.S.S.R. as are the fingers to the palm of a hand. Charges of pro-Italianism, of reactionary sympathies, against the other (or, 'Western') Delegations are not for long allowed to remain absent from the lips of any of that *bloc*. For the onlooker, there is the sinister fascination of watching Russia create, by her own suspicions, a psycho-political situation that, actually, not only has not existed so far but need not, in spite of Russia, ever exist at all. (HRC 8.7)

The word 'West' that concludes *The Heat of the Day* resonates with the 'Western' delegations staving off Soviet hostility. Whereas the Russian army occupied Eastern Europe as far as the Elbe in 1945, the French, British and American armies occupied western Germany, most of Austria, and all of Italy. As Bowen notes, the cries of 'pro-Italianism' and 'reactionary sympathies' were propagandistic efforts to consolidate Russian influence and expand the Soviet bloc. Even a child could see through the Russians' ruses.

Bowen was not alone in imagining the future generationally. In *A Train of Powder*, Rebecca West conjures images of German children swimming or playing outside the courthouse in Nuremberg while the war trials take place inside (18, 23, 25, 322, 331). For West, the German children bode a sinister eventuality. She predicts the possibility of a future war (12), while recalling that 'People can become accustomed to committing acts of cruelty; recent Europe proves that' (96). Unlike West, Bowen sees the child as subject to the vicissitudes of history. Ominously, a child appears at the conclusion to 'Folkestone: July, 1945' as a sign of the treacheries that the past inflicts on subsequent generations. Bowen notes that 'military occupation is at an end' in July 1945 (*CI* 228), although soldiers are still about and not all houses have been derequisitioned. The essay contrasts pre-war beach-goers wearing espadrilles and swilling cocktails with postwar reality: 'For the child of 1945 Folkestone bristles with barbed wire' (*CI* 230). The child in 1945 cannot play on beaches strewn dangerously with the relics of war. The generation that has no memory of the war lives out its consequences nonetheless. Bowen dramatises this proposition in *The Heat of the Day*; when Stella tells her son that Robert was a traitor, Roderick can think of nothing appropriate to say. He calls his youth a 'disadvantage', and he expects that he will be, as he says, 'no good for another fifty years – because all I can do now is try and work this out, which could easily take my lifetime' (*HD* 337). Young enough to fight but not old enough to understand why someone would betray the national cause by acting as a Nazi spy, Roderick feels the burden of posterity; more specifically, he bears the burden of construing the meaning of war and its treacheries. To work out the conundrum of culpability – which Roderick imagines will take his entire lifetime – is to suspend judgement in the present. In part, Roderick means that he, or his generation, cannot separate the war from its aftermath. The war and postwar form a continuum, in which culpability has no single meaning. Literary explorations of this continuum point to the possibility, or perhaps inevitability, of intermodernism.

The passage to the end of the war is equally fraught for Stella. Travelling to Ireland, she momentarily experiences the 'exciting sensation of being outside war' (*HD* 185). Being outside the war relieves the pressure of determining who is and who is not trustworthy. Back in England, Stella reassures Robert, '"You have no enemy anywhere in me!"' (209). Doubt shades her negative formulation. She does not say, 'You have a friend in me'. In a way, she challenges Robert to find some speck of treachery that she has not suspected in herself. More disturbing still, Stella adds the exculpatory 'anywhere' to her sentence. She means that she hides nothing of herself from Robert; her love for him conceals no enmity whatsoever. But the phrase 'no enemy anywhere' expands the dimensions of enmity beyond Stella to all nooks and crannies of wartime Britain. By contrast, he turns out to be inimical to her in that he betrays his country. By not telling Stella about his treachery, he implicates her in treason.

Numerous readers thought that Bowen erred by making Robert a Nazi spy (Lee 237 n.41). In a letter dated 14 February 1949, Rosamond Lehmann wondered 'whether Robert's being a "traitor" is sufficiently, clearly motivated, and what he believes about strength and law – is it in the Nietzschean sense?' (HRC 11.6). After reading *The Heat of the Day* again, Lehmann elaborated her concern in a letter on 4 March 1949: 'I cannot see why he shouldn't have been a Communist & therefore pro-Russian, & therefore pro-Ally, rather than pro-Germany' (HRC 11.6). Bowen's decision to make Robert a Nazi sympathiser is motivated by her critique of middle-class British complacency. In Bowen's view, the war heightens the sense of treachery implicit within complacency. Not wanting to lose its entitlements, the middle class prefers to calumniate and betray national interests. In a review of John Lehmann's edited collection *New Writing in Europe* published in January 1941, Bowen, discussing the revolutionary zeal of writing in the 1930s, mocks 'the norm of most writing in England', which condoles with and flatters 'middle-class sensibility' ('Advance' 65). She calls the middle-class home 'claustrophobic', because it breeds a class of people who feel themselves 'special, intensive, charged with personal feeling' ('Advance' 65). Robert Kelway, as the product of such an environment, perpetrates treachery out of self-interest and out of belief in his class-entitled superiority. Although generally reluctant to make accusations, Bowen indicts Kelway and his class for its hypocritical and narrow smugness. Such complacency has political consequences, which are dire during warfare.

In 'Britain in Autumn', Bowen explicitly links middle-class complacency with fascism, as two forms of culpability:

> When you stand by to die every night you see, if only in moments, what life was meant to be. You ask, what stopped life being like that? You grow enemy-conscious. Nazis make a name and front for the Enemy, but we have bred our own, and deadlier, enemies. These are waiting, these may try to come back: *laissez faire*, subservience, smugness, habit-of-mind. (HRC 2.2)

The war permits some chink in complacency because it levels distinctions between classes as it levels distinctions between those who will live and those who will die; neither civilian nor soldier is immune to death during war. Bowen interprets this levelling as a political evolution in a favourable direction in 'Britain in Autumn': 'We have almost stopped talking about Democracy because, for the first time, we *are* a democracy. We are more, we are almost a commune' (HRC 2.2). Fascism is not just a malevolent political regime abroad, but a tendency to interpret any kind of otherness as intolerable. Petra Rau sums up the inevitability of Robert's fascist sympathies: 'The old order of the British Empire and the new Nazi regime appeared to share a preference for clearly defined forms of otherness as opposed to the hodgepodge heterogeneity of democracy' (40).

After Robert's death – he may either 'fall or leap' from the roof of Stella's building (*HD* 327) – Stella has to speak for him at the coroner's inquest. In this interrogation, only Stella's answers to questions appear. The questions about Robert, his activities and their relationship can be inferred from her answers: '. . . On the contrary: I made every attempt to stop him . . . Yes; but what could I do? . . . I've already said so – I have already described him as being in an excitable state' (342). This one-sided interrogative technique recalls the elliptical style that Bowen uses in some of her short stories, such as 'The Disinherited', 'Oh, Madam', and 'The Dolt's Tale'. Like Stella's testimony in *The Heat of the Day*, these narratives usually imply unlawful activities of some sort: murder, trafficking in stolen goods, treachery. Each of these monologues, founded in talk, implies 'incomprehension' and 'conversational failure' (Mepham 67, 70) as characteristic intermodern tropes. Stella's testimony leads to false conclusions about her conduct and personality. The court creates the false inference that she drinks heavily and entertains 'other men friends' besides Robert in her West End flat (*HD* 340). The newspapers that report the inquest perpetuate these falsehoods. Reading the news, Louie concludes that Stella is as common, as treacherous, as any other outwardly respectable person: '[S]he had stood in court, telling them all. That was that; simply that again. There was nobody to admire' (*HD* 346). Louie's feeling that Stella has betrayed her conforms to a pattern of treachery that Robert raises: 'simply that again'. The court undermines Stella's credibility, for, as Louie wonders, what respectable woman would publicly expose her love affairs? Stella is culpable by association with Robert, yet her culpability, at least as Louie interprets it, pertains to sexual availability, not treason against the nation in time of war. Stella nevertheless faces possible accusation of guilt by association with Robert.

SHOW TRIALS AND WAR TRIALS

Stella's day in court, however unjustly concluded, anticipates Bowen's own thinking about the nature of trials and errors while working on the Royal Commission on Capital Punishment from 1949 to 1953. She was appointed to the commission, she thought, because her occupation as a writer gave her a perspective that differed from the eleven other jurisprudential and political appointees. She was one of only two women who served, the other being Florence May Hancock. Bowen told Blanche Knopf that she had 'a 4-day session of the Royal Commission on Capital Punishment' in Edinburgh in April 1950 (HRC Knopf 685.15). In a letter to Veronica Wedgwood on 10 April 1952, Bowen mentions her duties in passing: 'I've got to make one of my monthly Royal-Commission-on-Capital-Punishment dashes over to London' (Bodleian MS Eng. c. 6839). The commissioners visited prisons in Scotland, England and the United States. They heard submissions from dozens of experts. They saw gallows and cells where the condemned were confined. They did not, in the end, witness an execution. In their deliberations, they ultimately considered alternatives to hanging, such as lethal injection, electrocution and gassing, but concluded that none of these methods, 'on balance, [had] any advantage over hanging' (*Royal* 280).

Bowen's contributions to the findings of the commission merge with those of the other commissioners in the final report. Nonetheless, in a radio interview in 1959, she claimed to have argued during deliberations that 'continuous mental torture is equally provocative' in a case of murder as physical provocation ('Interview, 1959'). She also sought to redress the imbalance between men and women in *crimes passionels*. She objected to the fact that 'clemency is more likely to be extended to a man who finds his wife has been unfaithful to him, who finds her in the arms of somebody, whereas a man whose mistress distresses him in the same way is more likely to have the law against him' ('Interview, 1959'). In its final report, the commission specifically questions whether murder ought to be more narrowly defined, and 'manslaughter correspondingly enlarged' in definition (*Royal* 25). Although the deterrent effect of hanging was cited as the chief reason to retain the death sentence, the commission found this argument limited: 'It is therefore important to view the question in a just perspective and not to base a penal policy in relation to murder on exaggerated estimates of the uniquely deterrent force of the death penalty' (*Royal* 274). Overall, the commission was not charged with investigating the abolition of capital punishment; recommendations, therefore, were restricted to modifications of existing laws, including, as Bowen herself urged, to make 'no distinction between provocation by words and other forms of provocation' (*Royal* 274). In fact, the chief conclusion of the commissioners was that 'little more can be done effectively to limit the liability to suffer the death penalty, and that the issue is now whether capital punishment should be retained or abolished' (*Royal* 278). As a punishment for murder, the death penalty was abolished in the United Kingdom in 1964.

Feeling guilty about murdering someone is not the same as war guilt. In *The Heat of the Day*, Bowen speculates on the degree to which Stella's liaison with Robert makes her guilty. The situation can be stated as a paradox: how many people are required for a betrayal to occur? During a candid conversation about his culpability for passing information to the Nazis, Robert proclaims, '"Nothing I *can* break *is* law!"' (303). Breaking a law means that he sets the law, not in a Nietzschean way as Rosamond Lehmann speculates, but in the fascistic way of doing as one pleases without, in the doing, feeling any culpability. Robert Kelway intimates that he is a law unto himself, in an absolute and unbreakable sense. Embodying the law has the sinister implication of manipulating the law for one's own purposes. Intermodern writers such as Orwell and Bowen merge political culpability with the responsibility that ordinary citizens bear to uphold the law, especially in time of war, and their failure to do so. As Robert's plea in *The Heat of the Day* makes clear, not breaking the law is not synonymous with defending the law.

The postwar perplexity about law – at national and international levels – dates to the pre-war show trials in Russia. Stalin rejigged the definition of legal process by staging hearings for the sake of incriminating and purging undesirable elements from the governing party. Purges escalated to the point that no stalwarts of the revolution remained by 1938; anyone who might remember Lenin personally or recall the principles of the revolution was dead. In August 1936, 'The Trial of Sixteen' concluded in Moscow with the execution of all sixteen accused Communist Party members who denounced their own trumped-up, nefarious actions. André Gide, who spent the summer of 1936 in the USSR and who read the official transcript of the tribunal, later noted in his journal, 'What is one to think of those sixteen men under indictment accusing themselves, and each one in almost the same terms, and singing the praises of a régime and a man that they risked their lives to eliminate?' (1254–55).[2] The lamentable display of self-accusation did not abate. In 1937, another seventeen old Bolsheviks were executed or sentenced to long prison terms. In 1938, Bukharin and other rightists within the Central Committee were executed after further show trials. The Stalinist purges appropriated legal procedure to endorse a fiction of culpability.

International unease about Stalinist communism and its fast-and-loose application of justice found an outlet in Arthur Koestler's *Darkness at Noon*. The novel, translated from German, was published in English in 1940 by Jonathan Cape.[3] As Koestler specifies in an opening note to *Darkness at Noon*, the protagonist N. S. Rubashov 'is a synthesis of the lives of a number of men who were victims of the so-called Moscow Trials' (vi). The novel is structured not around chapters but around three 'hearings' and a coda. Having replaced the chapter as a unit of action, the 'hearing' assumes the form of an interrogation behind closed doors with limited opportunity for physical action. Relentless questions and answers constitute the plot. An atmosphere of Sartre's *Huis Clos* with the doctrine of Lenin's *The State and Revolution* predominates. Rubashov explains the mystery of how the prosecution obtains confessions from accused enemies of the party: torture. Trial novels, in fact, are closely allied to the representation of torture. Rubashov's first inquisitor, Ivanov, extols the necessity of public spectacle: 'For the public, one needs, of course, a trial and legal justification. For us, what I have just said should be enough' (*DN* 70). In the Stalinist context, the trial justifies liquidation on the grounds that a confession, no matter how it is extorted, incriminates absolutely and without recourse.

In *Darkness at Noon*, trials require no rationale; the trial exists to prove that ideology has its impurities, and those who sit in judgement place themselves above those impurities. For instance, the loyal party member Bogrov is executed over a quibble about submarine size. Rubashov meets his fate on the gallows for no discernible reason except that his old friend, Number 1 (a cipher for Stalin), wants him executed. Explaining a nuance of procedure that also underlies *Animal Farm* and *The Spy Who Came in from the Cold*, Ivanov parses the effects of public and administrative trials: 'In a public trial [Bogrov] would only have created confusion among the people. There was no other way possible than to liquidate him administratively' (*DN* 123). Instead of concentrating on the deterrent effects of a public hanging, the public trial prolongs punishment and places the responsibility for guilt squarely on the shoulders of the accused. Once the defendant confesses, the state, by the logic of the show trial, has no choice but to execute him. The execution is merely the culmination of protracted hypocrisy.

In an essay on Koestler written in 1944, George Orwell praises the 'atmosphere of nightmare' that prevails in *Darkness at Noon* and Koestler's other works (236). Recognising that Koestler writes about the Moscow 'frame-up trials', Orwell comments on the reaction to those trials in insular England:

> [T]here exists in England almost no literature of disillusionment about the Soviet Union. There is the attitude of ignorant disapproval, and there is the attitude of uncritical admiration, but very little in between. Opinion on the Moscow sabotage trials, for instance, was divided, but divided chiefly on the question of whether the accused were guilty. Few people were able to see that, whether justified or not, the trials were an unspeakable horror. ('Koestler' 235)

Sentiment, whether for or against communism, ought not to cloud the humane conviction that torture-induced confessions and the consolidation of power through fake tribunals are travesties of justice. Orwell implies that, viewed from the position of enlightened internationalism, laws should not be bent for the purposes of condemning those who want to think for themselves. Whereas Orwell adheres to a belief in law as the enshrinement of individual freedoms in a universal sense, Stalin applies the law as a punishment for those who think independently in a milieu of doctrinal revolutionary politics. The law protects; the law oppresses.

Orwell echoes his anti-Soviet sentiment in a cancelled preface to *Animal Farm*, written at nearly the same time as the essay on Koestler: 'At this moment what is demanded by the prevailing orthodoxy [in Britain] is an uncritical admiration of Soviet Russia' (*AF* 99). In *The Heat of the Day*, Bowen seconds this observation, but applies it to September 1942 in London, 'the summer when the idealisation of Russia was at its height' (*HD* 8). Especially as she wrote and revised *The Heat of the Day* through the late 1940s, Bowen was deeply suspicious of the ostentatious and naive solidarity that some British citizens felt for Russia.

In both *Darkness at Noon* and *Animal Farm*, excessive, vigilante punishment is rampant. Secret hearings, torture and summary execution on the suspicion, rather than the confirmation, of guilt do not add up to due legal process. In this regard, fiction converges with historical events. Representations of trials sometimes grew out of historical precedent. During World War II, seventeen people in England were executed for offences under the Treachery Act of 1940 (*Royal* 5). The arrival of peace in Europe heralded a period of judicial and quasi-judicial proceedings that often ended in death by hanging. The carnage of war, measured by millions of dead, produced the symbolic, if not cathartic, postwar execution of military and political figures deemed responsible for destruction and bloodshed. Some people may have been guilty, but immediately after the war, no established parameters for judging war crimes existed. Across Europe, judgements proceeded swiftly: 110,000 people were punished for collaboration in Holland (Huyse 65); approximately 9,000 people were executed summarily in France (Rousso 119); 668 people were convicted of war crimes in Romania (*Report* n.p.).

After careful if legally unprecedented deliberation by international judges, verdicts at the Nuremberg Trial in 1946 condemned twelve of the twenty-three accused Nazi officials to death; Martin Bormann was tried in absentia and sentenced to hang, but he had disappeared in 1945 (Marrus 258–60). Denazification courts set to work to punish or absolve Germans who had served Hitler's Third Reich. The application of due legal process for monstrously culpable figures like Adolf Eichmann or Hermann Wilhelm Göring created doubt about the efficacy of the law when confronted with the enormity of wartime crimes. As Arendt states, the Nuremberg Trials 'gave the illusion that the altogether unprecedented could be judged according to precedents and the standards that went with them' (Arendt 135). The resolutions of the 1928 Kellogg–Briand pact made aggressive warfare a crime, and this definition of criminal acts among nations gave some purchase on the bringing to justice of offenders. After the war, 'there had to be a trial' (*TP* 17), even if the Soviet Russians disagreed with what legal apparatus should be used to judge Nazi criminals and who should preside; and the accused Germans, unaccustomed to the combination of English and American legal procedures adopted, found the system incomprehensible.

At the Nuremberg Trials, the Russians energetically bullied their peers and devised stalling tactics over procedure. They wore uniforms to the trials to indicate that judgement was a prerogative of military victory. In their view, military rule trumped all laws, including international law. Thus, even as Nazi war criminals were tried and convicted at Nuremberg, the lines of the Cold War emerged. In full awareness of these early conflicts between the Soviets and the West over the meaning and arbitration of justice, Bowen's postwar essays touch on the understanding of futurity. Specifically, Bowen wonders if the future develops from personal motivations and actions, or if the future will be national or international. Whereas communist Russia in the 1930s held out the promise of a utopian future for many in the West, communist Russia in the 1940s had lost its political credibility and its status as a model of egalitarianism. Bowen believed with many other intermodernists that the future lay with international tribunals, not international political parties.

FUTURITY: INTERNATIONAL INTERMODERNISM

In contrast to Orwell's castigations and Koestler's disaffection with the internationalist conception of communism, Bowen approached the Cold War through impressions gleaned from travels in Europe and from first-hand witnessing of diplomacy. She believed in a personal connection with politics. In the 1940s and 1950s, she spent a great deal of time on the Continent. Between July and September 1946, she travelled twice to the Paris Peace Conference, which was busy redrawing national frontiers in postwar Europe. The Paris negotiations afforded her an understanding of the stakes in international law and the conduct of nations, whether obstructionist or co-operative. Approaching the Paris negotiations with an eye to atmosphere and unspoken tensions, Bowen gathers impressions rather than data. In the three newspaper articles that she published in the *Cork Examiner* about the conference, she emphasises the touchiness of Russian delegates regarding their desire to extend the boundaries of the Soviet bloc. Bowen observes about the tireless Russian delegates, 'Their irritability arises from quite another source: their by now palpable persecution-mania – which, I was told, even takes the form of a touchy childishness on the subject of seating accommodation, etc' ('Paris 2' 7). She complains of the irksome 'Russian voice going unintelligibly on and on' like 'an electric drill' ('Paris 2' 7) and attributes moral qualities to the Russians' physical appearance:

> Molotov's absolute greyness of speech and person sent out a sort of fume whenever he was present and rose to speak. He seems to be the one hundred per cent bureaucrat, sub-acid in mind and person, incapable of any impulse of the heart, even anger. One could feel him strongly antipathetic to the majority of the persons there. ('Paris 3' 4)

Observing the tense negotiations, Bowen applies the strategies of fiction to the forms and purposes of political reportage.

Between 1946 and the mid-1950s, Bowen travelled throughout Central and Western Europe, often under the auspices of the British Council; she gave lectures on literature at various universities and cultural associations. She visited Prague early in February 1948, mere days before the communists consolidated power there, and she toured Hungary in October of the same year. During her travels, Bowen observed that Russian communism awoke the ghosts of fascism. Scarcely had Nazi occupiers withdrawn from Eastern Europe than Russian occupiers moved in. Consequently, the political regimes appeared to merge with each other.

In 'Without Coffee, Cigarettes, or Feeling,' a 1955 essay about West Germany, she reverts to her theme of futurity as an answer to the dilemmas of Cold War influence and foreign occupation. Students in Germany offer prospects for the future: 'First [. . .] of the postwar German enigmas which confronted me was that of the outlook, intellectual interests, psychological background, plans, hopes and intentions of present-day German youth. To which was added my own personal, human, I suppose essentially feminine query, "How does it feel?"' (175). According to Bowen, both German and Hungarian students shy away from fascist and communist allegiances. German students tell her that they despise clubs in which one or two people dominate because such youth organisations recall Nazi authoritarianism (221). Unlike Rebecca West who worried about a resurgence of Nazism in 1946, Bowen allayed her doubts about recidivist, fascistic nationalism:

> When I say that ambition seemed to be national more than personal, I in no way mean that these girls and boys struck me as tinged by a dangerous nationalism. Their concern is for their country and its recovery – hence, I think, the stress they lay on security: the greater number of secure persons Germany contains, the more secure as a country she will be. Also, they witness the ruin left by the excessiveness of the Nazi daydream. (222)

Contradictorily, she concludes that 'national boundaries don't mean much' to German students, even though they tell her that, with regard to the future, 'they often speak of "the time when Germany shall again be whole"' (223). Despite students' reassurances, Bowen worries that transmogrified fascist politics are grafted onto communist politics, either because the young resist the fascist past and seek alternatives or because they endorse communism as a sensible approach to the future.

She notes the embers of Nazism in Prague, but sees no danger of their being fanned into flames:

> It was to be wondered at that Prague was not more deeply stultified by its years of the Nazi reign of terror. As things were, I could see what my friends there meant when they said: 'We are not fully awake from that nightmare yet; we have not fully recovered'. I was in flats where any unexpected ringing of the doorbell had – and how lately! – been heard with terror; where any footstep on the stone staircase outside might be carrying doom. ('Prague' 195)

While the 'nightmare' as a metaphor for history, especially the traumatic history of warfare, recalls both Bowen's characterisation of 'the nightmare aspects of enforced Communist government' in 'Hungary' (HRC 6.2) and Orwell's reference to the nightmarish miscarriage of justice in Moscow, Bowen also posits a moment when the nightmare ends and the future, less anguished, arrives; if not yet fully awake, one day 'we' will be. In this regard, she praises the Czech people, who are 'full of integrity, courage, strength and promise' ('Impressions' HRC 2.3). The Czech soldier who listens to music in Regent's Park in *The Heat of the Day* passingly attests to Bowen's sense of the urgency of the European situation in the late 1940s (6–7). The ghosts of Nazism have not been entirely laid to rest, even as some European countries appear resigned to Soviet occupation and militarisation.

In the immediate postwar years, Bowen's essays promoted ways to think about the overlay of historical epochs, specifically the unresolved legacies of fascism and the escalating militarism of Soviet communism. From the perspective of the late 1940s, the future was a zone of unclaimed, and sometimes unclaimable, legacies. Picking up on the view that Europe required some sort of unified front if not a single European government, Bowen focuses her third Paris Peace Conference article on Russian dodges. Predicting the Cold War implacability of Russian leaders, she observed the widening 'East-West split' ('Paris 3' 4). If anything, Cold War tensions reinforced her allegiance to European countries and cultures. Documenting dread in Prague and mistrust in Budapest, Bowen concluded that resistance to oppression emerges from an active commitment to peace and culture. Resistance is an individual choice. As she claims about Hungarians, '[T]he temperament of the people seemed in itself to constitute an *unformulated* resistance to the régime' ('Hungary' HRC 6.2).

Soviet show trials and postwar hangings, as symptoms of a preoccupation with the nature of justice and guilt from the 1930s to the 1960s, led to a rethinking of the efficacy of punishment for offenders who commit murder and offenders who commit crimes that surpass the ability of the law to impose suitable punishment. To punish an individual does not extirpate guilt, especially when those who are guilty engage in aggressive warfare or commit crimes against humanity. Like Koestler, Orwell and West, Bowen contributes substantially to the intermodern discourse about treachery and guilt. Culpability was an inescapable preoccupation within interwar, wartime and postwar culture. Bowen, treating the human aspect of culpability in *The Heat of the Day*, demonstrates that truth and error combine in any judgement, whether juridical or personal. Without exceeding the bounds of truth, Stella misrepresents the complications of Robert's espionage activity and Harrison's barging into her life during the coroner's inquest. Error arises from judgement: everyone misunderstands Stella, in part because she misunderstands how she ought to comport herself when faced by the dilemma of having to judge and condemn others, or more specifically Robert. Not just a matter of public trials and punishment, judgement occurs in the realm of human relations, where the consequences are, for all that, no less absolute.

NOTES

1. Acronyms for some titles have been used in this essay for the sake of clarity and brevity: *Animal Farm* (*AF*); *Collected Impressions* (*CI*); *Darkness at Noon* (*DN*); *The Heat of the Day* (*HD*); *A Train of Powder* (*TP*). Bowen's four articles on the Paris Peace Conference are referred to as 'Paris draft', 'Paris 1', 'Paris 2', and 'Paris 3'. 'HRC' refers to the Elizabeth Bowen archives at the Harry Ransom Center by box and folio numbers. Other archives consulted at the HRC, such as the Knopf papers, are indicated by name.

2. In *André Gide: A Life in the Present*, Alan Sheridan gives a lucid account of Gide's response to the USSR (492–503). Gide's book *Retour de l'U.R.S.S.* caused a furore when it appeared in 1936 because it boldly criticised the Soviet bureaucratic classes and Stalin's dictatorship. I use Sheridan's apt translation of the passage from Gide's *Journal*.
3. Although Koestler wrote *Darkness at Noon* in German, the novel was first published in English in Britain. I cannot prove absolutely that Bowen read *Darkness at Noon*, despite the faint resonance with the title of her novel, *The Heat of the Day*. She did, however, review Koestler's *Thieves in the Night* in the *Tatler* (4 December 1946), 328–29. Bowen's lover, Charles Ritchie, read *Darkness at Noon* six years after its publication, as he notes in his diary on 26 August 1946. He calls the book 'a terrifying picture of the evil courses into which the Soviet bureaucracy has turned' (Ritchie 9). Bowen saw a great deal of Ritchie between July and October of 1946 in Paris; more than likely, they discussed the novel at that time.

Works Cited

Arendt, Hannah. *Eichmann in Jerusalem: A Report on the Banality of Evil.* 1963. New York: Penguin, 1994.

Bowen, Elizabeth. 'Advance in Formation'. Rev. of *New Writing in Europe*, by John Lehmann. *Spectator* 17 January 1941: 65.

—. *The Bazaar and Other Stories*. Ed. and intro. Allan Hepburn. Edinburgh: Edinburgh University Press, 2008.

—. 'Britain in Autumn'. Ten-page essay [1940]. HRC 2.2.

—. *Collected Impressions*. London: Longmans Green, 1950.

—. *The Collected Stories of Elizabeth Bowen*. Intro. Angus Wilson. New York: Ecco Press, 1981.

—. 'The Disinherited'. Bowen, *Collected Stories* 375–407.

—. 'The Dolt's Tale'. Bowen, *Collected Stories* 741–47.

—. 'English Fiction at Mid-Century'. *The Arts at Mid-Century*. Ed. Robert Richman. New York: Horizon, 1954. 209–13.

—. 'Folkestone: July, 1945'. *Collected Impressions* 225–30.

—. *The Heat of the Day*. 1949. New York: Anchor, 2002.

—. 'The Heat of the Day'. Publicity note. HRC 5.5.

—. 'Hungary'. Ten-page essay dated 29 November 1948. HRC 6.2.

—. 'Impressions of Czechoslovakia'. Three-page essay dated 15 March 1948. Broadcast 16 March 1948 on BBC European Service. HRC 2.3.

—. 'The Informer'. Rev. of *Witness* by Whittaker Chambers. *Observer* 19 July 1953: 9.

—. 'Interview, 1959'. Conducted by John Bowen, William Craig and W. N. Ewer. Broadcast 11 September 1959 on BBC. Transcription. HRC 2.3.

—. Letter to Blanche Knopf. Dated Sunday, 2 April, 1950. HRC 685.15.

—. Letter to Veronica Wedgwood. Dated 10 April 1952. Oxford University, Bodleian Library MS Eng. c. 6829, fols 2–49.

—. 'London, 1940'. Bowen, *Collected Impressions* 217–20.

—. 'Oh, Madam'. Bowen, *Collected Stories* 578–82.

—. 'Paris Peace Conference: 1946. An Impression'. Seven-page draft for subsequent published articles. HRC 8.7.

—. 'Paris Peace Conference – Some Impressions 1'. *Cork Examiner* 12 October 1946: 9.

—. 'Paris Peace Conference – Some Impressions 2'. *Cork Examiner* 15 October 1946: 7.

—. 'Paris Peace Conference – Some Impressions 3'. *Cork Examiner* 22 October 1946: 4.

—. 'Prague and the Crisis'. *Vogue* 1 April 1948: 156, 195–96.

—. 'The Unromantic Princess'. *The Bazaar and Other Stories*. Ed. and intro. Allan Hepburn. Edinburgh: Edinburgh University Press, 2008. 99–110.

—. 'Without Coffee, Cigarettes, or Feeling'. *Mademoiselle* February 1955: 174–75, 221–23.

Elster, Jon, ed. *Retribution and Reparation in the Transition to Democracy*. Cambridge: Cambridge University Press, 2006.

Gide, André. *Journal 1889–1939*. 1951. Paris: Pléiade, 1970. 345–46.

Hepburn, Allan. *Intrigue: Espionage and Culture*. New Haven and London: Yale University Press, 2005.

Huyse, Luc. 'Belgian and Dutch Purges after World War II Compared'. Elster 164–80.

Koestler, Arthur. *Darkness at Noon*. Trans. Daphne Hardy. 1940. London: Penguin, 1964.

Le Carré, John. *The Spy Who Came in from the Cold*. 1963. London: Penguin, 1989.

Lee, Hermione. *Elizabeth Bowen*. Rev. ed. London: Vintage, 1999.

Lehmann, Rosamond. Letters to Elizabeth Bowen. Dated 14 February 1949 and 3 March 1949. HRC 11.6.

MacKay, Marina. *Modernism and World War II*. Cambridge: Cambridge University Press, 2007.

Marrus, Michael, ed. *The Nuremberg War Crimes Trial 1945–46: A Documentary History*. Boston: Bedford, 1997.

Mepham, John. 'Varieties of Modernism, Varieties of Incomprehension: Patrick Hamilton and Elizabeth Bowen'. *British Fiction after Modernism: The Novel at Mid-Century*. Ed. Marina MacKay and Lyndsey Stonebridge. Basingstoke: Palgrave Macmillan, 2007. 59–76.

Orwell, George. *Animal Farm: A Fairy Story*. 1945. London: Penguin, 1987.

—. 'Arthur Koestler'. *As I Please: Collected Essays, Journalism and Letters*. Ed. Sonia Orwell and Ian Angus. Vol. 3. New York: Harcourt, Brace and World, 1968. 234–44.

—. *Nineteen Eighty-Four*. 1949. London: Harcourt Brace Jovanovich, 1983.

Rau, Petra. 'The Common Frontier: Fictions of Alterity in Elizabeth Bowen's

The Heat of the Day and Graham Greene's *The Ministry of Fear*'. *Literature and History* 14.1 (2005): 31–55.

Report of the International Commission on the Holocaust in Romania. Submitted to President Ion Iliescu on 11 November 2004. Online at www1.yadvashem.org. Accessed 26 August 2007.

Ritchie, Charles. *Diplomatic Passport: More Undiplomatic Diaries, 1946–1962*. Toronto: Laurentian Macmillan, 1981.

Rousso, Henry. 'The Purge in France: An Incomplete Story'. Elster 89–123.

Royal Commission on Capital Punishment 1949–1953 Report. London: Her Majesty's Stationery Office, 1953.

Sheridan, Alan. *André Gide: A Life in the Present*. Cambridge: Harvard University Press, 1999.

West, Rebecca. *The Meaning of Treason*. New York: Viking, 1949.

—. *The New Meaning of Treason*. New York: Viking, 1964.

—. *A Train of Powder*. London: Macmillan, 1955.

8

REBECCA WEST'S PALIMPSESTIC PRAXIS: CRAFTING THE INTERMODERN VOICE OF WITNESS

Debra Rae Cohen

Was Rebecca West an intermodernist? Is this the right question? It's certainly a tempting one, in the way it's always been tempting to find a name for the vast oeuvre, the long and knobby sprawl, of West's seventy-year career. Like the blind men confronted with the elephant, critics often categorise her by selective dismemberment, dubbing her, variously, Vorticist, socialist, feminist, modernist, Manichaean, sentimentalist, essentialist, anti-communist – even, most recently and awkwardly, proto-postmodernist – by referring to a novel here, a decade there, a swatch of invective or cant. Such criticism duplicates rather than illuminates West's paradoxical positioning with regard to 'modernist' and political groupings, in which temporary identification was often only mobilised as a mode of critique[1] – but such positioning, in its moment, was always contingent, determined by both the institutionalisation of canonical discourses and the resistance to it.

My own instinct is that all this labelling is futile – or rather, that it's more valuable as historiography than as history, that it tells us more about the various labelling agents and institutions, their assumptions and agendas, than it does about West herself. To label West ensures that we know how to read her 'story', to parse it within the reassuring limits of a history already known.[2] It renders her, in a sense, generic.

Yet if dubbing West, *tout court*, an intermodernist, seems like more of this sort of pigeonholing, viewing her through the lens of intermodernism as practice, as retrospective methodology, proves the reverse. Kristin Bluemel's evocation of the liminal space of intermodernism as 'a cultural and critical bridge or borderland whose inhabitants are always looking two ways' (2 above) resonates intriguingly with the modalities of West's own practice during the period with which Bluemel is primarily concerned, and indeed for her practice as a whole. Much as the doubling lens of intermodernism disrupts conventional taxonomies of periodisation and affiliation, West, by 'looking two ways' (or more) at once – by employing multiple subject positions and generic lenses – disrupts those readerly certainties that attach to genre and implicitly interrogates the cultural apparatuses that produce them. This palimpsestic use of genre, as West deploys it both in *Black Lamb and Grey Falcon* and later in her postwar Nuremberg reportage, enables her to construct a multiple witnessing persona, both historian and historical subject, Cassandra and collaborator, within texts deliberately open-ended and interventionist. Like intermodernism itself, she turns perspective into praxis.

In describing West's frustration of taxonomy and the distinctive voice that results, I'm deliberately employing the terminology of genre so as to underscore the interactivity of her process and the way aesthetic categories take on, for her, explicit political freight linked to the need to polemicise: the intermodernism, in fact, of her formal choices. Though Elizabeth Maslen has claimed that 'choice of form . . . is in itself amoral' (24), such choices are always distinctly *ideological*; we can term them intermodern when they become specifically *political*. Given the peculiarly regulatory character of genre – James Frow terms it 'a shared convention with a social force' (*Genre* 102) – it's not surprising that it proved fertile ground for intermodern exploitation, manipulation and fracturing. While exploiting the political possibilities of undervalued and popular genres was a distinctively intermodern technique – as Phyllis Lassner explores in her essay for this volume – West's own manipulation of their subversive potential dates back to her earliest fiction, and reflects a sensitivity to multiple, distinct and subornable audiences cultivated by her immersion in the journalistic marketplace. Thus *The Return of the Soldier* (originally published for an American magazine audience) served up a socialist anti-patriarchal critique folded neatly into a romance package, like a file baked into a cake, while *Harriet Hume* did much the same in the form of a lapidary fantasy.

Such single-genre subversiveness, however, gave way, in the heightened political climate of the late interwar period, to more ambitious attempts to craft a distinctive multigeneric or intergeneric voice – a voice for the public intellectual (the *female* public intellectual) that would formally reflect its political content. West's deliberate outraging of generic models for the critical essay in the 1928 'The Strange Necessity' serves as the clearest signpost toward what she would attempt in *Black Lamb and Grey Falcon*; as Laura Heffernan has argued, her compositional practices in that essay represent a mode of interpretation that recognises aesthetic categories as themselves relations of power.

Responding in April 1941 to her friend Alexander Woollcott's praise of *Black Lamb and Grey Falcon*, West wrote:

> The Yugoslavian book now seems to me a preternatural event in my life. Why should I be moved in 1936 to devote the next five years of my life . . . to take an inventory of a country down to its last vest-button, in a form insane from any ordinary artistic or commercial point of view – a country which ceases to exist? I find the hair raising on my scalp at the extraordinary usefulness of this apparently utterly futile act. (*Letters* 169)

While West's use of the word 'inventory' here recalls the workings of colonial epistemology, the assembling of an 'imperial archive', her methodology involves, on the contrary, the dismantling of conventional taxonomies.[3] The 'insane' form to which she refers – most often delineated by critics in a kind of hypertrophic epic catalogue of genres (for example, 'characters, dramatic scenes, dialogue, description, reportage, autobiography, literary criticism, philosophy, theology and feminism' (Rollyson 209), or 'history, politics, archaeology, anecdote, conversation, polemic, prophecy, and jokes' (Glendinning 32)) – may have prompted the awed confusion that marked the book's initial reception.[4] In the past two decades, by contrast, such 'transgressive' – or, glibly, 'genre-bending' – hybridity has been central to its celebration, but still largely undertheorised. In focusing on the book's intended propaganda function ('to persuade [West's] own people through Yugoslavia's example that they must strive to stave off the sleep of death which would both induce and follow Nazi conquest' (Colquitt 78)) rather than the dispute over genre, critics tend to miss its significance *to* that propaganda function. The deliberate manipulation West imposes on the 'laws' of genre renders structural the thematics of her anti-fascist, anti-imperial critique.

The subtitle of West's text, *A Journey through Yugoslavia*, foregrounds from the outset her testing of generic expectations, wryly saluting a literary marketplace attuned to the 1930s travel literature boom.[5] This double doorstop of an opus was surely an uncomfortable shelf-fellow for the works of Peter Fleming, J. R. Ackerley, Evelyn Waugh and Robert Byron, unlikely to deliver the expected dollop of comfortable vicarious vagabondage. Even a genre so capacious, unstable and historically multiple as the travel narrative – which covers so many sins that it seems perhaps unnecessary for it even to be 'bent'[6] – seemed an inadequate container, cornucopia rather than corset. Yet as her subtitle indicates, West paradoxically exploits the centrality and recognisability of interwar travel writing as a genre in order to emphasise her breaking of its 'rules'. Like Auden and MacNeice's pastiche in *Letters from Iceland*, but with a far less playful aim, West's display of generic mash-up in *Black Lamb* is strategic – clearly stylised, purposive and overt.[7] Through it she creates a model for authoritative pronouncement that serves her purposes beyond the bounds of this single massive project, into the postwar era.

What Frow describes as 'the couplet of law and transgression' model ('Reproducibles' 1627) of generic rule-breaking underpins West's narrative; yet it operates deliberately, hinged to the other looming binaries that shadow the text: man's 'bright nature', at war with his 'yeasty darkness' (1102), nationalism and imperialism, and 'idiocy' and 'lunacy', West's terms for the female and male 'defect' – respectively, the overabsorption in private affairs, the obsession with the public. The foregrounding of this last binary opposition on page three of West's gargantuan tome prepares one for the same juxtaposition of the philosophical and the homely that so outraged early critics of 'The Strange Necessity'; West highlights the opposition to call attention, as she did in that essay, to her textual mixing of domestic and the panoramic – 'sweeping', that is, in both senses of the word.

West's strategic deployment of the idiot/lunatic distinction is central to her case for the incorporation of women into public life as one means of combating the fascist threat – as Marina MacKay has argued, West sees gender as 'a public as well as a private category, and therefore implicated in public violence' ('Lunacy' 142). But it's also central to the way she constructs the authority for herself to make such a case. Steve Clark has pointed to the way the 'perennially marginal position' of the travel narrative 'allows the production of a self in the course of writing by means of perpetual detours into communal utterance, public codes' (1). West exploits this play between public and private in order to reverse its terms, inverting the 'disinterested, mobile, subjective freedom' of what we might call the Fussell-oid traveller (privileged, white, male) to render the travel narrative itself interventionist (Caesar 195). At the same time West distinguishes *Black Lamb* from the comparatively 'plain-speaking itinerant political writing' (MacKay, *Modernism* 52) of intermodern contemporaries like Naomi Mitchison, James Hanley or even Orwell, the craftedness of whose personae is instrumental rather than formally overt.

The interplay between public and private discourses is enacted in the complex portrayal of the West-protagonist herself as multiple and contradictory: rational and emotive, petty and philosophical, both the limited and quotidian product of the vast historical processes she describes and their Cassandra-like observer. As with 'The Strange Necessity', West's strategic use of genre in *Black Lamb* has often prompted the unwitting reproduction of the very gendered generic expectations she seeks to exploit and critique. The tone of thinking aloud that sometimes marks *Black Lamb* has tempted some critics to tease out this single strand of the complex braid to pronounce it the book's most salient element. Vesna Goldsworthy, accepting at face value John Gunther's compliment to his former lover that 'it somehow pleased me that it was not so much a book about Jugoslavia as a book about Rebecca West' (*Letters* 175), sees West approvingly as a woman writer availing herself of the 'self-legitimizing' genre of travel writing in order to 'gain a deeper knowledge of herself. . . . Introspection is the essence of West's journey' (87, 91–22). Goldsworthy quotes to support this a well-known passage that begins with West's declaration that there is a natural 'coincidence' between the shapes and colours of Yugoslavia and those of her own mental landscape. West continues,

> [M]y journey moved me also because it was like picking up a strand of wool that would lead me out of a labyrinth in which, to my surprise, I had found myself immured. It might be that when I followed the thread to its end I would find myself faced by locked gates, and that this labyrinth was my sole portion on earth. But at least I now knew its twists and turns, and what corridor led into what vaulted chamber, and nothing in my life before I went to Yugoslavia had ever made plain these mysteries. (*Black Lamb* 1089)

Goldsworthy seems unaware of the implications of her interpretation here – that Yugoslavia serves as a convenience for the bootstrapping of West's subjectivity, her journey thus recapitulating the very colonial and imperial processes she wrote *Black Lamb* to condemn. And she ignores the passage that immediately follows, which makes clear that the 'labyrinth' here is not merely that of West's own selfhood, but (in a feminised version of the 'contrived corridors' of 'Gerontion') that of modern history:

> This experience made me say to myself, 'If a Roman woman had, some years before the sack of Rome, realized why it was going to be sacked and what motives inspired the barbarians and what the Romans, and had written down all she knew and felt about it, the record would have been of value to historians. My situation, though probably not so fatal, is as interesting'. Without doubt it was my duty to keep a record of it.
> So I resolved to put on paper what a typical Englishwoman felt and thought in the nineteen-thirties when, already convinced of the inevitability of the second Anglo-German war, she had been able to follow the dark waters of that event back to its source. (1089)

West the historian, in other words, is here interrogating West the historical subject; the splitting of the subject foregrounds her manipulations of public and private discourses, and thus her construction of a compound authority, an intermodern form of the public intellectual.[8] Often, indeed, the relation between these elements is projected onto the stylised conversations between West (or 'West') and her husband Henry Andrews, who 'does double duty', as Carl Rollyson puts it, 'as her other half' (214). Indeed, perhaps the central speech of the 'present-day' narrative – the long disquisition on 'the sense of process' that serves as a kind of manifesto for the text itself – is voiced through the figure of Henry, with 'West' herself making only brief and personal interruptions. Once again the public/private juxtaposition is deliberate, part of an illustrative dialectic; for in this long slab of argument West takes on the imperial mindset writ small, in the person of Gerda, German wife of her Serbian guide, Constantine, whose insensitivity, egotism and greed stun those who encounter her. Henry diagnoses Gerda's 'moral somnabulis[m]' (Rosslyn 116) as both endemic and incurable, the result of a lacuna in her makeup: 'Gerda has no sense of process' (*Black Lamb* 799).

The disquisition that follows moves from the domestic (Gerda's rudeness, her refusal to do the work of marriage, her proud inability to bake bread) to the consequences of such a mindset on an international scale:

> 'This is the conqueror's point of view. . . . Everybody who is not Gerda is to Gerda "a dog of an infidel" to be treated without mercy. If she could get hold of our money by killing us, and would not be punished for it, I think she would do it, not out of cruelty, but out of blankness. . . . She has shut herself off from the possibility of feeling mercy, since pain is a process and not a result. This will give her a great advantage in any conflict with more sensitive people, and in fact it is not her only advantage'. (800)

Thus 'there is no way to be safe from her except to treat her as if she were, finally and exclusively, a threat to existence' and to resist the coming of 'Gerda's empire', fascist empire, with every fibre of one's being (800, 805).

Gerda's worldview is first revealed, notably, at her first meeting with the couple, in *generic* terms. She literally judges a book by its cover, slotting it into a particular category over West's explanatory protestations: 'She took my book from my hand, looked at the title, and handed it back to me with a little shake of the head and a smile, full of compassionate contempt' (458). Through Gerda, West ties generic taxonomising, 'the discourse of total order, where everything has its place' (Owen 1393), to the imperial assumption of 'advantageous difference' (*Black Lamb* 458). She thus attributes to and displaces onto the figure of Gerda (rather than herself embodying) the 'confident commitment to a norm' (170) that Fussell cites as the distinguishing characteristic of 'real' British literary travelling, once more manipulating genre markers within her own text in order to sound doubly her anti-imperial tocsin.

Though it's a cliché these days that, as Bruce Robbins puts it, 'when genre is discussed the metaphor of the police is everywhere' (1646), it's exactly this prescriptive notion of genre that West connects with the figure of Gerda, and that she sets up in order to disavow. If genre is Law, it is also Order, and thus can serve as a kind of consoling, reassuring fiction – the kind of consolation that West, as far back as *The Return of the Soldier*, consistently refuses her readers. Indeed, in a key metaphor, she figures the Western response to the salutary small-state nationalism she celebrates – the same mind-set that led to the 'cataleptic quiet' of appeasement (1114) – as a kind of anomic readerly tunnel vision:

England and France and America turned away, for what lived disgusted them; they wanted a blanched world, without blood, given over to defeat.

They would not interfere, therefore, with the marginal activity that ran parallel to the continuous national effort which I was chronicling. From time to time out of the text there emerged little black figures which postured on the page beside it, achieved a group which was magical, an incantation to death, and ran back into the text, which carried on its story. (1103)

The effects of such disruption, says West, were at first 'almost invisible save to the specialist eye' – not that of the passive or complacent reader, of the nations that *would not* look beyond the main text on the page.

By contrast, in her epilogue West depicts her own process as necessarily interactive, intertextual, intergeneric; she can read the lesson of modern passivity in the face of fascism 'in the pages of my own book if I spread out the newspaper beside it' (1123). The very text she writes, then, deliberately enacts and reinforces its emphasis on *process*, historical, dialectical, interactive, creative, the blindness to which is so evident in Gerda. West deliberately constructs a text that seems (in the words of historian Lewis Namier) to have 'no more system or completeness in it than in the colour-scheme of wild flowers in a field'. 'How I worked to get that effect,' wrote West to Namier. 'Again and again I broke sequences and relaxed tension to get the lethargic attention of the ordinary reader along the road' (qtd in Rollyson 215). The very success of West's text as propaganda, then – its utility outside itself – is tied to its intratextual manipulation of genre. In this regard, one need only recur to West's reference to the 'extraordinary usefulness' of her 'insane' form to register the importance of both the plasticity of the travel genre and her deliberate homage to its status *as* genre for crafting the intermodern witnessing voice. Even in its transgressiveness, West's approach has much in common with the contemporary notion that that genre serves as a necessary set of standards for making 'history in the ambitious sense' possible (Robbins 1649) – in other words, less as philosophy than as praxis.

And yet the special significance of *Black Lamb*'s function as propaganda is that it calls for an action at once necessary and impossible. The witnessing voice is at once the voice of Cassandra – always correct in her urgings and always too late – and that of the loving eulogist. West knows it's impossible to save the South Slavs from the 'fountain of negativism [that] plays in the centre of Europe, killing all living things within the reach of its spray' (1083); it's impossible, too, to rewrite the history of British imperial 'roguery and stupidity' (1090) or the drugged indolence of appeasement. A book conceived as a goad to British policy can only, finally, allude to the awakening of its 'honor' under attack (1129). Where is the venue for praxis then, the 'ground for hope' where man might, in West's shockingly blunt term, 'disinfect' himself (1126)? In the crudest sense, it is America, where the volume first appeared in 1941 as an unlikely, unwieldy slab of interventionist appeal. But more crucially, it's in the volume's own status *as* art, an 'uncertain instrument' that nevertheless serves as 'a small white star', that can change the tide of men's minds (1126–27). Art provides not simply a model for action or inaction – though that is the danger implied in the myths of the title, myths that provide a double model for submissive sacrifice[9] – but the possibility of continued process and continued interaction with the things of time implied in the act of reading and reinterpretation.

It's not *Black Lamb*'s weightiness as artistic object that represents its significance as intervention, then, so much as West's recursive and historiographic process, which necessarily foregrounds its own provisionality. As she argues of one of the book's discomfiting title myths, the poem of Tsar Lazar and the grey falcon – reread in 1941 as a sign of the very resistance its text denies[10] – art shapes (and misshapes, since 'art cannot talk plain sense'), but is itself palimpsestic. It is thus subject to reinterpretation, often manifesting as different readings of the tension between the idea in the work that is 'expressed with the greatest intensity' and that 'which has determined its narrative form' (1145).[11] Indeed, it's exactly this quality of tension within West's own writing, the way the fervency of her judgements, the slash of her condemnations, often emerge in strained relation to their complexly crafted palimpsestic surroundings, that makes her writing so difficult to describe and leads so often to its miscategorisation; if one responds only to the surface barrage one is likely to miss the sappers, tunnelling beneath.

Nowhere are these contradictions and tensions more salient than in West's reporting on the Nuremberg trials, where the momentous events that she attempts to chronicle test to breaking point any commitment to open-endedness. The challenge to the writer at Nuremberg is the challenge of Nuremberg itself: to continue a commitment to *process* in the face of crimes that seem to demand summary judgement – which if enacted would only accede to the taxonomic mindset that lay behind the crimes themselves. What Lassner has perceptively recognised as West's 'antireligious, critical ambivalence toward a Manichaean political philosophy of good and evil' (43) – not the simple Manicheanism many critics ascribe to her – demands a stance as public witness that refuses the simple gratifications of us/them thinking, at a historical moment where such gratifications are perhaps the only ones possible, and in fact seem absolutely necessary.

In *Black Lamb and Gray Falcon*, West's hybrid mingling of genres serves as her formal endorsement of the perpetually self-revising process of understanding that resists the taxonomies she identifies with the exclusions and prescriptions of imperial and fascist thought. In her Nuremberg reportage, West extends and adapts this pragmatic work with genre in order to construct a voice that might adequately respond to Nuremberg's challenge. The homely guidebook moments that stud her texts naturalise a traveller's responsive interiority – the equivalent of *Black Lamb*'s emotive 'typical Englishwoman' – even as the solemn historical context seems to demand the suppression of such interiority in favour of dispassionate witness. The play with and fracturing of generic frames allows West continually to interrogate both the mindset that allowed the rise of Nazism and the impulse to disown that mindset as necessarily, definitively 'other'.

As in *Black Lamb and Grey Falcon*, then, West both depicts Nuremberg's historic challenge and acts it out on the level of form. Yet this depiction is itself a divided one. West's original *New Yorker* articles duplicate closely the narrative discontinuities of *Black Lamb* – circuitously juxtaposing the anecdotal and first-person with long set-pieces of social observation. The 'personal' voice is distinctly gendered,[12] often equivocal, sometimes oddly playful, and given to snarky one-liners – evoking, in context, a purposeful discomfort, tied to the overtly expressed difficulties of decoding Nuremberg itself. These articles, however, were profoundly recast – not merely edited down – to create the piece 'Greenhouse with Cyclamens I' in West's 1955 collection *A Train of Powder*. Though this piece is identified with the date '1946', and has usually been treated by critics as if it represented her contemporaneous rendering of the trials, it was actually recreated in light of her subsequent revisiting, in 1949 and 1954, of Nuremberg's legacy, reformed as part of a new minatory arc designed to highlight the Soviet threat. Constructed to support a new version of interventionist witnessing, the reworking serves as another enactment of formal judgement – thus illustrating the strains of West's palimpsestic process.

Both versions of West's 1946 travels centre on the impossibility of completely 'reading' Nuremberg. Evocations of generic form here serve as tentative mechanisms, alternative frames, for decoding the surpassing strangeness of the trials, the town and postwar Germany itself, that falter at the blurred border between 'us' and 'them'. As in *Black Lamb and Grey Falcon*, the mode of the travelogue first (in both versions) sets the terms of the discourse: West chronicles the journey, the accommodations, the shopping, the available sights. Yet this stance is immediately interrupted and problematised. In West's first *New Yorker* piece we enter Nuremberg with her (in the present tense), like tourists, from above: 'There rushes up towards the plane,' West begins, 'the astonishing face of the world's enemy: pine woods on little hills, grey-green, glossy lakes, too small to be anything but smooth, gardens tall with red-tongued beans, fields striped with red-gold wheat, russet-roofed villages with high gables and pumpkin-steeple churches that no architect over seven could have designed' ('Extraordinary' 3). The landscape is multiply defamiliarised – shrunk from above at once into guidebook mapping and to the dimension of fairy tale, at once 'rushing up' and thrust away, rejected as morally other. The phrase 'the world's enemy' marks out a touristic space that is, paradoxically, visitable and impossibly distant, natural and artificial, homely and, literally, other-worldly.[13]

This defamiliarisation evoked by the cascade of conflicting generic markers only accelerates as West swoops from plane to courtroom: the defendants' desire for the trial's timeless tedium to last 'for ever and ever' – deferring mortality – marks this once again as a fairy tale, with the defendants self-ensorcelled Snow Whites, victims of their own fantasy. Indeed, West throughout the piece returns repeatedly to the stuff of fairy tales in characterising the national tendencies that formed the 'world's enemy'.[14] The Schloss Faber, now serving as housing for journalists covering the trials, looms fantastically over the factory that funded it, the bloated childish dream of its builders: 'Its turret windows were quite useless,' writes West 'unless Rapunzel was to let down her hair from them; its odd upper rooms, sliced into queer shapes by the intemperate steepness of the tiled roof, could be fitly occupied only by a fairy godmother with a spinning wheel; the staircase was for the descent of a prince and princess that should live happily ever after' (A Train 24). In this context, the defendants' preservation in the trial's imperfect bell jar, their bodies decaying before the spectator like the Cumaean Sybil, seems the familiar vision from Black Lamb and Gray Falcon – an object lesson in the dangers of mythic hypertrophy. Yet West does not allow us – we the readers, we the judges – to fall into our own comforting fantasy that fantasy can be so easily rendered other. Her initial fairy-tale framing of the defendants' position is fractured by the intrusion of a new frame: now they seem a portrait gallery, in the postures that 'historical characters, particularly in distress, assume in bad pictures'; like 'Mary Queen of Scots at Fotheringay or Napoleon on St Helena in a mid-Victorian Academy success' (A Train 3–4), they are suspended in a historical judgement that itself, she implies, is equally mythifying.

Such generic collisions – stylised shorthand truncations of the excursions and detours of Black Lamb and Grey Falcon – recur throughout West's texts, the conflicting markers of stage, fairy tale, Baedeker, documentary, museum, suggesting a host of incompatible narratives in which the lines between actor and observer blur. Are visitors 'housed in a German fairy tale' (A Train 25), reduced by the fracturing of their touristic expectations to 'ghost[s] among the living' (A Train 10) really so different from those other 'ghosts' (A Train 46), the defendants themselves? What does it mean, then, to read in the landscape of Nuremberg, in the 'strange pattern printed on this terrain', a 'call for punishment' (A Train 17, 16)? West's formal disruption of the narrative of judgement underscores her conviction that the 'nostra culpa' of the trial itself might have been its most important element, 'a step farther on the road to civilization' (A Train 49). Indeed, whereas in Black Lamb and Grey Falcon West constructed a multiple 'I' that was both chronicler and subject, historian and housewife, here she decants that multiplicity into the impersonality of an 'us' that strains against its multiple subject-positions. This 'us' is a shifting thing – journalists, British, allies, observers – even, in the piece's opening, 'the world'.

This is an 'us' commodious enough, potentially, to accommodate 'them' – and yet 'they' are definitively not-'us', 'the world's enemy'. The play of pronouns and subject positions enacts the need for a new language of process equivalent to Nuremberg's new language of law.

The terms here are, as West means them to be, disturbingly contradictory, and they're inevitably tied to the impulse to 'order'. On one hand, 'order' throughout this text is reassurance, a long-lost desideratum, seemingly impossible to realise in a postwar landscape littered with incongruities and administered by overlapping mutually interfering authorities and contradictory processes. In this sense, 'order' as desideratum is necessarily aligned with the Allies against the bloody fantasies of the Nazis, with the urge to create legal order in the trials themselves. But order is also, at its limit, destructive taxonomy: the fixed idea, the monomania that built the Schloss Faber and the death camps. There are unmistakable implications here for West's own compositional practice: the human urge to find order that we all share (whether to close the frame, to leave a myth or metaphor unquestioned, or to embrace the consolations of genre) is in some measure linked to the denial of process that produced the Final Solution. Indeed, one central, almost inconceivably difficult, aim of the Nuremberg trials themselves was to find a way to honour judicial process in the face of undeniable and overwhelming guilt.

Similarly, the refracting uncertainties of West's '1946' piece, echoing formally in the impossibility of finding an effective mode of *reading* Nuremberg, the supreme difficulties of its effective administration, question the limitations of both law and literature to *conjure* what West calls 'reality' while resisting the use of either to *impose* it. Yet, as I've suggested, the extent to which 'Greenhouse with Cyclamens I' underscores this difficulty needs to be understood as a feature of West's retrospective rearrangement; neither the '1946' 'Greenhouse with Cyclamens I' nor the '1949' instalment (recast from dispatches in the *Evening Standard*) actually acquired its current form until 1954. Margaret Stetz has argued that the 1954 'Greenhouse with Cyclamens III' serves as a self-reflexive commentary on West's 1946 journalism, 'her own imperfect attempts' to render the trials 'comprehensible' (229). But I'd go much further than this: when one compares the original *New Yorker* pieces to the very different '1946' 'Greenhouse with Cyclamens I', the three pieces in *A Train of Powder* reveal themselves as a carefully crafted commentary on the process of reading order into history – a retrospective arc that formally restages, and yet finally, inevitably, exposes, West's own imposition of historical meaning.

By 1954, for West, Nuremberg was no longer a necessary enigma allied to, yet uncontained by, every possible generic mode of defamiliarisation, but 'an unshapely event, a defective composition, stamping no clear image on the mind of the people it had been designed to impress' (*A Train* 246); the Germans, she says, have derived the wrong lesson from the trials, and from their new prosperity, once again pursuing 'fantasy' without an animating ethic. West imposes this 'defective' shape, the shape of wrongness, on her earlier impressions of Germany, not simply with historical perspective – but also in compositional retrospect. The myriad and contradictory 'oddities' – both anecdotal and formal – of the *New Yorker* pieces resolve, in *A Train of Powder*, into a single overarching symbol, the 'Greenhouse with Cyclamens' of the title. Indeed, it's important to recognise that West's anecdote of her 1946 encounter with a one-legged gardener whose dedicated, unwearying industry amid the grey deprivation of Nuremberg serves as a harbinger of German economic rebirth, didn't provide the title for either of her *New Yorker* articles; in fact, it doesn't appear in there at all. It's only mobilised in West's redesign for the book, a clear equivalent to the titular myths of *Black Lamb and Grey Falcon* that is allowed, in its development over the course of the three articles, to take on a similar proleptic, ominous significance.

In fact, the first version of the gardener – incongruously, in a Nuremberg described as economically scarred by the war, growing cyclamens for sale to the occupiers – is a remarkably complex and nuanced one, as multiply and variously readable as Nuremberg itself; while there is 'something different and peculiarly German and dynamic in his self-dedication' (29), he is not – or not yet – figured as 'frighteningly tenacious', 'monomaniacal' or 'obsessed' (Stetz 231–22). Though his drive may prove as overblown as that of the builders of the Schloss, he proves, in 1946, a bright corrective, 'industrious to the point of nobility' (29). Indeed, given West's formulation of the observer's plight – that 'The traveller does not feel he has made terms with the country he visits till the people have sold him their goods. Without that he is like a ghost among the living' (10) – the gardener is both a touristic highlight, and a supernatural reanimator of the dead. By the opening of the second, '1949' 'Greenhouse with Cyclamens', however, his dedication has already become distended, 'repellent', vaguely perverse, and halfway through it he is a 'nightmare figure', whose industry is itself an amoral juggernaut that threatens to produce more nightmares still. In 'Greenhouse with Cyclamens III' he has become the emblem for the failure of Nuremberg to bind German energies to any larger faith, to 'religion or philosophy or art' (248).[15] Such faith is now, in 1954, for West, visibly achievable through the struggle of Berliners against the categorical imperatives of Russian totalitarianism. The progression performs a staged distillation of the nuanced complexity of '1946' (a date when the gardener's maiming must invariably remind us of other, absent and fragmented bodies) into totalising metaphor. And thus West's emphatic 're'-reading during the Cold War is paradoxically tied to her own implacability in the face of this new version of 'Gerda's empire'.

Many of the other details of revision work as well to support West's 1954 interpretation of Nuremberg as 'one of the first fronts of the Cold War' (Hirsch 726). In West's first *New Yorker* dispatch, the fact that the Russian judges wear military uniform is remarked as an oddity – 'the strangest choice for officers of a tribunal set up in hope of superseding war by law' ('Extraordinary' 40), but perhaps no odder than the looks of the French judges, who 'immediately recall the drawings of Daumier' (a description immediately preceding that of the Russians). And she notes, too, that the Russian judges are well-liked, 'one of them, General Nikitchenko, as well as almost anyone in Nuremberg'. In the revision, all reference to likeability is removed, and the choice of uniform becomes ominous: 'The Russian judges sat in military uniform as a sign that this was no tribunal at all' (A Train 16).[16] While in the earlier version *all* the judges believe that the imperfections of the trial process are remediable by 'strict adherence to a code of law' ('Extraordinary' 40), in the revision the uniforms serve in retrospect as a pre-emptive foreclosing of Nuremberg's significance, a denial of process equivalent to Gerda's.

Lassner's recognition that 'West's reportage of these trials represents a catalytic moment in her writing, where she sees that personal and public history and psychology match her worst fears' (56), pushing her toward a more complete acceptance of Manichaean evil, is thus borne out formally in West's writing. Lassner is referring only to the restaged *Train of Powder* versions and thus the 'moment' to which she refers is a proleptic one, retrospectively rendered. The 'Greenhouse with Cyclamens' pieces in *A Train of Powder* chronicle West's own (and thus 'our') irresistible urge to foreclose process, to relax into the easy 'us' and 'them' that totalising metaphor and the comforting order of genre allow. Indeed, the 'Greenhouse with Cyclamens' image is employed precisely to detail the process by which this occurs – a self-reflexive self-exposure that renders that process deliberately incomplete.

The recursive looping and meandering trajectory of *Black Lamb and Grey Falcon*, the emphasis on self-interruption and multiple perspective, the book's paradoxical insistence on both storytelling and the danger of codifying such stories, vested the witnessing voice with additional urgency and authority. In contrast, the revision of West's Nuremberg pieces into their 'Greenhouse with Cyclamens' form reminds us that such authority is itself always at risk of becoming codified; in her own movement to conform her observations retroactively to a new minatory narrative, West, again paradoxically, foregrounds this dangerous process. If, as I've noted above, she saw Nuremberg by the time of revision as 'an unshapely event, a defective composition, stamping no clear image on the mind of the people it had been designed to impress' (246) – a formulation that seems to disavow the openendedness of her earlier praxis in favour of a more simplified notion of effective propaganda – the very terms in which she articulates her judgement call attention to the discomfort behind such new and aestheticised rigour.

Key here is an anecdote near the end of 'Greenhouse with Cyclamens I' – a passage that, like the image of the one-legged gardener, West added to the text revised for 1954 publication. During the hiatus between the pronouncing of sentence on the Nuremberg defendants and its imposition, members of the legal and journalistic corps take a brief sojourn to Prague. Asleep in the audience at a showing of *Brief Encounter*, 'one of the American lawyers' – actually West's lover, Nuremberg judge Francis Biddle – awakens to the sight of a minor character, and exclaims, 'By God, that man looks just like Göring'. Most critical mentions of this anecdote centre on West's following summary phrase, that the screen had become 'a palimpsest, with the great tragedy imposed upon the small' (65), and thus see it either as an example, in Carl Rollyson's terms, 'of her own tendency to conflate the . . . public and the private in her own life and career' (256), or else as a demonstration, like *Black Lamb and Grey Falcon*, of West's belief that such superimposition, such conflation, is necessary to a moral understanding of history.

But the incident alludes symbolically as well to the palimpsest, cited in *Black Lamb and Grey Falcon*, of the artistic and interpretive process. Indeed, the scene is fraught with repeated and contradictory interpretive gestures based on conflicting definitions of 'us' and 'them'. The Czechs who watch the movie, in a British Film Festival, as a gesture of solidarity see not heart-rending romance, but 'drab' inhibition; the trial lawyers and journalists who have dispersed in search of refreshing new sights – 'like going off on a cruise' (65) – find 'drowsiness in the air' at the rehearsing of the familiar; in the darkness, finally, fiction is read as documentary: 'By God, that man looks just like Göring'. West evokes the palimpsest 'with the great tragedy imposed upon the small', and then goes on: 'The trial had begun its retreat into the past'.

If this moment is an example of West's 'prophetic witnessing' (167) as Victor Sage has recently claimed, what is it that's being prophesised? It's not, I think, as Sage would have it, that the film represents the nostalgic British past innocently prescient of its swallowing up by the forces of darkness. West is neither that nostalgic nor, at this stage of her narrative arc, that Manichean. Rather, what we see – in embryo – is that dangerous moment where metaphor happens, when equivalence is imposed on the disparate, and self-challenging interpretation ceases, the moment when history turns to myth – an exposure of historiographic processes that is deeply intermodern. Like the anecdote of the one-legged gardener, West added this scene to *A Train of Powder* to illuminate the process of retrospective judgement: the 'palimpsest' here is 'Greenhouse with Cyclamens' itself. Through the black marks of West's own increasingly fervent categorisations, we can see – as she wants us to – the nuances of the past.

NOTES

1. An early and famous example is her disparagement by A. N. Orage in his *New Age* review of *Blast I* as *the* arch-Vorticist who embodies (unlike Wyndham Lewis himself) 'all the vices of the "Blast" school' ('Readers and Writers').
2. Though I think it's fundamentally flawed in its embrace of the myth of literary progress, which helps evade – as the lens of intermodernism does not – a

renegotiation of the ground of modernist institutionalisation (see Pitchford in this regard), Bernard Schweizer's recent work in this area has the virtue of foregrounding West's process rather than her positions.

3. The need to undo such taxonomies had been both the political message and the aesthetic basis of West's 1929 novel *Harriet Hume*, itself, as I've argued in *Sheepish Modernism*, a riposte against unfriendly reactions to 'The Strange Necessity' that stressed the essay's categorical and generic violations.

4. See for example Colquitt 77.

5. That the language of travel dominated the 1930s even beyond the confines of the dedicated travel narrative has been massively documented by Valentine Cunningham and numerous others; but such signposting marks the critical discourse on the period as well. Tyrus Miller's formulation of 'late modernism', significantly, borrows the language of travel to plot the trajectory of those writers under the shadow of (as per Miller's epigraph from Noel Annan) 'modernism and collectivism' (Miller 13, 1). Viewed through an intermodernist lens, detour becomes main line, rendering 'seasonable' what Fredric Jameson famously deems the 'unseasonable forms' (305) of the period. Indeed, to deploy the lens of intermodernism is to turn literary history into a figure/ground illusion.

6. Even Paul Fussell, whose delineation of the interwar anti-guidebook is exactly as prescriptive as it pretends not to be, locates the 1930s travel narrative at the point of hyphenation, metaphorising the genre as itself uncharted territory in order to shore up the credentials of his canonical 'explorers' (202).

7. Relevant here is John Frow's description of texts as 'transformative instantiations of genres' rather than dwellers within them ('Reproducibles' 1633); West's reartiulation of the travel genre, in a sense, remaps the world.

8. And, as Marina MacKay has noted, an explicitly anti-Bloomsbury model (*Modernism* 52–53). See *Black Lamb* 1100–01. Useful in understanding West's doubled narration is John Marx's identification of *Black Lamb* as a precursor of recent 'failed-state fiction', in which the 'unaccredited expert' emerges as the alternative to official professional, credentialed expertise. While Marx focuses his brief treatment of the book on Constantine as potential (and failed) 'unaccredited expert', I'd argue that West's bifurcation of persona allows her to fulfil both roles, in relation first to Yugoslavia, and then to England itself.

9. Both myths support West's reading of Christianity as detrimentally infatuated with submission: the black lamb serves as the 'necessary' sacrifice in a fertility rite, the grey falcon offers Tsar Lazar, before the 1389 battle of Kosovo at which the Serbs fell to the Ottoman Empire, the choice of an earthly kingdom (victory) or a heavenly (martyrs') kingdom.

10. Schweizer was the first to seize on the significance of these multiple renderings, though he sees West's exegesis, wrongly, I think, as 'self-absolving' (141); West never apologises and only implicitly explains.

11. Though I'd argue that this tension marks, to one degree or another, most of West's writing, it is most apparent and germane during that period Bluemel identifies with the intermodern. I thus am sceptical of MacKay's recent formulation that identifies West's rendering of the book's title myths with Eliot's 'mythical method'. Not only are these, as she herself notes, 'antimythological' myths (*Modernism* 67) but West's formal practice itself resists the enshrinement of myth. Notably, it's MacKay's desire to name West as *modernist* that leads her to push this identification in what is otherwise a convincing and suggestive treatment of the book.

12. 'When I saw . . . my Army orders, in triplicate, I knew that I was entering a man's world, in the pejorative sense' ('Birch Leaves' 93). Later she describes the guards at the courts as 'confused male children' (103).

13. Forty years later she was to write that 'to arrive at Nuremberg was like stepping on to the set of a science fiction film: the extreme of unreality, and at that extremely prosaic' (Foreword 7).
14. This is especially true in the revision, where the theme of fantasy acquires prophetic weight.
15. Peter Wolfe long ago noted that the valence of the gardener symbol shifts over the course of the three essays: at first he is a symbol of energy and renewal, but then 'she changes her mind' (76). Wolfe misses the extent to which the 'change' is itself a fictionalised formal construction – and indeed maintains that *A Train of Powder* is not 'self-consciously' written (71, 70).
16. It's salient in this connection that American judge Francis Biddle's memoir includes a detailed record of the discussions about the choice of dress, in which Nikitchenko actually suggested the wearing of dark suits as preferable to the 'medieval' robes on which the French insisted (Biddle 382). West was likely privy to this information, as Biddle was her lover during her visits to Nuremberg.

Works Cited

Annan, Noel. *Our Age: English Intellectuals between the World Wars*. New York: Random House, 1991.

Biddle, Francis. *In Brief Authority*. Garden City: Doubleday, 1962.

Caesar, Terry. *Forgiving the Boundaries: Home as Abroad in American Travel Writing*. Athens: University of Georgia Press, 2005.

Clark, Steve. 'Introduction'. *Travel Writing and Empire: Postcolonial Theory in Transit*. Ed. Steve Clark. London and New York: Zed, 1999. 1–28.

Cohen, Debra Rae. 'Sheepish Modernism: Rebecca West, the Adam Brothers, and the Taxonomies of Criticism'. *Rebecca West Today: Contemporary Critical Approaches*. Ed. Bernard Schweizer, Newark: University of Delaware Press, 2006. 143–56.

Colquitt, Clare. 'A Call to Arms: Rebecca West's Assault on the Limits of "Gerda's Empire" in *Black Lamb and Grey Falcon*'. *South Atlantic Review* 51.2 (1986): 77–91.

Frow, John. *Genre*. London and New York: Routledge, 2006.

—. '"Reproducibles, Rubrics, and Everything You Need": Genre Theory Today'. *PMLA* 122.5 (2007): 1626–34.

Fussell, Paul. *Abroad: British Literary Traveling between the Wars*. New York and Oxford: Oxford University Press, 1980.

Glendinning, Victoria. 'In Memoriam: Rebecca West – A Woman for Our Century'. *New Republic* 11 April 1983: 28–32.

Goldsworthy, Vesna. 'Rebecca West's Journey of Self-Discovery'. *Representing Lives: Women and Auto/biography*. Ed. Alison Donnell and Pauline Polkey. Houndmills: Macmillan, 2000. 87–95.

Heffernan, Laura. 'Reading Modernism's Cultural Field: Rebecca West's *The Strange Necessity* and the Aesthetic "System of Relations"'. *Tulsa Studies in Women's Literature* 27.2 (2008): 309–25.

Hirsch, Francine. 'The Soviets at Nuremberg: International Law, Propaganda, and the Making of the Postwar Order'. *American Historical Review* 113.3 (2008): 701–30.

Jameson, Fredric. *Postmodernism, Or, the Cultural Logic of Late Capitalism*. Durham: Duke University Press, 1992.

Lassner, Phyllis. 'Rebecca West's Shadowy Other'. *Rebecca West Today: Contemporary Critical Approaches*. Ed. Bernard Schweizer. Newark: University of Delaware Press, 2006. 43–63.

MacKay, Marina. 'The Lunacy of Men, the Idiocy of Women: Woolf, West, and War'. *NWSA Journal* 15.3 (2003): 124–44.

—. *Modernism and World War II*. Cambridge: Cambridge University Press, 2007.

Marx, John. 'Failed-State Fiction'. *Contemporary Literature* 49.4 (2008): 597–633.

Maslen, Elizabeth. *Political and Social Issues in British Women's Fiction, 1928–1968*. London: Palgrave Macmillan, 2001.

Miller, Tyrus. *Late Modernism: Politics, Fiction and the Arts between the World Wars*. Berkeley: University of California Press, 1999.

Orage, A. N. 'Readers and Writers'. *New Age* 16 July 1914: 253.

Owen, Stephen. 'Genres in Motion'. *PMLA* 122.5 (2007): 1389–93.

Pitchford, Nicola. 'Unlikely Modernism, Unlikely Postmodernism: Stein's *Tender Buttons*'. *American Literary History* 11.4 (1999): 642–67.

Robbins, Bruce. 'Afterword'. *PMLA* 122.5 (2007): 1644–51.

Rollyson, Carl. *Rebecca West: A Life*. New York: Scribner, 1996.

Rosslyn, Felicity. 'Rebecca West, Gerda, and the Sense of Process'. *Black Lambs and Grey Falcons: Women Travellers in the Balkans*. Ed. John B. Allcock and Antonia Young. 1991. New York and Oxford: Berghahn, 2000. 113–27.

Sage, Victor. 'The Greater Tragedy Imposed on the Small: Art, Anachrony and the Pleasures of Bohemia in Rebecca West's *The Fountain Overflows*'. *British Fiction after Modernism*. Ed. Marina MacKay and Lyndsey Stonebridge. Basingstoke: Palgrave, 2007. 166–83.

Schweizer, Bernard. *Radicals on the Road: The Politics of English Travel Writing in the 1930s*. Charlottesville and London: University Press of Virginia, 2001.

Stetz, Margaret. 'Rebecca West and the Nuremberg Trials'. *Peace Review* 13.2 (2001): 229–35.

West, Rebecca. 'The Birch Leaves Falling'. *New Yorker* 26 October 1946: 93–105.

—. *Black Lamb and Grey Falcon: A Journey through Yugoslavia*. 1941. New York: Penguin, 1982.

—. 'Extraordinary Exile'. *New Yorker* 7 September 1946: 34–46.

—. Foreword. *On Trial at Nuremberg*. By Airey Neve. Boston: Little, Brown, 1978. 5–9.

—. *The Return of the Soldier*. 1918. New York: New York: Penguin, 1998.

—. *Selected Letters of Rebecca West*. Ed. Bonnie Kime Scott. New Haven and London: Yale University Press, 2000.

—. *A Train of Powder*. New York: Viking, 1955.

Wolfe, Peter. *Rebecca West: Artist and Thinker*. Carbondale: Southern Illinois University Press, 1971.

PART IV
DOCUMENTS

9

THE INTERMODERN ASSUMPTION OF THE FUTURE: WILLIAM EMPSON, CHARLES MADGE AND MASS-OBSERVATION

Nick Hubble

Inez Holden's ironically titled 1944 novel, *There's No Story There*, the tale of a wartime factory told by a female narrator, is one of the paradigmatic examples of an intermodern text discussed in Kristin Bluemel's *George Orwell and the Radical Eccentrics: Intermodernism in Literary London* (2004). Bluemel remarks on the similarities between the approaches of Holden and the social-research organisation Mass-Observation, while describing how the blizzard scene in the novel pokes fun at Mass-Observation:

> Although Mass-Observation and Holden's version of documentary realism share common techniques and goals, Holden maliciously represents Mass-Observation in the form of the peculiar, horn-rimmed Geoffrey Doran who has been studiously recording the conversations and doings of the workers in a notebook (much the way we imagine Holden doing as she prepared to write *There's No Story There*). Doran loses his precious notebook in the blizzard and as he paws frantically through snowdrifts trying to find it, Holden enjoys a joke at Mass-Observation's (and her own) expense when another worker comments, 'There was a mass of workers observing him' (132).[1]

This joke highlights the central ambiguity of Mass-Observation: 'It is never wholly clear . . . whether the primary aim was observation *of* the mass or *by* the masses' (Calder xiii). The whole point, of course, was that it was simultaneously both. Mass-Observation argued that subjective individual observations were rendered objective because the subjectivity of the observer was always one of the facts under observation. On one level, this relationship is the truth behind literary production: authors and poets are legitimated through the act of being read. It is by foregrounding this relationship that Holden's novel is able to display one of the key features of intermodernism: the simultaneous promotion of 'the imaginative lives of readers and the interests of the workers themselves' (Bluemel 133). The characteristic montage technique of Mass-Observation publications, in which the observations of hundreds of individuals were quoted verbatim, goes further than this by allowing the masses to become writers as well as readers and workers. However, an inevitable consequence of this radical approach is the demystification of literary performance, as the Mass-Observation founders were perfectly aware:

> [Observers] produce a poetry which is, not at present, restricted to a handful of esoteric performers. The immediate effect of MASS-OBSERVATION is to devalue considerably the status of the 'poet'. It makes the term 'poet' apply, not to his performance, but to his profession, like 'footballer'. (Jennings and Madge, 'Poetic Description' 3)

As a general historical prediction, this has undoubtedly proved to be the case: the status of poets and literary authors has been devalued because the technological developments of modernity have allowed the masses to express themselves to themselves through an array of media. Unfortunately, mainstream literary studies, despite the efforts of postwar academics such as Raymond Williams, remains wilfully opposed to this reality and determined to preserve the status of 'a handful of esoteric performers'. Hence the necessity of new critical approaches such as intermodernism which attempt to recover a meaningful cultural history for the twenty-first century.

With its egalitarian tone and combination of the two traditions of socialist and women's writing, *There's No Story There* may be seen as part of the configuration, identified by Stuart Hall as surrounding 'The Social Eye of *Picture Post*', that developed the social-democratic consciousness of wartime Britain and so created the context for the 1945 political settlement. Hall's argument for the prime importance of *Picture Post* within this configuration is that from its launch in 1938 it photographically deconstructed the apparent antithesis between a passive people and active leaders and established the democratic equality of its mass readership (Hall 82–83). However, these techniques were anticipated more than a year earlier by Mass-Observation and, as I have argued elsewhere, 'there is a strong case for reconsidering the centre of the democratising movement as "The Social Eye of Mass-Observation"' (*Mass-Observation* 162).

Mass-Observation was officially launched as the culmination of scientific developments in anthropology and psychology in a letter to the *New Statesman* of 30 January 1937 signed by Tom Harrisson, Humphrey Jennings and Charles

Madge. However, four weeks earlier the same journal had published a letter written solely by Madge which makes it plain that the specific context for the organisation's foundation was a perception that the abdication of Edward VIII in December 1936 had triggered an unprecedented public emergence of the repressed desires of the masses. It is clear that Madge – a poet, communist and *Daily Mirror* journalist – had broad political objectives for Mass-Observation beginning with treating the coming coronation of George VI, scheduled for 12 May 1937, as an opportunity for a programme of mass observations. These mass observations would simultaneously lay bare the symbolic power of the monarchy and re-empower the masses by making them conscious of their own desires.

The result was *May the Twelfth: Mass-Observation Day Surveys 1937* written by over 200 observers, edited by Jennings and Madge with the assistance of their mutual friend William Empson, among others, and published as a result of T. S. Eliot's advocacy at Faber and Faber. Unfortunately, the book proved too expensive at 12/6 to reach the mass audience it deserved and only 'sold a bare 800 copies' (Calder and Sheridan 62). However, it did successfully subvert the intended public theatrical performance of the Coronation by switching the focus entirely onto the crowd and so demonstrating that the autonomy and agency that appeared to belong to the newly crowned king were really the property of the masses themselves. This achievement was complemented by the 'Worktown' project simultaneously run by Harrisson in the predominantly industrial and working-class town of Bolton. Here, the intensive participant observation undertaken by the Mass-Observation team – including Empson on occasion – entailed living in such close proximity to the local population that, as in Holden's satire, every observer had a mass of workers observing him or her. In practice, this situation led to the effective deconstruction of the dominant anthropological discourse of otherness and revealed the underlying relationship of mutual intersubjectivity between the townsfolk and the observers: no longer were they ethnographers and natives but rather everyone was revealed to be both ethnographer and native and, therefore, equal members of the same modern mass society.

In January 1939, two years after its launch, Mass-Observation was finally able to bring its insights to a wider audience with the publication of *Britain by Mass-Observation* in the bestselling Penguin Special series. This book was to have profound political consequences for two reasons. First, the editors, Harrisson and Madge, were able to use the reports of mass observers to put together a devastating account of the way public opinion had been manipulated during the events of the 'Munich Crisis' just four months earlier in September 1938. By analysing the way in which Chamberlain's three meetings with Hitler were represented in the press as the actions of a dynamic new leader, they exposed the 'crisis' as a British form of fascist public theatre in which 'the threat of war, while real enough, had been experienced at a fantasy level and then dissipated with a fantasy resolution which allowed what had been objectively unacceptable (the forced partition of Czechoslovakia) to become publicly acceptable' (Hubble, *Mass-Observation* 155). Thus, what a few lone voices had expressed in private was made obvious in public; the book can be seen as a crucial factor in the subsequent turn of British public opinion against appeasement.[2] Second, the book's analysis of the Lambeth Walk dance craze phenomenon offers, as Ben Highmore has noted, 'an alternative imaginary identification that can be seen as (effectively) resistant to Fascism' (109). This piece became a model for the eventual wartime popular representation of Britain as simultaneously socially heterogeneous and the site of a collective identity; it sustained the nation against the immense internal and external pressures of those years. The craze was inspired by the 1937 show *Me and My Girl* in which the Cockney comedian Lupino Lane played a Lambethian who 'inherits an earldom but cannot unlearn his cockney ways. At a grand dinner party he starts "doin' the Lambeth Walk" with such effect that duchesses and all join in with him and his Lambeth pals' (Madge and Harrisson 140). Empson's analysis of pastoral was invoked to point out that the show was essentially about 'the contrast between the *natural* behaviour of the Lambethians and the affectation of the upper class' (Madge and Harrisson 157). However, the real appeal of the craze, as Madge and Harrisson realised from their experience in mass-observing the Coronation and Worktown, was that it allowed participants to interchange and combine apparently opposing class roles in a manner that was immensely liberating. Normally such carnivalesque reversals are short-lived, but the performative image of the working class promoted by Mass-Observation in this manner not only enabled a wartime spirit of resistance – figured in the chirpy Cockney defying the Blitz – but also became one of the cultural props of the strange persistence of wartime Britishness throughout the postwar period up until at least 1979. While that state of affairs might appear bizarre to subsequent generations, its attraction can still be grasped from the prophetically-titled *Britain by Mass-Observation*:

> When you do the Lambeth Walk, you pretend to be a Lambethian. . . . One thing which the huge popularity of the Lambeth Walk indicates quite definitely is a very widespread 'wish to be these people', though of course that wish is not a simple or straightforward one, and includes elements of make-believe and ballyhoo. The upper classes wish to masquerade as Lambethians: sixteenth century lords and ladies played, in pastoral make-believe, as shepherds and shepherdesses. The middle classes wish to be Lambethians because it temporarily lets them off a sticky code of manners which they usually feel bound to keep up. The working classes wish to be Lambethians because Lambethians *are* like themselves, plus a reputation for racy wit and musical talent – partly they represent that

part of the working class which knows how to have a good time. (Madge and Harrisson 173–74)

Madge and Harrisson's use of Empson's concept of 'pastoral' can again be seen and it underlies much of the analysis in the Lambeth Walk chapter. The fact that Empson was, as we have seen, directly or indirectly involved in *May the Twelfth*, the Worktown project and *Britain* is not simply contingent on his friendship and shared Cambridge background with Madge and Jennings; his connection with Mass-Observation was far more significant than that. On 16 March 1936, some months before Madge had even thought of Mass-Observation, Empson wrote a letter to him, which included the following criticism of a long manuscript on Chaucer, Spenser and Milton that Madge had just finished writing:

> The shape of the book I think is bloody insolent. This idea that one must write very esoteric stuff because nobody will read [it] anyway seems to me nonsense – you get plenty of readers if you give anybody a chance. Surely even a communist can have a reasonable amount of democratic feeling; the point about writing as plainly as you can is that you are testing your ideas against somebody who is not a specialist and just knows about life in general . . . I feel I have some right to be rude about this because [I am] so much open to the same faults. You had much better imagine before you write anything that England has long been a settled communist state, and that the only difficulties before you are (a) making the comrades hear what you want to say (b) convincing them that you are not talking nonsense; assuming the future to have arrived is a piece of symbolism quite in your manner; you will find it works much better both as making you write better and making people buy your books (Empson, *Letters* 97).[3]

In his biography of Empson, John Haffenden characterises the relationship between Empson and Madge as akin to that of teacher and student: 'Empson began in the time-honoured and best pedagogical way, by highlighting what he thought the strengths of the work . . . But after a few more such comments on various good features of the text, he moved on to criticise what he considered the profoundly serious weakness of Madge's approach' (430). After quoting at length from Empson's letter, Haffenden cements the hierarchical impression he has created for the reader by concluding, 'Madge took the lesson well, and did not publish his typescript. He valued Empson's robust words so highly that he kept the letter by him till he died' (431). While hardly in the same league as Valentine Cunningham's brutal review of Madge's collected poetry in 1994, in which Madge was branded 'a second-hand merchant in verse' and living illustration of 'how a period of high cultural energy such as the 1930s can charge up the batteries of quite mediocre talents lucky enough to be in the right vicinity' (Cunningham 4), Haffenden's account is quite in keeping with a tendency within critical and academic orthodoxy to marginalise the importance of Madge in any consideration of the literary politics and culture of the 1930s and 1940s.[4] However, it is particularly significant in this case that Haffenden uses this exchange of 1936 to end his account of Empson's involvement with Mass-Observation in summer 1937 (when he went to China). Despite Haffenden's partial and parenthetical acknowledgement of real chronologies, his decision to place the 1936 letter after his discussion of subsequent events inevitably obscures the otherwise obvious possibility that Empson's letter was a significant catalyst for Madge's formation of Mass-Observation. When this possibility is combined with the implicit sense that Empson is suggesting to Madge a line of action which he has adopted to correct his own similar faults, it becomes arguable that Mass-Observation was not merely a brief interlude in Empson's career, but a concrete manifestation of the position he adopted in his criticism of the 1930s. In what follows, I shall discuss Empson's work, in its mixture of critical, imaginative and universal thinking orientated towards the future, as a theory of intermodernism; and, by examining Empson's influence on Madge, will reveal the intellectual prehistory of Mass-Observation, which can be seen as an exemplary intermodern project.

Empson, Madge and Richards's Theory of Value

To appreciate fully the significance of Empson's letter, it is necessary to understand the particular parallels between him and Madge. Madge, born in 1912 and therefore six years younger, replicated many of the nodal points of Empson's career: both won scholarships, first, to Winchester College and then to Magdalene College, Cambridge. Although Empson was originally reading maths and Madge science, both ended up studying English literature under I. A. Richards. They both left Cambridge in an unconventional manner: Empson notoriously sent down during his postgraduate studies for keeping condoms in his rooms (Haffenden, *Empson* 242–60) and Madge running away with Kathleen Raine, the wife of college fellow Hugh Sykes Davies (Raine 78–79). Both were recognised as significant poets at an early age and featured, respectively, in the two anthologies edited by Michael Roberts which have come to be seen as the manifestoes of the Auden generation, *New Signatures* (1932) and *New Country* (1933). Empson contributed six poems to the former and Madge's 'Letter to the Intelligentsia' graced the latter. Both also went on to become leading poets of the thirties but effectively stopped publishing after the war, having written two volumes apiece: Empson's *Poems* appeared in 1935 and *The Gathering Storm* in 1940, while Madge's *The Disappearing Castle* was published in 1937 and *The Father Found* in 1941 (the latter three volumes all published by Eliot at Faber and Faber). Other work of the thirties includes Empson's early books of literary criticism, *Seven Types of Ambiguity*

(1930) and *Some Versions of Pastoral* (1935) and Madge's Mass-Observation publications. Like many of the British literary intelligentsia, both spent the war years working for state institutions: Empson, alongside George Orwell, was a talks producer for the BBC and Madge worked in turn with the Ministry of Information, for John Maynard Keynes at the National Institute of Economic and Social Research, and with Michael Young at Politics and Economic Planning. Therefore, although both eventually went on to long and illustrious postwar academic careers – Empson as Professor of English at Sheffield University from 1953 to 1971 and Madge as Professor of Sociology at the University of Birmingham from 1950 to 1971 – it can also be seen that both were fully part of that distinctive and discrete cultural constellation of the 1930–45 period which is the especial focus of this volume.

However, the most significant parallel for our purposes is Empson and Madge's shared relationship with Richards and fascination with the psychological Theory of Value that he outlined. The rise of mass society had created a context in which 'the problem presented by the gulf between what is preferred by the majority and what is accepted as excellent by the most qualified opinion has become infinitely more serious and appears likely to become threatening in the near future' (Richards, *Principles* 36). If the critic wanted to avoid the awkward position of assuming him or herself better than the dissenting majority, Richards argued, it was necessary to have an overriding general theory of value. Following Freud, he contended that life consists of satisfying impulses – aversions and appetencies (Richards's preferred term to desires because it did not carry the same implication of conscious belief) – and so, consequently, the good life consists of satisfying as many impulses as possible: 'Anything is valuable which will satisfy an appetency without involving the frustration of some equal or more important appetency; in other words the only reason which can be given for not satisfying a desire is that more important desires will thereby be thwarted' (Richards, *Principles* 48). Those who could order their impulses with the maximum of satisfaction and minimum of suppression lived the most valuable lives because they were the most free and well-balanced. Not only was such a life a source of individual value but also of collective value because maximising satisfaction depends on 'due sensitiveness to the reciprocal claims of human intercourse' (Richards, *Principles* 53). This utilitarian argument was a genuinely radical stance entailing a prescient warning against the potential dangers presented by absolute value systems such as religion, morality and nationalism to the fragile modernity of the twentieth century. It was belief in the possibility of averting this coming crisis by the reordering of individual and collective impulses which led to Richards's inspirational rallying call that '[poetry] is capable of saving us; it is a perfectly possible means of overcoming chaos' (Richards, *Science and Poetry* 82–83). For it was poetry, which depended on the awareness and balancing of the widest range of impulses, that held open the promise of reorganising and systematising those impulses to ensure that the maximum number could be satisfied.

These were the ideas Richards was pursuing when Madge first contacted him to ask his advice about a predecessor to the Chaucer–Spenser–Milton manuscript that he called his 'Ideolexicon': a huge key to imagery in English poetry that was designed to guide readers to the hidden stores of knowledge in the poetic unconsciousness. Here Madge was following Empson's path in *Seven Types of Ambiguity*, which has been described as 'a kind of magical key to all mythologies' (Jackson 107). However, the significant difference was that Empson was concerned with showing that for poetry to work in the manner Richards suggested, the full range of poetical impulses had to be consciously apprehended not just to the point when meaning became ambiguous, but even – in the case of the seventh type of ambiguity – to the point when apparently opposite meanings were able to exist simultaneously. For instance, Keats's 'Ode to Melancholy' requires the reader to apprehend all the impulses expressed by a number of paired opposites – including death and the sexual act; pain and pleasure; woman as mistress whom one must master and to whom one must yield; ideal sensual beauty and fleeting eternal beauty – contained within the main opposition between melancholy and joy. The invitation to 'glut thy sorrow on a morning rose' allows a full freedom of emotion, whether unreined sorrow or the transfiguration of that sorrow into joy through excess, that is revealed by rationally following the various related arguments of the poem. Empson suggests that the poem is 'universally intelligible and admired [because] evidently these pairs of opposites, stated in the right way, make a direct appeal to the normal habits of the mind' (Empson, *Ambiguity* 215). He goes on to argue that this simultaneous presentation of apparently opposed alternatives enables maximum satisfaction of impulses at both individual and collective levels:

> Indeed the way in which a person lives by these vaguely-conceived opposites is the most important thing about his make-up; the way in which opposites can be stated so as to satisfy a wide variety of people, for a great number of degrees of interpretation, is the most important thing about the communication of the arts. (Empson, *Ambiguity* 221)

He points out, however, that these opposites are not always as obviously employed as in the Keats 'Ode' by turning to Richard Crashaw's 'Hymn to Saint Teresa', in which the saint is praised for chastity with subtle metaphors alluding to the sexual act. Empson describes the resulting effect as similar to Dryden's ribald 'Marriage à la Mode', in which the heroine's line 'Now die, my Alexis, and I will die too' is a plea for simultaneous climax; he suggests that these kinds of mutual comparisons are doubly beneficial, conferring dignity on the natural act and tenderness on the heroic one: '[T]he strongest resultant feeling . . . is . . . not far from the central sentiment of Christianity. "Pleasure is exhausting and fleeting . . . nothing is to be valued more than mutual forbearance"' (Empson, *Ambiguity* 220).

Although such interpretations could provoke outrage – either at the blasphemous content or the very idea that poetry could be rationally analysed in this way – this was not what Empson meant when he later described Madge's Chaucer–Spenser–Milton book as insolent. Madge's crime lay in his failure to reveal fully all the arguments in the poetry he was writing about; whereas at the opposite extreme, as we can see, Empson was fully committed to laying bare the device of ambiguity regardless of the consequences. Richards had been quite clear on the threat posed by a society whose values were based on satisfying one set of desires at the cost of suppressing another to any who demonstrated the possibility of successfully satisfying both of the apparently opposed sets of desires: '[T]he spectacle of other people enjoying both activities without difficulty, thanks to some not very obvious adjustment, is peculiarly distressing, and such people are usually regarded as especially depraved' (Richards, *Principles* 55–56). Empson, who had experienced this type of social condemnation firsthand in his expulsion from Magdalene, understood exactly what Richards meant and yet, at the same time, he realised that his sending down had liberated him. Fortunately, he rejected Richards's more cautious stance and chose to pursue his own path (which would go on to wind its way through original poetry, brilliant literary criticism, the Far East, bisexuality, open relationships and generally eccentric behaviour into one of the great examples of a life lived freely and fully). However, Empson's aim was never to go out and deliberately flout the veneer of respectability which covered the repressive nature of pre-war Britain's rigidly hierarchical society, but rather to orientate behaviour and arguments to the values of a more liberated society to come. This is what Empson meant when he advised Madge to assume the viewpoint of the future in his writing. Of course Madge was particularly responsive to Empson's thinking because he had experienced his own moment of exclusion and subsequent liberation, and it is this intent to promote a liberated heterodox society that underlies Mass-Observation's initial aim of making the masses conscious of their own desires.

PROLETARIAN LITERATURE

For all the brilliance on display in *Seven Types of Ambiguity*, it is nonetheless somewhat esoteric in places and appears to fall foul of Empson's later objection to

> the idea that poetry is good in proportion as it is complicated, or simply hard to construe; it seems quite a common delusion, and always shocks me when expressed. And yet I suppose it is very near my own position;

in any case it joins on to I. A. Richards' Theory of Value as the satisfaction of more impulses rather than less, and T. S. Eliot's struggle to
find a poetic idiom adequate to the complexity of modern life (qtd in
Haffenden, *Empson* 185).

However, as Haffenden suggests, Empson's own position actually offers the
way out of this poetic impasse, because he shows ambiguity as the means
by which a poet can express complexity in the simplest form of language.
Once Empson had fully worked out this concept, the ground was laid for the
subsequent analysis of *Some Versions of Pastoral*; a sharper and more disciplined study focusing on 'the pastoral process of putting the complex into the
simple' (Empson, *Pastoral* 25). His own act of 'assuming the future' is visible
in the shift from the individualist stance of the earlier work to the more self-
consciously collective and democratic tone of the latter, established at the
outset by his opening chapter on 'Proletarian Literature'.

Empson argues that the proletarian literature of the 1920s and 1930s is part
of a historical series, including works as wide ranging as *The Beggar's Opera*
and *Alice in Wonderland*, displaying the pastoral 'trick of thought' he calls
'Comic Primness' and which he defines as 'double irony in the acceptance of a
convention' (Empson, *Pastoral* 170). An example of this is 'Ironical Humility,
whose simplest gambit is to say "I am not clever, educated, well born" or what
not (as if you had a low standard to judge by), and then to imply that your
standards are so high in the matter that the person you are humbling yourself
before is quite out of sight' (Empson, *Pastoral* 171). The effect of classing the
most valuable with the 'lowest' in this manner is to create plenty of space below
the ironically accepted conventions for life to be lived freely. Proletarian literature functions as a variant of this: on the one hand, it appears as an acceptance
of the lowest position in society but, on the other, it lays claim to a revolutionary historical agency so that the effect of simultaneously combining the two is to
create plenty of space below the ironically accepted conventions of hierarchical
society for the holder of such attitudes to stand up and act freely.

Empson was not just arguing that proletarian literature was a version of
pastoral but rather that it was the culmination of the genre into a form in
which the constituent double irony of the plot overlapped with the material
processes that turned it into printed texts written by authors for a mass readership. Members of this readership were not simply confronted with themselves
in the texts they read but with the 'double attitude of the artist to the worker,
of the complex man to the simple one ("I am in one way better, in another
not so good")' (Empson, *Pastoral* 19); this double attitude also generated,
as we have seen, a proletarian performative agency. It is this combination
of the pastoral form and the historic emergence of a mass readership which
enables the intermodern possibility we examined at the start of this chapter, of

simultaneously promoting the imaginative lives of readers and the interests of the workers themselves in books such as Holden's *There's No Story There* – a novel that clearly fits Empson's definition of proletarian literature.

Empson understood that showing real and imaginative human interests to coincide was a necessary condition for social transformation, as he demonstrated by quoting approvingly from Maxim Gorki's speech to the 1934 Soviet Writers' Congress:

> To invent means to extract from the totality of real existence its basic idea and to incarnate this in an image; thus we obtain realism. But if to the idea extracted from the real is added the desirable, the potential, and the image is supplemented by this, we obtain that romanticism which lies at the basis of myth and is highly useful in that it facilitates the arousing of a revolutionary attitude towards reality, an attitude of practically changing the world (Empson, *Pastoral* 21).

Although Empson noted that this description would apply to any good literature, he also concluded that 'revolutionary proletarian literature, in intention at any rate, is obviously a product of transition' (Empson, *Pastoral* 21) – that is, in transition to a future liberated society. Orwell was to make this point more bluntly: 'I believe we are passing into a classless period, and what we call proletarian literature is one of the signs of change' (Orwell 297).

POPULAR POETRY

There is another clear link running from Richards through Empson to Madge. While it is possible to see how Richards generally established the context for the alliance between poetry and political purpose which dominated the 1930s, it is also clear that Michael Roberts's preface to *New Signatures* refines Richards's position by locating the promise of salvation in a specifically '"popular" poetry', characterised by symbolism 'of exceptionally wide validity' (Roberts, 'Preface' 11). His examples of such a poetry were not only Auden, Spender and Day-Lewis but also Empson, whose 'obscurity' was due to a 'necessary compression' of the logical analogy between ideas and the corresponding emotional responses: 'In Mr Empson's poetry there is no scope for vagueness of interpretation, and its "difficulty" arises from this merit. Apart from their elegance, their purely poetic merit, they are important because they do something to remove the difficulties which have stood between the poet and the writing of popular poetry' (Roberts, 'Preface' 12).

On one level, Empson's 'Camping Out', with its opening line 'And now she cleans her teeth into the lake', reads like an updated version of one of Wordsworth's Lucy poems, in which, rather than being restricted to 'earth's diurnal course' (Wordsworth 147), the subject occupies 'a straddled sky of stars'. Empson later explained the relationship of the vulgarly modern and the transcendent divine in his notes on the poem: 'She gives the lake its pattern of reflected stars, now made of toothpaste, as God's grace allows man virtues that nature wouldn't' (Empson, *Poems* 44). However, in keeping with the pastoral stance of double irony in the acceptance of a convention, the 'vaults' of space are not opened 'to achieve the Lord' but for us – humans camping out in the Cosmos – to soar and explore galaxies:

> Our bullet boat light's speed by thousand flies,
> Who moves so among stars their frame unties,
> See where they blur, and die, and are outsoared.
>
> (Roberts, *New Signatures* 71)

Here, the popular symbolism includes the idea of space flight as 'integrity and independence: . . . a bid for freedom from authority and institutionalism' (Haffenden, 'Introduction' xxxvii–xxxviii); the central ambiguity links the sexual act with faster than light travel so that, as Empson once noted of the poem, 'The idea is that a great enough ecstasy can make the common world unreal' (Empson, *Complete Poems* 205). It is this economical precision by which Empson was able to present complex ideas – in this case, almost the whole of his sophisticated philosophy in two seven line stanzas – that were also inherently modern and democratic, which enabled Roberts to endorse his work as an exemplary version of 'popular poetry'.

Although it is possible to trace the influence of Empson's 'popular poetry' on Madge's own verse, it is considerably more obvious in other fields of Madge's work. For example, Madge used the term 'popular poetry' to describe a story run by the *Daily Mirror* about a 'Human Mole' (161). This story of a recluse, who was living in poverty in order to save enough money to launch an invention, was singled out by Madge both for its 'affinities with poetic tradition' and as an example of the way it was created by the collaboration of reporter, sub-editor, photographer and caption-writer: 'the mass-produced character of the modern newspaper is its supreme virtue' (Madge 162–63). It was this combination that allowed the press, for all its faults, to demonstrate the potentially liberating process of freely expressing mass desires. As Madge noted, 'the Press has put us in a dream world' (Madge 151) and thus, ambiguity analogous to Freudian 'condensation' could reach a mass audience with its possibilities of adjustments allowing the reconciliation of opposed sets of desires:

> I was told on entering a Fleet Street newspaper office as a reporter that it would be my job to concentrate on 'Sex, Scandal and Crime.' Beyond these three grisly abstractions, I glimpsed the afterglow of another trio in whose names much confusion has been wrought: Beauty, Truth and Goodness. Sex, Scandal and Crime are the poetry of modern journalism (Madge 153–54).

Madge saw the press as providing a challenge to an official policy in Britain that amounted to the organised sexual repression of the masses – a challenge that finally expressed itself in full with the *Daily Mirror* headline of 3 December 1936:

THE KING WANTS TO MARRY MRS SIMPSON:
CABINET ADVISES 'NO'

As he commented, 'No amount of negative advice from cabinets or archbishops could nullify the effect of that openly expressed wish. Millions saw the emergence of their own thwarted and concealed desires' (Madge 160).

The 'Human Mole' story appeared on 26 October 1936; but that was not the first time Madge found a use for the term 'popular poetry'. In the wake of Empson's letter of admonishment in March of that year, he chose 'Popular Poetry' as the working title of his plans for the democratic future-orientated movement, which would emerge immediately after the Abdication as Mass-Observation:

> A series of notes under [the] title, 'Popular Poetry', in one of Madge's notebooks, calls for 'Coincidence Clubs: groups in colleges, factories, localities' to study the press and advertisements, and be involved in 'exercises for imagination'. Under a list of 'Plans for PP' come 'First Text Book of PP', lectures, training courses, 'mimeographed record sheets', delegate conferences and 'PP Newspaper on mass basis'. Possible slogans include 'Newspaper Active' and 'Mass Science'. A list of potential contacts includes Empson [and] Richards . . . (Hubble, *Mass-Observation* 77)

The bold declaration, 'Movt can cut the Gordian Knot', that ends these notes suggests Madge shared Empson's desire to resolve the crisis of modernity in which the growing number of impulses possible in modern life seemed to require responses of ever growing complexity.

THE INTERMODERN SHIFT

Popular poetry and proletarian literature became linked ideas at the 1934 Soviet Writers' Congress, where Karl Radek confirmed that 'we in the Soviet Union, in our handling of our proletarian writers, have discarded the old "Proletcult" method . . .' (qtd in Croft 42). As Andy Croft notes:

> Radek's use of the term 'proletarian' indicates his impatience with previous ultra-left theorising and his eagerness to encourage writers who were neither working-class nor socialist, but whose imaginative achievements he wished to claim for the side of humanity against fascism. On the one hand he used the term 'proletarian' to apply to all Soviet literature, on the other he used it specifically to denote 'socialist realist' writers. Then again

he used the term synonymously with any working-class writing *and* to hail the 'beginning of proletarian literature in England' (by which he meant the poetry of the *New Signatures* Group, writers like Auden, Spender and Day-Lewis). As William Empson noted at the time, Radek's vocabulary 'is meant to shift from a political idea to a universal one'. (44)

Croft interprets this 'shift' as a deliberate and tactical stretching of the term 'beyond the point of usefulness', which allowed the introduction of 'more specific and encouraging terms' and opened the way to the Popular Front (44–45). In Britain, as he goes on to note approvingly, the impact of the Soviet Congress, and the successful establishment of *Left Review* soon afterwards, marked the point at which the term 'proletarian literature' was 'dropped from general use on the Left, as a sectarian and unhelpful term' (46). However, such a reading ignores the point Empson was trying to make, which, as we have seen, is that the true universal applicability of proletarian literature – the capacity, like any good literature, of changing the world – is dependent precisely on the maintenance of a 'double attitude of the artist to the worker' rather than the blurring created by first combining worker writers with writers who supported the workers and then characterising them collectively as 'the best friends of humanity' (43–44). The implied unity of the Popular Front suppressed the necessary conditions for the pastoral concept of Comic Primness:

> For this pleasure of effective momentary simplification the arguments of the two sides must be pulling their weight on the ironist, and though he might be sincerely indignant if told so it is fair to call him conscious of them. A character who accepts this way of thinking tends to be forced into isolation by sheer strength of mind, and so into a philosophy of Independence. (Empson, *Pastoral* 171)

Once the British Left abandoned the concept of 'proletarian literature', aesthetic representations of workers began to appear which no longer embodied difference and, while this seemed appropriate for projecting images of solidarity, the long-term consequence was that they lost their transformative capacity. This is why, despite inspiring tremendous enthusiasm initially, the Popular Front aesthetic disappeared from view relatively quickly once the war was over.

However, there was a group of writers who remained true to the transformative possibilities of proletarian literature and related versions of mass pastoral. Although Empson joined the group of friends Bluemel has labelled the intermodern 'radical eccentrics' only after his return from China in January 1940, they had already independently produced a number of versions of pastoral. For instance, both Stevie Smith, in *Novel on Yellow Paper* (1936) and Orwell, in *Coming Up for Air* (1939), combined authorial privilege with suburban everydayness in their main characters to present modern life as a puzzling ambiguity and then invited their readership to 'Work it Out for Yourself' (Bluemel 34–36, 62–63; Hubble, 'Intermodern Pastoral' 131–35). Both novels were orientated more to the emergent society of the future than the hierarchical pre-war world in which people knew their place, which explains their continuing contemporary feel and relevance for twenty-first century readerships. A form of intermodern pastoral closer to orthodox proletarian literature was adopted by Orwell's *The Road to Wigan Pier* (1937), which managed to be both a biting satire of Popular Front documentary and a deliberately perverse reiteration of class difference designed to tempt a sinking middle class into losing their aitches in spite of themselves (J. Roberts 66; Hubble, *Mass-Observation* 100–01). *Wigan Pier's* technique of doubly ironic (almost parodic) acceptance of the conventions of social class – by which the working-class interior is celebrated only in order to open it up and so spread its freedoms out into the public sphere – can also be found in Mass-Observation's *May the Twelfth*, in which the beer drinking, singing and good humour of the crowd is separated from its official occasion and allowed to signify the possibility of a liberated society. As we have seen, these techniques were subsequently used for considerable political effect in *Britain by Mass-Observation*.

The rapid changes in British life that occurred during the first years of the war bear out the validity of Empson's (and Orwell's) understanding of 'proletarian literature' as a literature of social transition. Slavoj Žižek has observed that 'in the class struggle between bourgeoisie and proletariat, the proletariat stands for the struggle as such' (42). Similarly, 'proletarian literature' stands for the struggle to get away from bourgeois social realism – to move from a literature that describes the world to one that changes it – rather than the expression of an authentic proletarian existence. In general literary discourse proletarian literature is regarded as another species of social realism and the opposite of social realism is usually considered to be modernism. It would, therefore, be logical to label the literature of social transition as 'modernist literature' if it weren't for the fact that modernism has been hypostatised into a monumental presence – partly by the ideological exclusion of writers such as the 'radical eccentrics' – and used to signify a timeless authentic being. In reality these terms are not the signifiers of absolute meaning they seem to be but merely unifocal snapshots of a parallax shift. The advantage of introducing the term 'intermodernism' into literary discourse is that it suggests transition rather than authentic presence. From now on, it will make more sense to consider the old categories such as modernism and proletarian literature as elements of a greater intermodern shift.[5]

The different intermodern interventions examined in this chapter were united by personal networks and a shared commitment to the maintenance of a double attitude. Much of the apparent eccentricity of the radical eccentrics lies in their resistance to easy labelling: they were always situated both inside and outside conventional groupings. The process by which bourgeois writers 'went over' to the working class in the 1930s is sometimes described pejoratively as one of 'negative identification'; by way of contrast, the process adopted by the radical eccentrics might be described as one of non-identification, of refusing any single imposed identity. Žižek argues that the observed difference in an object undergoing a parallax shift is not subjective but reflects an ontological shift in the object itself so that what is revealed is the object's non-coincidence with itself (Žižek 17). This non-identity lies at the heart of the (parallax) Real, which unlike the Lacanian Real, 'accounts for the very multiplicity of appearances of the same underlying Real – it is not the hardcore which persists as the Same, but the hard bone of contention which pulverises the sameness into the multitude of appearances' (Žižek 26). Similarly, the process of discerning the seventh type of ambiguity, which depends on the simultaneous awareness of all the opposed tendencies operating at one particular moment, also reveals the 'hard bone of contention' of the Real; and, in fact, Empson himself compared it 'to the difference of sound heard by the two ears, which decides where the sound is coming from, or to the stereoscopic contradictions that imply a dimension' (Empson, *Ambiguity* 193). It is this fundamental core of non-identity, revealed by the 'stereoscopic contradictions' of the dual perspective of writers like Orwell and Holden, which underwrites the intermodern capacity to satisfy apparently opposed impulses simultaneously and thereby hold open the promise of full human agency – by showing, variously, how being a Mass-Observer can lead to the pleasure of being observed by the mass; how everyday routine can become the possibility of performative transformation; and how the limits of social class can leave infinite space in which to live freely.

Notes

1. Mass-Observation has gone through several incarnations including a current project that has been running continuously since 1981 based in the Mass-Observation Archive at the University of Sussex. The original organisation (1937–49) entered popular consciousness almost from its inception but its particular notoriety at the time of Holden's writing was due to its work for the Ministry of Information during the early part of the war. A number of historical accounts provide further details (Highmore 75–112). See also Hubble, *Mass-Observation*; Jeffery; Sheridan, Street and Bloome.
2. A version of the Munich Crisis chapter was broadcast on BBC radio in June 1939 (Highmore 107).
3. The date of composition in the *Selected Letters* is given as '?1937' but in his biography of Empson, Haffenden identifies it as 16 March 1936 (430).
4. In similar vein, Julian Symons dubbed Madge 'the ideal intellectual revolutionary simpleton of the [Thirties]' (88) and Anthony Easthope, seemingly unconcerned by the actual nature of Madge's poetry, cited him as proof of the thesis that the more hardline the communist poet, the greater the slavish adherence to traditional metre (333). What all these accounts miss – or, rather, what they ideologically obfuscate – is Madge's significance as an unsung architect of the Welfare State, one who carried

the political and aesthetic values of the 1930s into the postwar period (Hubble, 'Charles Madge' 76–89).
5. For a fuller discussion of the relationship between social realism, modernism and intermodernism, see Hubble, 'The Origins of Intermodernism' (167–70).

WORKS CITED

Bluemel, Kristin. *George Orwell and the Radical Eccentrics: Intermodernism in Literary London*. New York and Basingstoke: Palgrave Macmillan, 2004.

Calder, Angus. Introduction. *Britain by Mass-Observation*. Ed. Tom Harrisson and Charles Madge. London: Cresset Library, 1986. vii–xv.

— and Dorothy Sheridan, eds. *Speak for Yourself: A Mass-Observation Anthology, 1937–49*. London: Jonathan Cape, 1984.

Croft, Andy. *Red Letter Days: British Fiction in the 1930s*. London: Lawrence and Wishart, 1990.

Cunningham, Valentine. 'Marooned in the 30s'. *Times Literary Supplement*, 19 August 1994: 4–5.

Easthope, Anthony. 'Traditional Metre and the Poetry of the Thirties'. *1936: The Sociology of Literature, Volume 2 – Practices of Literature and Politics*. Ed. Francis Barker, Jay Bernstein, John Coombes, Peter Hulme, David Musselwhite and Jennifer Stone. Colchester: University of Essex, 1979. 324–43.

Empson, William. *The Complete Poems of William Empson*. Ed. John Haffenden. Harmondsworth: Penguin, 2001.

—. *Poems*. London: Chatto and Windus, 1935.

—. *Selected Letters of William Empson*. Ed. John Haffenden. Oxford and New York: Oxford University Press, 2006.

—. *Seven Types of Ambiguity*. 1930. Harmondsworth: Penguin, 1961.

—. *Some Versions of Pastoral*. 1935. Harmondsworth, Penguin, 1995.

Haffenden, John. 'Introduction'. *The Complete Poems of William Empson*. Ed. J. Haffenden. Harmondsworth: Penguin, 2001. xi–lxv.

—. *William Empson: Among the Mandarins*. Oxford and New York: Oxford University Press, 2005.

Hall, Stuart. 'The Social Eye of *Picture Post*'. *Working Papers in Cultural Studies* 2 (1972): 71–120.

Highmore, Ben. *Everyday Life and Cultural Theory: An Introduction*. London: Routledge, 2002.

Hubble, Nick. 'Charles Madge and Mass-Observation Are at Home: From Anthropology to War, and After'. *New Formations* 44 (2001): 76–89.

—. 'Intermodern Pastoral: William Empson and George Orwell'. *New Versions of Pastoral: Post-Romantic, Modern, and Contemporary Responses to the Tradition*. Ed. David James and Philip Tew. Madison: Fairleigh

Dickinson University Press; London: Associated University Press, 2009, 125–35.

—. *Mass-Observation and Everyday Life: Culture, History, Theory*. London: Palgrave, 2006.

—. 'The Origins of Intermodernism in Ford Madox Ford's Parallax View'. *Ford Madox Ford: Literary Networks and Cultural Transformations*. Ed. Andrzej Gasiorek and Daniel Moore. Amsterdam and New York: Rodopi, 2008. 167–88.

Jackson, Kevin. *Humphrey Jennings*. Basingstoke: Picador, 2004.

Jeffery, Tom. *Mass-Observation: A Short History*. Birmingham: Centre for Contemporary Cultural Studies, 1978.

Jennings, Humphrey and Charles Madge. 'Poetic Description and Mass-Observation'. *New Verse* Feb.–March 1937: 1–6.

— and Charles Madge, T. O. Beachcroft, Julian Blackburn, William Empson, Stuart Legg and Kathleen Raine, eds. *May the Twelfth: Mass-Observation Day-Surveys 1937*. London: Faber and Faber, 1937.

Madge, Charles. 'Press, Radio and Social Consciousness'. *The Mind in Chains: Socialism and the Cultural Revolution*. Ed C. Day Lewis. London: Frederick Muller, 1937. 147–63.

— and Tom Harrisson, eds. *Britain by Mass-Observation*. Harmondsworth: Penguin, 1939.

Orwell, George. 'The Proletarian Writer'. 1940. *The Complete Works of George Orwell, Volume XII: A Patriot After All 1940–1941*. Ed. Peter Davison. London: Secker and Warburg, 2000. 294–99.

Raine, Kathleen. *The Land Unknown*. London: Hamish Hamilton, 1975.

Richards, I. A. *Principles of Literary Criticism*. 1924. London: Routledge and Kegan Paul, 1960.

—. *Science and Poetry*. London: Kegan Paul, Trench, Trubner and Co., 1926.

Roberts, John. *The Art of Interruption: Realism, Photography and the Everyday*. Manchester: Manchester University Press, 1998.

Roberts, Michael, ed. *New Country*. London: Hogarth Press, 1933.

—. *New Signatures*. London: Hogarth Press, 1932.

—. 'Preface'. Roberts, M. 7–20.

Sheridan, Dorothy, Brian Street and David Bloome. *Writing Ourselves: Mass-Observation and Literacy Practices*. Cresskill: Hampton Press, 2000.

Symons, Julian. *The Thirties: A Dream Revolved*. Rev. ed. London: Faber and Faber, 1975.

Wordsworth, William. *William Wordsworth: The Oxford Authors*. Ed. Stephen Gill. Oxford and New York: Oxford University Press, 1984.

Žižek, Slavoj. *The Parallax View*. Cambridge and London: MIT Press, 2006.

10

'THE CREATIVE TREATMENT OF ACTUALITY': JOHN GRIERSON, DOCUMENTARY CINEMA AND 'FACT' IN THE 1930S

Laura Marcus

The film theorist and documentary film-maker Paul Rotha, at the opening of his 'informal history' of the documentary film movement between 1928 and 1939, *Documentary Diary* (1973), made a significant claim. 'The movement of documentary film-making in Britain in the 1930s' was, prior to 1940, the 'only one real coherent movement in the young art of the cinema which was destined to have an influence on Western-film making and to attract world attention among critics and audiences' (xii). He also suggested that the group of authors most strongly associated with the 1930s – Auden, Isherwood, Day Lewis, Warner, Spender, Graham Greene, Calder-Marshall and others – had less social influence in their time than the documentary film-makers. Rotha saw the writers as a parallel cultural formation to the film-makers, but argued that there was little dialogue between the two 'movements'. In this chapter, I take up Rotha's large claim for the significance of documentary film in the 1930s, while also suggesting that the interchange between documentary film-makers and thirties writers was more complex and dynamic than his account suggests.

Historians and analysts of British cinema have researched and explored the documentary film movement extensively, and there is a large critical literature on the topic, including recent anthologies of the writings of both Rotha and the most significant figure in the movement, the director and producer John Grierson. The question of documentary cinema's impact on writers of the inter-war period has also received critical attention, with a particular focus on the work of George Orwell and J. B. Priestley, and their production of 'documentary' writing in the 1930s. This chapter also takes up these dimensions of the literature-film relationship, addressing the ways in which texts such as Priestley's *English Journey* and Orwell's *The Road to Wigan Pier* negotiated and incorporated, implicitly or explicitly, documentary film's ways of seeing. Beyond this, the chapter argues that the literature-film relationship is central to the documentary movement's self-definitions and, more broadly, that the connections and contestations between writing and cinema played a crucial role in concepts of aesthetics, politics and culture in the early decades of the twentieth century.

The first part of the chapter will explore the films and writings of the most prominent figures of the documentary movement, in particular those of Grierson and Rotha. It will also look at a number of largely forgotten writings from the journal *Cinema Quarterly*, which ran between 1932 and 1935, and which was very substantially devoted to discussion, and indeed promotion, of the documentary film movement in Britain. Edited from Edinburgh by Norman Wilson, the journal's reviews editor was Forsyth Hardy, who would become Grierson's biographer and an editor and anthologist of his writings. The second part of the chapter turns to the question of 1930s writers and the relationship of their new modes of realism to documentary film, with discussion of J. B. Priestley, George Orwell and Storm Jameson.

'We relied,' wrote John Grierson, 'beyond renter and exhibiter alike, on the people, and their superior taste in realism' (Grierson, *Documentary* 77). He was referring to the documentary films of the late 1920s and 1930s with whose making he had been involved. The term 'documentary' was defined by Grierson as 'the creative treatment of actuality' (Paul Rotha's gloss on the term in 1936 was 'the use of the film medium to interpret creatively and in social terms the life of the people as it exists in reality' (Rotha, *Documentary Film* 5)) and it was first used in a film sense in 1926, when Grierson wrote of the Canadian anthropologist turned film-maker Robert Flaherty's *Moana*: 'Being a visual account of the daily life of a Polynesian youth, [the film] has documentary value' (Grierson, *Documentary* 11).

The Scottish-born Grierson became involved with film – as critic, director and producer – after a degree in literature and moral philosophy at Glasgow University at the beginning of the 1920s and postgraduate studies on a Rockefeller Foundation scholarship at the University of Chicago. He was drawn to the latter city, he would assert, by the writings of Vachel Lindsay and Sherwood Anderson, and, in particular, by the 'public' urban poetry of Carl Sandburg, which was equivalent, in Grierson's later formulation, to the 'symphonic form' in documentary film, 'concerned with the orchestration of movement' (Grierson, *Documentary* 43). At the University of Chicago, Grierson undertook research on the press and public opinion in relation to immigration. He spent time in New York in 1925, turning to research on film-going and public opinion after meeting the journalist and political commentator Walter Lippmann, whose study *Public Opinion* had been published in 1922. Lippmann's work in the emerging field of 'mass media' and 'mass communications' studies guided Grierson's research on film audiences and 'box-office records of success and failure'. Grierson based this research 'on two essential factors: the observation of the ordinary or the actual, and the discovery within the actual of the patterns which gave it significance for civic education' (Grierson, *Documentary* 290–91).

While researching in the US, Grierson began to write articles on cinema-going and film criticism, and gained experience of post-production film work, contributing to the English subtitling of Sergei Eisenstein's *Battleship Potemkin* for US distribution and to critical commentary on the film. Grierson returned to Britain in 1927, taking up employment under Stephen Tallents at the recently established Empire Marketing Board (whose role was to promote trade and economic relations between Britain and the countries of the Empire) with an initial commission to explore international developments in film-making and to set up screenings of documentary and narrative films, including the Soviet cinema that was banned from public exhibition in Britain and a number of other European countries at this time.

In late 1927 Grierson was himself given the commission to make a film on the home fishing industry. This was the film that would become *Drifters*, a documentary on the Scottish herring fleets, on which both Flaherty and Eisenstein were major influences. Combining Flaherty's representations of the natural world with the dynamic editing and symphonic structure of Eisenstein's *Potemkin*, '*Drifters*', Grierson wrote, 'is about the sea and about fishermen, and there is not a Piccadilly actor in the piece':

> The life of Natural cinema is in this massing of detail, in this massing of all the rhythmic energies that contribute to the blazing fact of the matter. Men and the energies of men, things and the functions of things, horizons and the poetics of horizons: these are the essential materials. And one must never grow so drunk with the energies and the functions as to forget the poetics. (Grierson, *Documentary* 20)

Drifters was premiered at the Film Society in London, in a programme in which it preceded *Battleship Potemkin*, whose screening in Britain had been long awaited: it is said that Eisenstein perceived Grierson's alleged act of homage to be more a theft of his thunder. Most significantly, perhaps, Grierson's indebtedness to Eisenstein and other Soviet film-makers, and the milieu of the screening – the Film Society had a strong commitment to avant-garde and experimental cinema – helped situate *Drifters*, one of the first 'documentary' films, in the context of European avant-garde film culture.

In a number of his writings on film of the late 1920s and early 1930s, which included extensive discussions of *Drifters*, Grierson invoked, as one of the frameworks for his film, the 'city symphonies' of the period. These included Walter Ruttmann's *Berlin: Symphony of a Great City* and Alberto Cavalcanti's *Rien que les heures*, which charted 'a day in the life' of Berlin and Paris respectively. Such films were part of the complex history whereby film-makers in the 1920s sought to renew the medium, and to turn away from commercial and narrative cinema, by returning to cinema's origins in the documenting of reality, but with the particular twist given by the perspectives and angles of modernism. Grierson's focus on 'symphonics' stressed the importance of tempo, rhythm and 'the orchestration of movement' in film form, while, in articles such as 'First Principles of Documentary' (1932) he emphasised the relationship between poetry and cinema, exploring the importance of the image and imagery in documentary film.

Even in these early writings, however, Grierson was distancing himself from what he perceived as form without content in a film such as *Berlin*:

> What more attractive (for a man of visual taste) than to swing wheels and pistons about in ding-dong description of a machine, when he has little to say about the man who tends it, and still less to say about the tin-pan products it spills? And what more comfortable if, in one's heart, there is avoidance of the issue of underpaid labour and meaningless production? (Grierson, *Documentary* 41–42).

Grierson became increasingly alienated from concepts of 'film art', to the point at which, in 1942, in 'The Documentary Idea', he was defining documentary as, from the beginning, 'when we first separated our public purpose theories from those of Flaherty – an "anti-aesthetic" movement' (Grierson, *Documentary* 112). Statements and attitudes such as these have been used as evidence, in numerous critical accounts, of Grierson's deleterious influence on British film culture and the thwarting of its experimental and poetic possibilities in the postwar period. Yet this failure does not take away from the achievements of the early years, nor from the fertility of the seeds sown by the Griersonian 'imagist' documentary.

In the 1920s and 1930s, as my discussion so far has intimated, literature and poetics played a significant role in Grierson's definititions of, and prescriptions for, documentary cinema. On occasion, he expressed ambivalence towards poets and poetry, as essentially at odds with social and political purpose and as failing 'in the business of ordering most present chaos', but for the most part 'poetics' operated as a term of value in his accounts of documentary cinema. At other points, literary categories were deployed as ways of defining distinctions within film: '[T]he choice of the documentary medium is as gravely distinct a choice as the choice of poetry instead of fiction . . . the young director cannot, in nature, go documentary and go studio both' (Grierson, *Documentary* 37).

The correlation made here between literary 'fiction' and 'studio' (as opposed to a documentary–poetry pairing) is indicative of Grierson's contempt for the perceived artificialities of studio-made fiction film, and for 'the lily-fingered interpretations of the metropolitan actor' (Grierson, *Documentary* 37). On the one hand, he would pit against this effete figure in his manufactured world 'the living scene and the living story', the 'original (or native) actor' and materials and stories 'taken from the raw'. On the other, he would place, running counter to the conventions of 'fiction', the possibilities of 'poetry and prophecy': '[R]ealist documentary, with its streets and cities and slums and markets and exchanges and factories, has given itself the job of making poetry where no poet has gone before it' (Grierson, *Documentary* 41). At times, Grierson was prepared to acknowledge that poets – such as Sandburg – had produced and were continuing to produce in literature the representations of modern life he sought in documentary film; at others, as in the last quote, he seemed to suggest that it was only the 'poetics' within cinema that were in any way adequate to the movements of the modern world. Literature was thus at times perceived as a model for, and an ally of, the film; at others, as having signally failed to rise to challenges which were being triumphantly met by cinema.

Grierson's views, on the topic of film and literature as in every sphere to which he turned his attentions, were strongly held but not altogether consistent. In situating his comments in their times, it is helpful to read his articles from the early 1930s in the broader context of *Cinema Quarterly*, where a number of his most significant writings on documentary film made their first appearance, alongside other writings by his contemporaries on documentary and on film in relation to the other arts. Over the three years of its publication, the journal ran articles by the art historian and aesthetician Herbert Read, and by writers including Lewis Grassic Gibbon, Campbell Nairne and Hugh MacDiarmid. Norman Wilson, in his editorials, which ran under the byline 'The Spectator', frequently addressed the question of literature's relationship to film and, furthermore, constructed a discursive stance for the journal. The function of *Cinema Quarterly* was, Wilson stated, to present 'the spectator's point of view', which he defined in the terms of 'detachment' and 'disinterestedness': 'Our role, as far as possible, will be that of the detached spectator' (Wilson, 'Spectator' 1932 5). This, with its Kantian echoes, may appear to be a traditional aesthetics of autonomy. The doctrine of spectatorial disinterest would also, however, seem to imply the 'impersonality' of the documentary camera-eye as well as the 'objective' recording of social realities by writers so valorised by Storm Jameson, in her significant discussion of 'Documents', to which I will return.

Like Grierson, Wilson was keenly interested in the contested claims of film and literature to artistic primacy. He noted 'that certain modern poets such as W. H. Auden and C. Day Lewis are coming to regard the film as a medium worth consideration' ('Spectator' 1935 132). 'When they get to grips with it in their experiments,' he continued, 'they may discover that its technique is not greatly different from that of their own poetry. It may even transpire that what they have been attempting to do in verse will achieve finality in film' (132). We move, then, from the suggestion of parallel developments in poetry and film to the postulation that film will be able to complete what poetry had only begun.

In an earlier editorial, Wilson had commended an essay by the writer G. W. Stonier. 'We have long complained of the influence of literature and the stage on the film,' Wilson writes, noting, of Stonier's discussion, 'It was refreshing therefore to come across . . . a brief consideration of the influence of the film on literature and drama' ('Spectator' 1933–4 76). Campbell Nairne, in his article for *Cinema Quarterly* on 'The Writer's Approach to the Cinema', also cited Stonier, whose long-forgotten but very suggestive essay 'The Movie' (published in his 1933 collection of literary essays *Gog Magog*) had explored the ways in which modern literature was emulating film's visuality; its 'momentaneity'; its focus on the accidental detail; its substitution of part for whole; its 'elasticity of size and distance', so that in writers such as Joyce, Wyndham Lewis, Dos Passos and Celine, 'the puppets do not move in uniform scale'; and its silence, locatable in 'the absence of the voice in what is written', which Stonier perceived as a quality of modern literature (Stonier 187–88). The importance of the discussion for Wilson, in particular, was that literature was learning from film (thus displacing an aesthetic hierarchy in which literature was the prior and, by extension, the higher art). Read, in his essay 'The Poet and the Film', made some similar points to Stonier, though Read was concerned with the equivalence between literature and film, rather than with the impact of the one on the other:

> If you ask me to give you the most distinctive quality of good writing, I would give it you in this one word: VISUAL. Reduce the art of writing to its fundamentals and you come to this single aim: to convey images by means of words. But to *convey images*. To make the mind see. To project on to that inner screen of the brain a moving picture of objects and events, events and objects moving towards a balance and reconciliation of a more than usual state of emotion with more than usual order. That is a definition of good literature – of the achievement of every good poet – from Homer and Shakespeare to James Joyce or Ernest Hemingway. It is also a definition of the ideal film. (202)

Read's interests were not especially turned towards the question of documentary film, but his nuanced writings for the journal focused more fully on film aesthetics than those of most other contributors. His insistence on the conveyance of 'images' was in line with Grierson's definitions of the 'imagist' or poetic approach in documentary – 'by imagism I mean the telling of story or illumination of theme by images, as poetry is story or theme told by images' (Grierson, *Documentary* 42) – which itself has important connections to the focus in the 1930s Mass-Observation movement on 'dominant images'. The 'image' was, in particular, central to the ideas of the poet, painter and documentary film-maker Humphrey Jennings, for whom it acted, in the words of Charles Madge, one of the founders of Mass-Observation, as a way of turning the written world into its 'visual complement' and of connecting inner, hidden patterns of thoughts and ideas into visible forms. We can identify a shared project in this period of different modes of translation: from verbal to visual forms, and from inner to outer, private to public representations. It was within this project that the relationship between literature (often allied to inward, subjective forms) and film (conceived in terms of externality) was to be formulated.

Read's discussion in 'The Poet and the Film' rested on the essentially and irreducibly 'visual' nature of the film aesthetic. Yet it was the coming of sound that made discussion of the film–literature relationship, as well as developments in documentary cinema such as the commentary and voice over, particularly charged. Sound came relatively late to the British documentary film movement, occurring soon after the point at which Grierson and his team had moved from the recently defunct Empire Marketing Board to the General Post Office film unit. In 1934 the GPO unit acquired a sound studio in Blackheath, and the Brazilian-born director Alberto Cavalcanti was brought in as an expert on sound technology and the use of sound in film.

In 1934, Grierson published an article for *Cinema Quarterly* entitled 'The G.P.O Gets Sound', in which he described in detail the use of 'authentic sound' in the film *6.30 Collection* and plans for a film on the Savings Bank: '[O]ver the mechanical visuals we propose to put a chorus indicating – it may be in short snatches of confession, or in plain objective record, or in *vers libres* – the human reference behind the slips of the filing cabinet' (218). To a certain extent, Grierson and his contemporaries followed the Soviet directors' call for 'contrapuntal sound', or sound montage, in which sound would be deployed in counterpoint to the image (rather than in dialogue or as a sound-effect merely to accompany the visual image). Grierson was also drawn to the associations made between poetics and film sound, though he suggested a move beyond Eisenstein's correlation between interior monologue and voice-over: 'The larger possibilities lie beyond monologue, I believe, in the poetry which, in the case of streets, say, will arrange some essential story in the mumble of windows, pub counters and passers-by' ('G.P.O.' 221). The 'essential story', narrated in the 'mumble' of the street, the city and the public sphere, returns us to the concept of 'the common life' and a 'common culture'.

Grierson's discussion appears to have been strongly influenced by an article written by the Scottish poet Hugh MacDiarmid, published in the previous issue of the journal as 'A Poet Looks at the Cinema: Poetry and Film'. MacDiarmid made the argument that the complexity and concentration of poetry – by contrast with prose – made it a natural ally for the cinema. Poetry's 'unrivalled quality of memorableness', a product of its 'economy of presenting experience', creates 'the desirability, even the need, of associating this quality with the cinema by every possible means' (MacDiarmid 146). MacDiarmid's central argument was that cinema sound should follow the realities of human communication, which is not composed of 'grammatical sentences and a logical progression' but 'is a thing of verbal fragments and expressive sounds, needing no continuity of utterance because it is supplemented by all manner of gestures, looks, understandings and what not' (146). Cinema, already possessing 'that essential supplemental substance of expression as printed literature has not', should therefore turn its back on 'the unlifelike verbal continuity which the disabilities of the latter [printed literature] necessitate' (146–47). By contrast, cinema, in its use of sound, should ally itself, as a modern art, with the experiments of modernist literature, which 'depends upon a realization of the revelation of personalities less in speech than in sound' (147): MacDiarmid gives as evidence here recent Russian literature's use of *skaz* (inter-sense) and *zaumny* (local and personal intonations), as well as the more general use of 'stream of consciousness'. He makes the argument that the 'difficulty' of modernist writing – that of T. S. Eliot, Joyce, MacDiarmid himself – should not be seen as exclusionary or elitist, because its use of 'pure onomatopoeia' (which comes to the fore when the work is heard rather than read) renders it as a 'universal language' of sound, and it is this language which cinema (defined by numerous early critics in its silent years by the 'universalism' of its modes of expression) should be speaking:

> A great deal of work in modernist poetry consists in the exploitation of pure sound, and, alike from the psychological and purely aesthetic sides, it is with the poets that the verbal future of the cinema lies, since prose remains the language of logical discourse and most of its context is redundant to the film, whereas poetry has not only maximum economy, supreme relevatory power, and capacities, equal to its unrivalled power of penetrating reality, for soaring away from it altogether but of associating itself with music. I agree with Hitchcock that the music must be specially composed; so must the poetry. (MacDiarmid 147–48)

MacDiarmid's arguments are a suggestive reformulation of familiar understandings of popular and elite culture in the 1930s. They are also part of a widely-shared view that 'high' and 'popular' culture, the artist and the public, would exist in a far more productive relationship without the interventions of, in MacDiarmid's words, 'a parasitical and misleading "interpreting class"' (148). This widespread disdain for the critical 'middleman' (at times associated, as it was for Virginia Woolf, with the 'middlebrow') bears in important ways on questions of cultural reception, and the desire, acute amongst writers like MacDiarmid, whose 'experimental' poetics were inseparable from his far-left politics, for the artist to be brought 'into direct contact with the vast public' (148). The cinema's public in this period made it an arena in which poets might, as MacDiarmid claimed, have 'jump[ed] at the opportunity for next to nothing' (148).

The audiences for documentary cinema in the 1930s were by no means vast. Grierson, however, would certainly seem to have followed MacDiarmid's prescriptions in producing two films for the GPO for which poetry and music were 'specially composed': *Coal Face* (1935) and *Night Mail* (1936). Cavalcanti directed *Coal Face* with Stuart Legg and Basil Wright, and was largely responsible for the collaborative contributions of W. H. Auden and Benjamin Britten (then a student at the Royal College of Music) to the film. Of the two films, *Coal Face* offers the more radical experiment with sound, with its layerings of 'Voice of God' commentary, producing 'facts' about the mining industry (though at no point referring to the major recession and unemployment by which it had been hit), music and poetry. The commentary, however, also becomes a kind of chorus, repeating terms and phrases: at the very close of the film, the lines 'Here is the mine, here is the miner' seem to belong more to the realms of verse rather than the voice-over commentary.

Coal Face was first shown at the Film Society in London on 27 October 1935, along with Arthur Elton and Edgar Anstey's documentary film *Housing Problems* and Dziga Vertov's 1934 film *Three Songs of Lenin*, for which Auden worked on the English translations of passages in the songs, producing verse sub-titles. The Film Society programme notes described *Coal Face* as the presentation of 'a new experiment in sound':

> A very simple visual band was taken and an attempt made to build up, by use of natural sound, music and chorus, a film oratorio. The usual method of speaking commentary to a background of music was avoided and commentary and music were composed together. The effect is to incorporate commentary more clearly in the body of the film. To this foreground of sound were added a recitative chorus of male voices and a choir of male and female voices. The recitative chorus was used to fill out, by suggestion, the direct statement of the commentary. The choir was used to create atmosphere. (*Film Society Programmes* 330)

Coal Face was followed by *Night Mail*, directed by Harry Watt and produced by Basil Wright and Grierson. The film represented the sorting and delivery of mail on the night-train from London to the North of Scotland. Figures for documentary audiences are difficult to establish, in part due to the non-commercial venues in which they are often shown, but it would seem that *Night Mail* achieved the widest public circulation of any GPO documentary. As in *Coal Face*, verse by Auden accompanies the images of the final part of the film. The idea for a verse commentary came quite late in the film's conception, brought about by Grierson's sense that the early film assemblage of the mail train's journey from London to Scotland failed to 'say anything about the people who're going to get the letters' (Hardy 76).

As Auden composed the verse, it was cut to fit the visuals. The passages which were timed to the beat of the train's wheels were spoken by Stuart Legg, while Grierson spoke the slower-paced passages, including the final lines:

> And none will hear the postman's knock
> Without a quickening of the heart,
> For who can bear to feel himself forgotten.

In the sequences accompanied by Auden's verses, there is a play with the notion of the 'sleeper' train, reversing the usual relations of sleeping and wakefulness: there are no 'sleepers' on this train, but the country sleeps, oblivious to the labour that goes into the fulfilment of its wishes. Auden's verse (and the rhythms of Britten's sound score) are at once mimetic of the sound-rhythms of the train and speak of the world of dreams and desire, even as the film virtually evacuates the world of human subjects and indeed, as Marsha Bryant suggests, of images of industrialism, thus 'forming an industrial unconscious of Britain's "other country"' (48). There are no observers to see the train moving through the empty dawn landscape. It is visually at its most purely impersonal – pointing up the ways in which the world of the film is one that is complete without us and from which we are absent – even as the verse articulates the 'personality' of correspondence.

Auden's involvement with the documentary film movement was to be short-lived: in 1936 he left the GPO Film Unit and travelled to Iceland, with a commission from Faber to write a travel book. In that same year he used the occasion of a review of Rotha's *Documentary Film* (published in *The Listener*) to criticise the British documentary film movement itself, arguing that the creative and political freedoms of film-makers within government outfits such as the EMB and the GPO Film Units were severely compromised, that the schedules of film-making required directors to 'turn out a film in a ridiculously short period', and that the documentary directors would not be able to 'deal more than superficially' with characters outside of their own upper-middle-class backgrounds (Auden 354). Above all, he took issue with the documentary film's concentration on what Grierson later called 'an aesthetic of the person in public' (Grierson, 'Story').

The relationship between private and public and the question of individuals and individualism was central to conceptions and constructions of documentary film in Britain, and to its supporters' rejections of the 'story-film' and the film star. Grierson's disparaging comments on 'Piccadilly actors' were echoed by Rotha throughout his writings on documentary, in which, in his words: 'If there are human beings they are secondary to the main theme. Their private passions and petulances are of little interest . . . They are types selected from the many, portraying the mind and character of this or that social group' (Rotha, *Documentary Film* 142). 'Documentary', Rotha asserted, 'relies exclusively on the belief that there is nothing so interesting to ourselves as ourselves' (142), a claim which chimed with the Mass-Observation founders' account of the movement's 'new method': 'the observation of everyone by everyone, including themselves' (Madge and Harrisson, *Mass-Observation* 10).

There was, in fact, something of a contradiction, though one rarely openly acknowledged, between the documentarists' insistence on the secondary importance of the human being in the films, and their assertions of the primacy of the fascination with 'the common man' and the ordinary life as the underpinning of documentary culture. Rotha continued to critique the star-system, while increasingly coming to argue that the human being would need to take centre stage, if documentary were to be a significant influence as a popular form: '[I]f the masses are interested in seeing individuals and following their emotions on the screen, then documentary must embrace individuals . . . We must go into the streets and homes and factories to meet them' (Rotha, *Documentary Film* 181). Yet he also noted the difficulty in persuading 'natural people . . . to assume this or that expression, or feel this or that emotion according to our requirements' (Rotha, *Documentary Film* 182).

The issue had become a pressing one, with the growing move towards a conjunction of 'story film' and documentary. In an article on 'Films of Fact and Fiction', Rotha noted the emergence of 'the personal interview with camera and microphone', first used in *Housing Problems* in 1935: 'Here were human beings spontaneously speaking and gesturing right into the lens and microphone. This was not acting but normal behavior as far as a consciousness of the camera would permit. Sociologically, this was important; but the method deprived the documentary film of much of its cinematic quality' (193). The 'handling of natural actors in documentary' was developed in more individualising and fictionalising ways in Harry Watts's *The Saving of Bill Blewitt* (1936) and *North Sea* (1938), and *Today We Live* (1937), directed by Ralph Bond and Ruby Grierson. There was a clear perception, from the mid-1930s onwards, that audiences would be far more fully engaged by documentary cinema which focused on individuals and their stories. Nonetheless, Rotha and others continued to express uncertainties about the relationship of fact and fiction in film: 'Is it possible to bring about a blending of the two methods; or should the fact film and the fiction film pursue their divergent courses?' (Rotha, 'Films of Fact and Fiction' 196).

The further question that continued to trouble Rotha was that of the use of 'symbolism' as against 'fact' in documentary films: 'It is in the nature of the method to search for symbols which will express an idea, rather than an interpretation of facts by more analytical research. The use of a smoking factory chimney to symbolise Industry, or of a parade of revolving wheels to express Power, is a dangerous escape from facts into superficial impressions for sensational effect' (Rotha, *Documentary Film* 227). Rotha saw a connection between this issue and that of 'the interpretation of the human being in films': he looked to a synthesis of 'the impressionist and reporting methods' (Rotha, *Documentary Film* 228), as he had called for a possible conjoining of fact and fiction, the representation of the external world and the focus on the individual. These concerns were central not only to those in the documentary film movement but also to the literary writers of the period, for whom documentary raised crucial questions of representation, identification, politics and 'the condition of England'.

1930s WRITERS AND DOCUMENTARY CINEMA

Graham Greene, in a 29 August 1937 broadcast discussion on 'The Cinema' for the BBC National Service, celebrated the 'small documentary companies' for producing films depicting 'ordinary life', made by those who were 'still living the common life' (Greene 515). The documentary film-makers were, for Greene as for many of his contemporaries in the 1930s, the heroes of the commitment to cinematic realism, although (a fact somewhat occluded in Greene's account) their backgrounds were for the most part remote from those of the working men and women whose lives and labour they represented. The concept of 'the common life' was at one with the aspiration for a 'common culture', the nature of which lay at the heart of debates about art and politics in the interwar period.

In his 1939 memoir, *Rain upon Godshill*, J. B. Priestley included a brief chapter on the documentary film movement, writing of 'Grierson and his young men' who, 'with their contempt for big easy prizes and soft living, their taut social conscience, their rather Marxist sense of the contemporary scene, always seemed to me figures representative of a new world, at least a generation ahead of the dramatic film people' (81). In his view, however:

> Nearly all documentary film seems to me a very romantic heightening of ordinary life, comparable not to the work of a realistic novelist or dramatist, but to the picturesque and highly-coloured fictions of the romancer. It is not the raw material but the treatment that counts. . . . The film cannot help dropping out all the dull passages, beautifying and heightening the rest, and then giving the whole a sort of glitter and excitement. . . . For plain truth they cannot compete with the printed word. . . . In short, their very medium compels these young men to be romantic in practice, no matter how realistic they may be in theory. (81–82)

Priestley, despite his expressed admiration for the cinematic documentarists, and his substantial engagement with the film-world at a number of levels, made the claim for writing's greater powers of capturing reality and, by implication, the more significant 'documentary' value of the literary. To a certain extent Grierson might well have concurred with Priestley's attribution of 'a heightening of ordinary life' to documentary film, one function of which, in this period was, indeed, to show that 'ordinary life', when perceived as the camera eye was said to perceive it, in its richness and strangeness, already possessed heightened qualities to which habitual perception was, on the whole, blind. In a number of his writings of the 1920s and 1930s, Grierson had expressed a commitment to a form of 'realism' that went beyond or behind 'actuality', and to the use of 'poetry' and 'symbol' in reaching for this deeper and complex understanding of the real.

There were other strong connections between Priestley and the film documentarists (including, in 1937, his writing and narrating the commentary for the GPO film directed by Cavalcanti, *We Live in Two Worlds*). John Baxendale and Chris Pawling make the argument that they 'were part of the same cultural and political current', linked by a 'common project: to reunite a fractured nation around a more inclusive conception of itself, one which rested above all on defining and constructing "the people" as the real Britain' (46). We see the signs of this shared cinematic-literary goal in Paul Rotha's *The Face of Britain* (1935), which was significantly influenced by Priestley's *English Journey* of 1934. Recalling his making of the film *Shipyard*, Rotha would note in his retrospective *Documentary Diary* that Priestley's description of the mining village of Shotton in East Durham 'cannot be equalled. It was just as he wrote' (103). Rotha the film-maker would seem to be agreeing with the view that writing could replicate reality just as it was.

English Journey was commissioned by the publisher Victor Gollancz, two years before the creation of his Left Book Club, founded to sell radical books at low prices and, in the words of its first advertisement, to 'help in the struggle for world peace and a better social and economic order, and against fascism'. Orwell's *The Road to Wigan Pier* was commissioned by Gollancz some months before the launching of the club, and was a retrospective inclusion whose descriptions of the northern working class and political attack on Marxist intellectuals famously caused Gollancz and his associates significant embarrassment. In his foreword to the Left Book Club edition, Gollancz protested against Orwell's political and class critique in the second half of *Wigan Pier*; the first half of the book he unequivocally praised in terms of documentary 'record', admiring its 'first-hand account of the life of the working class population of Wigan and elsewhere' (Gollancz xiii).

The thirty or so photographs in the Gollancz edition of *The Road to Wigan Pier* were not selected by Orwell and they included no images of the northern English towns – Wigan, Liverpool and Sheffield – that Orwell visited. The images of miners and their homes in Wales nonetheless have a connection to Orwell's text, with its focus on the bodies of the working men; they also suggest the political energies, and the desperation, of the miners conducting stay-in strikes underground. Many of the photographs are those of slum dwellings and districts in East London. Here the titles render any human subjects generic and depersonalised: an image of a woman with a baby in a basement flat is titled 'Bethnal Green'; a family in a room, 'Overcrowding'. A number of the photographs focus on the rotting fabric of buildings, with or without human subjects in the frame; in a few the titles indicate a 'before' and 'after'. The massive crack in a scullery wall is 'now reconditioned'; the captioning of a photograph of a derelict house in Stepney elicits the viewer to 'compare the new housing in the background'. These ameliorative temporalities bring the photographs into the frame of documentary films such as Elton and Anstey's *Housing Problems* (sponsored by the British Commercial Gas Organisation) whose 'iconic image' is that of 'new flats rising behind an old row of slum houses in Stepney' (Birchall 15). The photographs and their presentation, however, reveal little or no attempt to individuate the human figures presented, while the innovatory qualities of *Housing Problems* (on which Ruby Grierson acted as production assistant) lay in its use of direct address to camera by working-class men and women from the East End.

Orwell made no comment in *The Road to Wigan Pier* on the ways in which documentary cinema was addressing and representing the living conditions he described. As in Priestley's *English Journey*, however, the words of the documentary writer are in dialogue with the images of the documentary film-maker. While Priestley's journey through England did not take him down into the mines, Orwell's experiences of going down into the coal-mines and watching the miners at work were at the heart of his text. The mines were, Orwell stated, 'like hell', and the way in which he described the descent and journey through the under-ground suggests that he was taking on something of the role of guide to the Inferno: 'You can never forget that spectacle once you have seen it – the line of bowed, kneeling figures, sooty black all over, driving their huge shovels under the coal with stupendous force and speed' (20). The image of the 'heroic worker' inflected Orwell's highly visual descriptions of the miners but it was accompanied by a powerful sense of the literally back-breaking nature of the work and the horror of the place. His account intersected with a number of documentary films, including *Coal Face*, but was able to go beyond them in political commentary and satire.

Both the opening and the close of the first chapter of *The Road to Wigan Pier* exist in a complex dialogue with documentary cinema. The first lines of the text – 'The first sound in the mornings was the clumping of the mill-girls' clogs down the cobbled street. Earlier than that, I suppose, there were factory whistles which I was never awake to hear' (3) – open onto a sensory world in which sound can be rendered separately from sight. The working-day thus dawns in the seeming absence of a perceiving consciousness, creating a link to the documentary 'city symphonies' which became so central to cinema in the 1920s. The chapter describes Orwell's stay in a filthy lodging-house 'in the North'; he departed when its noxious conditions began to overwhelm him. The train bore him away, Orwell wrote at the chapter's close, through the 'monstrous' industrial scenery and rows of slum houses on a cold March day. Here he described the now-iconic image of

> a young woman . . . kneeling on the stones, poking a stick up the leaden waste-pipe which ran from the sink inside and which I suppose was blocked. I had time to see everything about her – her sacking apron, her clumsy clogs, her arms reddened by the cold. She looked up as the train passed and I was almost near enough to catch her eye. She had a round pale face, the usual exhausted face of the slum girl who is twenty-five and looks forty, thanks to miscarriages and drudgery; and it wore, for the second in which I saw it, the most desolate, hopeless expression I have ever seen . . .
>
> But quite soon the train drew away into open country, and that seemed strange, almost unnatural, as though the open country had been a kind of part; for in the industrial areas one always feels that the smoke and filth must go on for ever and that no part of the earth's surface can escape them. (15)

This scene strongly suggests documentary perspectives. It is viewed, as in a film, through the window of a moving train. As Keith Williams has noted, the human figure is represented in sections, as if in a series of 'close ups', which move from the apron to the clogs to the reddened arms before reaching the face (171). The modes of synecdoche and metonymy, in which parts stand for wholes, lie at the heart of the grammar of the medium, as contemporary writers were defining it: not only is vision fragmented into new parts and wholes but the single image can be imbued with symbolic and representative status. In Orwell's account, vision and cognition – the spectator's image of the girl's face and the comprehension of its 'most desolate, hopeless' expression – are staged in the instant before the train draws away, leaving behind the girl who is thus transfixed in the endless performance of her 'hopeless' task. There is no visual reciprocity in the scene, though it is narrowly missed: 'I was almost near enough to catch her eye'.

Orwell was in fact reworking a passage from his diary entry of 15 February 1936 which formed the basis of the published text. Orwell described the woman in his diary, whom he sees as he is 'passing up a horrible squalid side-alley': 'At that moment she looked up and caught my eye, and her expression was as desolate as I have ever seen; it struck me that she was thinking just the same thing as I was' (Orwell, *Diary* 203). In the published work, Orwell abandoned

the meeting of eyes and the shared acknowledgement of the woman's hopeless situation and introduced the view from the moving train. Bernard Crick
notes the symbolic status of the train leaving Wigan, and its representation of
'the writer's almost desperate pain at being merely an observer . . . carried off
remorselessly and mechanically simply to write about "what can be done"'
(287). The detachment of the observer, however, is also inseparable from the
filmic nature of the scene, with its heightened symbolic status, which further
calls upon a historical and conceptual intertwining of the train, the cinema and
the modes of perception they bring into being. The scene also suggests Orwell's
own 'framings' of his observations as inflected by the documentary films of the
time, as well as the inevitably 'constructed' nature of perception and representation in film and in writing.

Storm Jameson, in an article on 'Documents' for a special issue of the journal
Fact, Writing in Revolt, discussed the trend whereby writers were going in
search of the smell and feel of poverty. She condemned such journeys when
they were undertaken by the writer 'for his own sake, for some fancied spiritual
advantage to be got from the experience', and may well have intended a jibe at
Priestley, in her criticism of writers' 'visits to the distressed area in a motor-car'
(15). They could only be justified, she argued, when they were undertaken by
the writer 'for the sake of *the fact*, as a medical student carries out a dissection,
and to equip himself . . . . he must be able to give an objective report' (12).
The first half of Orwell's *The Road to Wigan Pier* was placed in this category.
Throughout the article, Jameson suggested that the necessary objectivity and
clarity could only arise with knowledge of working-class lives untrammelled
by either sentiment or disgust, born of sustained experience of ways of life on
the margins, but without the distortions of the writer's subjective responses to
his or her experiences. Sociological case studies, she argued, retained critical
distance but were lacking in detail and inwardness: we do not have

> the essentials of speech and action . . . We do not *see* the woman stripping
> the filthy, bug-ridden wallpaper from the thin wall of her attic . . . nor the
> workless man looking at the soles of his shoes when he comes home. It
> is necessary that a writer should have lived with these things for him to
> record them as simply and coldly, even brutally, as if he chooses he can
> describe what has been familiar to him from his infancy. (13–14).

Jameson's terms, which render understanding as a question of perception
and vision, clearly invoke the visuality of cinema and she may well have
had in mind documentary films such as *Housing Problems*. Throughout
'Documents', Jameson makes explicit reference to documentary cinema as
the model for writers to follow, in their pursuit of the necessary combination
of the seemingly contradictory qualities of objectivity, proximity, inwardness
and impersonality:

> Perhaps the nearest equivalent to what is wanted already exists in another form in the documentary film. As the photographer does, so must the writer keep himself out of the picture while working ceaselessly to present the *fact* from a striking (poignant, ironic, penetrating, significant angle . . . We may stumble on the solution in the effort of trying to create the literary equivalent of the documentary film. (18).

The literature of the future, she concludes, will also take from the model of the documentary film a form of connectivity also present in poetry and in dreams: a way of expressing 'the relations between things (men, acts), widely separated in space or in the social complex' (18).

Jameson's arguments for a literature which would be an 'equivalent' of the documentary film were as much, or more, a matter of perspective than theme, and, like so many of the debates of the period – in literature, film, anthropology, sociology, history – they revolved around the relationship and the tension between 'objectivity' and 'subjectivity', 'fact' and 'fiction', 'proximity' and 'distance'. Such debates and perspectives reached a particular point of intensity in the projects of documentary cinema, and to this extent we can endorse Paul Rotha's large claim, quoted at the opening of this chapter, for the impact of 'the movement of documentary film-making in Britain in the 1930s', regardless of actual audience figures. We might also note, however, Grierson's assertion, in 'The Documentary Idea: 1942', that 'the documentary idea was not basically a film idea at all . . . The medium happened to be the most convenient and exciting available to us' (Grierson, *Documentary* 132). I have, in this chapter, focused on the relationship between literature and film in the 1930s and in the context of 'documentary culture'. It is also important, however, to note that 'the documentary idea' not only intersected different media but created new terms for an interdisciplinary synthesis. 'Documentary', in conclusion, offers one of the most significant and complex constellations for intermodernism, in its intertwinings of a modernist aesthetic and a realist imperative, a poetics and a politics.

Works Cited

Auden, W. H. Rev. of *Documentary Film*, by Paul Rotha. *The Listener* 19 Feb. 1936. Reprinted in *The English Auden: Poems, Essays and Dramatic Writings 1927–1939*. Ed. Edward Mendelson. London: Faber, 1977. 354–56.

Baxendale, John and Christopher Pawling. *Narrating the Thirties. A Decade in the Making: 1930 to the Present*. London: Macmillan Press, 1996.

Birchall, Danny. Notes on *Housing Problems*. In *Land of Promise: The British Documentary Film Movement*, booklet accompanying BFI DVD box set, p. 15.

Bryant, Marsha. *Auden and Documentary in the 1930s*. Charlottesville: University Press of Virginia, 1997.

Crick, Bernard. *George Orwell: A Life*. Harmondsworth: Penguin, 1980.

The Film Society Programmes 1925–1939. New York: Arno Press, 1972.

Gollancz, Victor. 'Foreword'. *The Road to Wigan Pier*. By George Orwell. Left Book Club Edition. London: Victor Gollancz, 1937. xi–xxiv.

Greene, Graham. 'The Cinema'. *Mornings in the Dark: The Graham Greene Film Reader*. Ed. David Parkinson. Harmondsworth: Penguin, 1993. 511–15.

Grierson, John. 'The G.P.O. Gets Sound'. *Cinema Quarterly* 2.4 (1934): 215–21.

—. *Grierson on Documentary*. Ed. Forsyth Hardy. London: Faber, 1979.

—. 'The Story of the Documentary Film'. *The Fortnightly Review* August 1939: 122–27.

Hardy, Forsyth. *John Grierson: A Documentary Biography*. London: Faber, 1979.

Jameson, Storm. 'Writing in Revolt, 1, Theory: Documents'. *Writing in Revolt*. Spec. issue of *Fact* July 1937: 9–18.

MacDiarmid, Hugh. 'A Poet Looks at the Cinema: Poetry and Film'. *Cinema Quarterly* 2.3 (1934): 146–49.

Madge, Charles and Tom Harrison. *Mass-Observation*. London: Frederick Mueller, 1937.

Nairne, Campbell. 'The Writer's Approach to the Cinema'. *Cinema Quarterly* 3.1 (1935): 134–38.

Orwell, George. *The Road to Wigan Pier*. 1937. Harmondsworth: Penguin, 1989.

—. 'The Road to Wigan Pier Diary'. *The Collected Essays, Journalism and Letters of George Orwell*. Eds. Sonia Orwell and Ian Angus. Vol 1. 1920–1940. Harmondsworth: Penguin, 1970. 194–242.

Priestley, J. B. *English Journey*. New York and London: Harper Collins, 1934.

—. *Rain upon Godshill: A Further Chapter of Autobiography*. London: Heinemann, 1939.

Read, Herbert. 'The Poet and the Film'. *Cinema Quarterly* 1.4 (1933): 197–202.

Rotha, Paul. *Documentary Diary: An Informal History of the British Documentary Film, 1928–1939*. New York: Hill and Wang, 1973.

—. *Documentary Film*. London: Faber, 1936.

—. 'Films of Fact and Fiction'. *Theatre Arts Monthly* 22.3 (1938): 186–96.

Stonier, G. W. *Gog Magog*. London: Dent, 1933.

Williams, Keith. 'Post/Modern Documentary: Orwell, Agee and the New Reportage'. *Rewriting the Thirties: Modernism and After*. Eds Keith Williams and Steven Matthews. London: Longman, 1997. 163–81.

Wilson, Norman. 'The Spectator'. *Cinema Quarterly* 1.1 (1932): 3–6.
—. 'The Spectator'. *Cinema Quarterly* 2.2 (1933–4): 75–77.
—. 'The Spectator'. *Cinema Quarterly* 3.3 (1935): 131–33.

APPENDIX: WHO ARE THE INTERMODERNISTS?

This listing of possible intermodernists includes basic information about writers' and artists' lives, cultural work and available archival sources. It is intended to function as a practical resource supporting future research and writing on British intermodernism. Readers might debate whether the most famous members of the so-called 'Auden Generation' should be included; I have opted to list those figures of Auden's generation who are not typically recognised as such and have not attracted significant treatment from scholars, or those whose chosen literary styles and genres, institutional and personal commitments and networks, correspond more closely to the intermodernism described in this book. Not only do I hope to encourage readers to look beyond the all-male, Oxbridge Auden Generation known through Samuel Hynes's work, for example, but also beyond the figures, genres and regions examined in depth in *Intermodernism*'s chapters. I invite readers to imagine other tables of contents for this volume or better yet, to write their own books on neglected intermodernists or on unexamined or underexamined aspects of intermodernism. For example, in an ideal world this volume would include chapters on children's literature and science fiction, or on the intermodern literature of Scotland and Wales. That it doesn't is a frank admission of its necessarily partial address of key questions surrounding intermodernism. Clearly this book, like this appendix, cannot aspire to total coverage or completion. 'Who Are the Intermodernists?' represents the hope that other scholars will join the contributors to this volume in the work of discovery and theorising that will expand and further define the field of intermodern study.

Margery Allingham (1904–66): Born Ealing, London, died Colchester. Popular writer of mystery and crime novels, famous for creation of detective Albert Campion who first appeared in *The Crime at Black Dudley* (1929). Biographies by Julia Thorogood (1991) and Richard Martin (1988).

Mulk Raj Anand (1905–2004): Born Peshawar, north-west India, died in Pune. A philosopher, Marxist and Indian nationalist who became famous for pioneering (with R. K. Narayan) the Indian novel in English. *Untouchable* (1935) launched his literary career in London, where he worked for more than twenty years. Critical studies by Saros Cowasjee, among others.

Stella Benson (1892–1933): Born near Easthope, Shropshire, died in Tonkin Province, Vietnam. Feminist, poet, novelist, travel writer. *Tobit Transplanted* (1931), published first in the US as *The Far-Away Bride* (1930), won the Femina Vie Heureuse Prize. Biography by Joy Grant (1987). Papers in Cambridge University Library's Department of Manuscripts and the British Library's Manuscript Collections, among other places.

John Betjeman (1906–84): Born Camden, London, died Trebetherick, Cornwall. Poet, journalist, architectural critic. Tutored at Oxford by C. S. Lewis. *Collected Poems* (1958), Queen's Medal for Poetry (1960), Poet Laureate (1972). Biographies by Bevis Hillier (2006) and Patrick Taylor-Martin (1983). Manuscripts and letters in the Library of the State University of New York, Buffalo, and the McPherson Library at the University of Victoria and British Library.

Dan Billany (1913–c.43): Born Hull, died in Italy in mysterious circumstances while trying to cross to Allied lines. Most famous for World War II novels of socialist sympathies *The Cage* (with David Dowie) (1949) and *The Trap* (1950) written while a POW in Italy. Biography by Valerie A. Reeves and Valerie Showan (1999). Manuscripts in Imperial War Museum archives.

Enid Blyton (known also as Mary Pollock, 1897–1968): Born East Dulwich, London, died Hampstead. Immensely popular and prolific children's writer famous for young readers series including The Famous Five (twenty-one novels, 1942–63). Official biography by Barbara Stoney (1974, 2007). There is an Enid Blyton Society that sponsors a journal.

Phyllis Bottome (Phyllis Forbes-Dennis, 1884–1963): Born Rochester, Kent, died London. Novelist, humanitarian and biographer of psychoanalyst Alfred Adler, whose theories greatly impacted her life and fiction. *The Mortal Storm* (1938) was an international best-seller that was made into an early anti-Nazi Hollywood feature film. Manuscripts and letters in the British Library, Manuscript Collections.

Elizabeth Bowen (1899–1973): Born Dublin, died Hythe, Kent. Anglo-Irish novelist, short story writer, essayist and critic, now sometimes heralded as a British modernist. She inherited Bowen's Court, County Cork, in 1930 but remained in England for most of her writing life. There she published *The*

Heat of the Day (1949), probably her best known novel. She received the James Tait Black Memorial Prize for *Eva Trout* (1969). Biography by Victoria Glendinning (1977). Majority of papers are at the Harry Ransom Center.

Vera Brittain (1893–1970): Born Newcastle-under-Lyme, Staffordshire, died London. Novelist, feminist, pacifist best remembered for her memoir of World War I, *Testament of Youth* (1933). Her memoir of her friendship with Winifred Holtby is *Testament of Friendship* (1940). Biographies by Deborah Gorham (2000), Paul Berry and Mark Bostridge (1995, 2001) and Hilary Bailey (1987). Papers and correspondence at Somerville College Library, Oxford University and Hull Central Library.

Christopher Caudwell (Christopher St John Sprigg, 1907–37): Born Putney, London, killed in action in the Jarama Valley, Spain. Marxist theorist, literary critic, poet, novelist. Joined the Communist Party of Great Britain and fought for the International Brigade in the Spanish Civil War. His best known work, published posthumously, is *Illusion and Reality: A Study of the Sources of Poetry* (1937). Papers at the Harry Ransom Center.

Ivy Compton-Burnett: (1884–1969): Born Pinner, near London, died London. Novelist known for humorous treatments of the dark secrets of domestic life, evident in her first celebrated novel, *Pastors and Masters* (1925), and nineteen subsequent novels. Biography by Hilary Spurling (1995). Letters and manuscripts in King's College Archive Centre of Cambridge University and the Special Collections of Olin Library at Washington University in St Louis, among other sites.

Barbara Comyns (Barbara Irene Veronica Bayley Comyns Carr, 1909–92): Born Bidford-on-Avon, Warwickshire, died Stanton-upon-Hine Heath, Shropshire. Artist and novelist. She exhibited her work with the London Group of artists in 1934. *Our Spoons Came from Woolworths* (1950) is a blackly comic, poignant, fictionalised version of this stage of her life. *The Vet's Daughter* (1959) is her most highly regarded novel. Criticism is virtually non-existent.

Cyril Connolly (1903–74): Born Coventry, Warwickshire, died Eastbourne, East Sussex. Author, influential critic and editor of *Horizon* from 1940 to 1950. Famous for the third, autobiographical part of *Enemies of Promise*, 'A Georgian Boyhood' (1938). Biographies by Clive Fisher (1995) and Jeremy Lewis (1995). Papers and library at the University of Tulsa.

John Cornford (Rupert John Cornford, 1915–36): Born Cambridge, died Lopera, Spain. Poet, communist, journalist and activist who was the first Englishman to enlist against Franco in the Spanish Civil War. He recruited for the International Brigade and died fighting on the Cordoba front. Correspondence and papers in Trinity College Library, Cambridge University, with additional letters in the Manuscript Collections of the British Library.

Noël Coward (1899–1973): Born Teddington, Middlesex, died Blue

Harbour, Jamaica. Comic actor, playwright, screenplay writer and prolific composer of popular songs. His best works are associated with the 1930s and 1940s. These include extravaganzas like *Cavalcade* (1931), witty social commentaries like *This Happy Breed* (1939), and the patriotic film *In Which We Serve* (1942). There is a multi-volume autobiography (1937, 1944, 1954, 1986) and a recent biography by Philip Hoare (1995). Papers are in Special Collections, University of Birmingham.

E. M. Delafield (Edmée Elizabeth Monica Dashwood, née de la Pasture, 1890–1943): Born Steyning, Sussex, died Kentisbeare, Devon. Prolific novelist best known for her very funny, autobiographical *Diary of a Provincial Lady* (1930), which began as a weekly column in *Time and Tide*. Biography by Violet Powell (1988). Letters and papers at the University of British Columbia Library.

Daphne du Maurier (1907–89): Born London, died Kilmarth, Cornwall. Famous for her popular suspense novels *Jamaica Inn* (1936) and *Rebecca* (1938), both of which were made into films by Alfred Hitchcock, as was her short story 'The Birds'. Made DBE (1969). There is a biography by Margaret Forster (1993) and a memoir, *Growing Pains* (1977). Papers are housed in various archives, including Exeter University Library's Special Collections and Warwick University's Modern Records Centre.

William Empson (1906–84): Born Hawdon, Yorkshire, died London. Literary critic, poet and professor. Famous for *Seven Types of Ambiguity* (1930) and *Some Versions of Pastoral* (1935). Two volume biography by John Haffenden (2005, 2006). Papers at Harvard University's Houghton Library and Sheffield University Library.

Ralph Fox (Ralph Winston Fox, 1900–36): Born Halifax, Yorkshire, killed in action with the International Brigade in Lopera, Spain. Novelist, journalist, biographer, translator and activist who helped found the Communist Party of Great Britain and later, with Montague Slater, Edgill Rickword and Tom Wintringham, *The Left Review*. Most famous for *The Novel and the People* (1937). For autobiographical information see *Ralph Fox: A Writer in Arms* (1937).

Pamela Frankau (1908–67): Born Windsor, died London. Popular novelist, short story writer, journalist and radio critic who came from an Anglo-Jewish literary family. Most famous for her novels *The Willow Cabin* (1949) and *A Wreath for the Enemy* (1954). She became the lesbian partner of pioneering American theatre director Margaret Webster in the 1950s. Frankau's early autobiography is *I Find Four People* (1935). Selected papers at Harry Ransom Center. Her nephew, the writer Timothy d'Arch Smith, has private papers.

Lewis Grassic Gibbon (James Leslie Mitchell, 1901–35): Born Arbuthnott, Scotland, died Welwyn, England. Novelist, short story writer, journalist, biographer, historian and soldier, most famous for his trilogy *A Scot's Quair* (1932, 1933, 1934). Biographies by Ian Campbell (1985) and Ian S. Munro (1966).

Manuscripts and correspondence in the Manuscripts Collection, National Library of Scotland. There is a Grassic Gibbon Centre in Arbuthnott.

Stella Gibbons (1902–89): Born and died London. Novelist, poet and short story writer. *Cold Comfort Farm* (1933), her most famous work, won the Prix Femina-Vie Heureuse. Biography by her nephew Reggie Oliver (1998). Manuscripts in Mugar Memorial Library Special Collections, Boston University.

Eric Gill (Arthur Eric Rowton Gill, 1882–1940): Born Brighton, died Uxbridge. Printmaker, sculptor, typeface designer and writer associated with the Arts and Crafts movement. A notoriously eccentric, controversial figure, of deep Catholic faith but leaning toward communism in the 1930s. Aesthetic pragmatism evident in his *Christianity in the Machine Age* (1940). Biography by Fiona McCarthy (1989). Papers and library at William Andrews Clark Memorial Library, UCLA.

Victor Gollancz (1893–1967): Born and died London. Founding publisher in 1927 of Victor Gollancz books, which published George Orwell, Betty Miller and Daphne du Maurier among others, and founder of the Left Book Club in 1936. Biography by Ruth Dudley Edwards (1987). Papers archived at the Modern Records Centre, University of Warwick Library.

Robert Graves (1895–1985): Born London, died Deyá, Majorca. Poet, novelist, classics scholar and translator. Famous for memoir of World War I, *Good-Bye to All That* (1929). Won James Tait Black Memorial Prize for *I, Claudius* and *Claudius the God* (1934). He founded, with Laura Riding, Seizin Press. One volume biographies by Martin Seymour-Smith (2nd ed. 1995) and Miranda Seymour (1995), and a three volume biography by nephew Richard Perceval Graves (1986, 1990, 1995). There is a Robert Graves Society and Robert Graves Trust. Papers and manuscripts are archived at St. John's College Library, Oxford University.

Henry Green (Henry Vincent Yorke; 1905–73): Born Tewkesbury, Gloucestershire, died London. Industrialist turned novelist noted for radical experiments with dialogue. He impressed critics with his representations of factory workers in *Living* (1929), Bright Young People in *Party Going* (1939), and Cockney servants in most acclaimed *Loving* (1945). Autobiography is *Pack My Bag* (1940). Critical biography by Jeremy Treglown (2001). Letters archived at Warwick University, Modern Records Centre.

Graham Greene (Henry Graham Greene; 1904–91): Born Berkhamsted, Hertfordshire, died Vevey, Switzerland. Popular novelist, famously leftist and Catholic. Known for his thrillers or 'entertainments' such as *Brighton Rock* (1938), literary novels such as *The Power and the Glory* (1940) and travel books such as *Journey without Maps* (1936). Awarded the James Tait Black Memorial Prize for *The Heart of the Matter* (1948). Three volume biography by Norman Sherry 1989, 1994, 2004). Manuscripts and papers at Harry Ransom Center.

Walter Greenwood (1903–74): Born Salford, Lancashire, died Douglas, Isle of Man. Novelist and playwright, most famous for *Love on the Dole* (1933), which was adapted for stage and screen. Autobiography is *There Was A Time* (1967). Manuscripts and papers are in the Walter Greenwood Collection, University of Salford.

John Grierson (1898–1972): Born Deanston, Scotland, died Bath, England. Father of documentary film whose leftist politics influenced his work, including *First Principles of Documentary* (1932–3). He is famous for leading the film unit of the Empire Marketing Board for which he produced *Drifters* (1929) and later for the film unit of the General Post Office, for which he produced *Night Mail* and *Coal Face* (1936). His papers are in the John Grierson Archive at Stirling University Library. There is a Grierson Trust.

Geoffrey Grigson (1905–85): Born Pelynt, Cornwall, died Broad Town, Wiltshire. Poet, journalist, critic, broadcaster best known for his editorship of *New Verse* (starting in 1933) and his many literary feuds. He compiled many poetry anthologies and authored thirteen poetry volumes of his own. Correspondence and manuscripts are at the Harry Ransom Center and Library of the State University of New York, Buffalo.

Rumer Godden (Margaret Rumer Godden, 1907–98): Born Eastbourne, England, died Dumfriesshire, Scotland. Author of over sixty books, including her famous novels *Black Narcissus* (1939) and *The River* (1946), both of which were made into successful films. Many of her books evoke the world of colonial India, where she lived for decades. Awarded OBE (1993). Autobiography (1989) and authorised biography by Anne Chisholm (1998). There is a Rumer Godden Literary Trust.

Patrick Hamilton (Anthony Walter Patrick Hamilton, 1904–62): Born Hassocks, Sussex, died Sheringham, Norfolk. Playwright and novelist famous for dark humour and illustrations of seedier aspects of interwar London life. His plays *Rope* (1929) and *Gaslight* (1938) were made into successful films. *Hangover Square* (1941) is his most famous novel. Biographies by Sean French (1993) and Nigel Jones (1991). Papers at the Harry Ransom Center and British Library.

James Hanley (1897 [not 1901, as he maintained]–1985): Born Liverpool, died London. Novelist and playwright of Irish descent who was known for his loosely autobiographical fictions of working-class and especially seamen's lives. The publishers of his *Boy* (1934) lost an obscenity case against the novel, which was not published in unexpurgated form until 1990. Correspondence and papers in the Liverpool Record Office, the Department of Collections at the National Library of Wales and Senate House Library, London University, among other places.

L. P. Hartley (Leslie Poles Hartley, 1895–1972): Born Fletton Tower, Northhamptonshire, died London. Novelist and short story writer, popular for his pastoral settings and domestic dramas. Best known for the nostalgic *The Go-Between* (1953). Awarded the James Tait Black Memorial Prize for the Eustace and Hilda trilogy (1944–7). Awarded the CBE (1956). Archives in the John Ryland Library of Manchester University and Special Collections of the British Library, among other places.

Harold Heslop (1898–1983): Born New Hunwick, Durham, died Taunton, Somerset. Proletarian novelist, miner, trade union activist known for his novels of mining life. *Goaf* (1926) is set in a fictionalised version of Harton Colliery in South Shields; *Last Cage Down* (1935) earned critical acclaim and is still in print. Autobiography is *Out of the Old Earth* (1994). Unpublished typescripts in Archives and Special Collections, Durham University Library.

Richard Hillary (1910–43): Born Sydney, Australia, died RAF Charter Hall, near the Scottish border. Pilot in the Battle of Britain known for his memoir, *The Last Enemy* (1942). Biography by David Ross (2004) and memoir by Lovat Dickson (1950). Correspondence and papers at the Trinity College Library, Oxford University.

Alfred Hitchcock (1899–1980): Born London, died Los Angeles. One of the world's best known film-makers, producers, directors and screenwriters who began his career in silent films in Britain and ended up a Hollywood legend. A pioneer of psychological thrillers, he is remembered for films such as the Gaumont-British picture *The 39 Steps* (1935), the Selznick-produced *Rebecca* (1940) and postwar masterpiece *North by Northwest* (1959). KBE (1980). Papers are in the Margaret Herrick Library of the Academy of Motion Picture Arts and Sciences.

Inez Holden (c. 1904–74): Born Warwickshire, died London. A bohemian adventuress turned socialist and documentary novelist, short story writer and film writer. Most famous for *Night Shift* (1942), which was made into a wartime film, for being one of the few women to be published in Cyril Connolly's *Horizon* and for her short stories in Basic English, C. K. Ogden's experimental, minimalist language that helped inspire *Nineteen-Eighty-Four*'s Newspeak. Her papers are held by the descendants of her cousin, Celia Goodman (now deceased).

Winifred Holtby (1898–1935): Born Rudston, Yorkshire, died London. Feminist, novelist, journalist who won the James Tait Black Memorial Prize for *South Riding* (1936). Life-long friend of Vera Brittain. Biography by Marion Shaw (1999). Manuscripts and letters at Hull Central Library and Fisk University Library in Nashville, Tennessee.

Elizabeth Jane Howard (1923-): Born London, lives in Bungay, Suffolk. Novelist and short story writer who started out as actress and model and whose third husband was Kingsley Amis. Won John Llewellyn Rhys Prize for first novel *The Beautiful Visit* (1951). CBE (2000). Autobiography is *Slipstream* (2002).

Aldous Huxley (1894–1963): Born Godalming, Surrey, died Los Angeles. Novelist, satirist and essayist, Huxley is thought to be one of his generation's leading intellectuals. *Antic Hay* (1923) is characteristic of his satires of postwar London bohemia, while the comic dystopia *Brave New World* (1932) is more famous. Biographies by Nicholas Murray (2003), Dana Sawyer (2002) and Sybille Bedford (1974). Correspondence and papers in Special Collections, Stanford University Library and the Harry Ransom Center.

Elspeth Huxley (1907–97): Born London, died Tetbury, Gloucestershire. Novelist, journalist, agriculturalist, administrator and conservationist, Huxley is famous for her lifelong connection to Africa and her literary explorations of the British colonial rule there. She is best known for *The Flame Trees of Thika* (1959). Biography by Christine S. Nicholls (2002). CBE (1962). Correspondence and papers in the Bodleian Library of Commonwealth and African Studies at Rhodes House, Oxford University.

Storm Jameson (Margaret Storm Jameson, 1891–1986): Born Whitby, Yorkshire, died Cambridge. Novelist, critic and journalist famous for her role as president of the English section of PEN (1938–44). Author of forty-five novels, including the famous Mirror of Darkness trilogy (1934–6). Her two volume autobiography is *Journey from the North* (1969). Biographies by Jennifer Birkett (2009) and Elizabeth Maslen (in progress). Papers at the Harry Ransom Center.

Pamela Hansford Johnson (1912–81): Born and died London. Novelist, playwright, poet, critic and professor, author of twenty-seven novels, fifteen of which were published between 1935 and 1955, starting with *This Bed Thy Centre* (1935). Her second marriage was to C. P. Snow. Her memoir is *Important To Me* (1974). Papers are at the Harry Ransom Center, correspondence at Cambridge University Library's Department of Manuscripts and University Archives, among other sites.

Arthur Koestler (Artúr Kösztler, 1905–83): Born Budapest, Austria-Hungary, died London. Multi-lingual Jewish-Hungarian journalist and activist who became a British subject. Writer of criticism, philosophy, politics, fiction. Ferocious anti-fascist and anti-communist who left the Communist Party after the Moscow trials. Stalin's purges are the subject of his most famous novel, *Darkness at Noon* (1940). CBE (1972). Biography by David Cesarani (1998). Correspondence and papers in Special Collections, University of Edinburgh Library.

Alexander Korda (Sándor Lászlo Kellner, 1893–1956): Born Puszta Túrpásztó, Austria-Hungary, died London. Jewish-Hungarian film director and producer who became a British national in 1936 and was the first film-maker to be knighted. He was a pioneer in the British film industry and founder of London Films. Among his many triumphs were *The Thief of Baghdad* (1940) and *The Third Man* (1949). Most recent biographies by Charles Drazin (2002) and Karol Kulik (1975, 1991).

Marghanita Laski (1915–88): Born Manchester, died London. Novelist and critic known for her atheism. *Little Boy Lost* (1949) and *The Village* (1953) are set in the postwar period. She was the first critic to treat Daphne du Maurier seriously. No biography and minimal criticism exist for Laski herself.

F. R. Leavis (Frank Raymond Leavis, 1895–1978): Born and died Cambridge. Scholar and critic known for advocating morality in literature. He co-founded with his wife, Q. D. Leavis, the literary journal *Scrutiny* and published nearly two dozen scholarly books. His major works include *New Bearings in English Poetry* (1932) and *The Great Tradition* (1948). He was made CH (1978). Biographies by Ian MacKillop (1997) and William Walsh (1980). Archives and papers are in various libraries, including Houghton Library of Harvard University, Eton College Library and Emmanuel College Library, Cambridge University.

Q. D. Leavis (Queenie Dorothy ('Queenie') Roth Leavis, 1906–81): Born Edmonton, North London, died Cambridge. Scholar and critic who famously published her revised PhD thesis, supervised by I. A. Richards, as *Fiction and the Reading Public* (1932). She co-founded *Scrutiny* (1932–53) with her husband, F. R. Leavis, although she did not serve on its editorial board. Her collected essays are available in three volumes published by Cambridge University Press

Rosamond Lehmann (1901–90): Born Bourne End, Buckinghamshire, died Clareville Grove, London. Popular novelist noted for her portrayals of young, upper-middle-class heroines. She achieved fame with her first novel, *Dusty Answer* (1927) and cemented it with *The Weather in the Streets* (1936) and *The Ballad and the Source* (1944). Her autobiography is *The Swan in the Evening* (1967). She was made a CBE (1982). Biographies by Selina Hastings (2002) and Gillian Tindall (1985). Papers are in King's College Archive Centre, Cambridge University.

C. Day Lewis (Cecil Day-Lewis, 1904–72): Born Ballintubbert, Ireland, died Hadley Wood, Hertfordshire. Most famous for his poetry, but successful also as a translator and detective novelist. His first collection of poetry is *Beechen Vigil* (1925) and most critically acclaimed volume is *Word Over All* (1944). Britain's Poet Laureate (1968–72). Autobiography is *Buried Day* (1960). Biographies by Peter Stanford (2007) and Sean Day-Lewis (1980). Correspondence and papers at Harry Ransom Center and Harvard University's Houghton Library.

C. S. Lewis (Clive Staples Lewis, 1898–1963): Born Belfast, Ireland, died Oxford. Novelist, scholar and poet best known for the children's book fantasy series, The Chronicles of Narnia (1950–6). Notable works include scholarly studies *The Allegory of Love* (1936) and *English Literature in the Sixteenth Century* (1954) and the popular *Screwtape Letters* (1942). Biographies by George Sayer (1994) and A. N. Wilson (1990). Correspondence and papers are in the Marion E. Wade Centre of Wheaton College and Special Collections of Oxford's Bodleian Library.

Jack Lindsay (Robert Leeson Jack Lindsay, 1900–90): Born Melbourne, Australia, died Cambridge. Prolific novelist, translator, biographer, playwright, art critic and publisher. Historical novels such as *1649: A Novel of a Year* (1939) led him to be regarded as one of Britain's most influential proletarian writers. He joined the Communist Party in the late 1930s, and was a bestselling writer (as Richard Preston) in the Soviet Union. Study by Paul Gillen (1993). Manuscripts and correspondence at the Harry Ransom Center. Additional papers at the British Library, Manuscript Collections.

Eric Linklater (1899–1974): Born Penarth, Wales, died Aberdeen, Scotland. Popular and prolific novelist, short story writer, fantasy writer and playwright. Many works such as *Juan in America* (1931) or *Private Angelo* (1946) are based on his world travels. Identified with Orkney Islands and Scotland. Three volume autobiography (1970) and critical biography by Michael Parnell (1984). Correspondence and papers in the National Library of Scotland, Manuscript Collections.

Malcolm Lowry (1909–57): Born Wallasey, Merseyside, died 'of misadventure', Ripe, East Sussex. Nomadic poet, short story writer and novelist, whose *Under the Volcano* (1947) has been recognised by the Library of America as one of the twentieth-century's best 100 novels. There is a two volume edition of the collected letters (1995–6), biographies by Gordon Bowker (1993) and Douglas Day (1973) and a memoir by Lowry's first wife, Jan Gabrial (2000). Papers in the University of British Columbia Library and the Harry Ransom Center, with additional letters in the Huntington Library.

Rose Macaulay (1881–1958): Born Rugby, died London. Novelist, biographer and travel writer who became DBE (1958). Most famous novel is *The Towers of Trebizond* (1956), which won the James Tait Black Memorial Prize. Mentor to Elizabeth Bowen, friends with Ivy Compton-Burnett, E. M. Forster and Rosamond Lehmann. Biographies by Sarah LeFanu (2003) and Jane Emery (1991). Manuscripts and correspondence at the Harry Ransom Center and the Trinity College Library of Cambridge University.

Hugh MacDiarmid (Christopher Murray Grieve, 1892–1978): Born Langholm, Scotland, died Edinburgh. Leading poet of the Scottish Renaissance, now claimed for a Scottish modernism. Best known for his book-length poem *A Drunk Man Looks at the Thistle* (1926). A member of the Communist Party of Great Britain and the National Party of Scotland, he wrote in English and literary Scots. Autobiography is *Lucky Poet* (1943). Biographies by Alan Bold (1988) and Gordon Wright (1977). Papers in the Special Collections of University of Edinburgh Library, the Harry Ransom Center and the National Library of Scotland, Manuscript Collections.

Helen MacInnes (1907–85): Born Glasgow, died New York City. Scottish writer of spy detection novels, the most popular of which, including *Above Suspicion* (1941) and *Assignment in Brittainy* (1942), were made into films.

Ethel Mannin (1900–84): Born London, died Teignmouth, Devonshire. Prolific, popular and politically activist working-class novelist, essayist and travel writer, whose representative books include *Late Have I Loved Thee* (1948) and *Connemara Journal* (1947). There are six memoirs, the last being *Sunset over Dartmoor* (1977), but no biographies. Papers are in the Boston University Library with additional correspondence in the Sligo County Library and London Metropolitan University, Women's Library.

Olivia Manning (1908–80): Born Portsmouth, died Isle of Wight. Novelist best known for two World War II trilogies, The Balkan Trilogy (1960, 1962, 1965) and The Levant Trilogy (1977, 1978, 1980), based in large part on her and her husband's experiences. CBE (1976). Biography by Neville Braybrooke (2004). Papers in the Harry Ransom Center.

Betty Miller (1910–65): Born Cork, died London. Biographer and novelist discovered by Victor Gollancz, who later dropped her. Most famous for Robert Browning biography (1952), wartime novel *On the Side of the Angels* (1945) and pre-war *Farewell Leicester Square* (published belatedly in 1941), which takes English anti-semitism as its theme. She gathered at her home a group of women writers including Stevie Smith, Olivia Manning and Marghanita Laski.

A. A. Milne (Alan Alexander Milne, 1882–1956): Born London, died Hartfield, Sussex. Playwright, humorist, poet and mystery writer whose success as creator of Winnie-the-Pooh children's books in the mid- and late 1920s overshadowed all else. The Pooh books were illustrated by *Punch* cartoonist E. H. Shepard. Biography of Milne by Ann Thwaite (1990). Manuscripts and correspondence at Harry Ransom Center and National Art Library, Victoria and Albert Museum.

Naomi Mitchison (1897–1999): Born Edinburgh, died Carradale, Argyll. Prolific writer and committed socialist and feminist. Famous for historical novels such as *The Corn King and the Spring Queen* (1931) and controversial realism such as the feminist, anti-fascist *We Have Been Warned* (1935). Made CBE (1981). Three volume autobiography (1973, 1975, 1979) and biographies by Jenni Calder (1997) and Jill Benton (1990). Manuscripts and correspondence at the Harry Ransom Center, Library of the State University of New York, Buffalo and the National Library of Scotland.

Nancy Mitford (1904–73): Born London, died Versailles. Aristocrat and socialist, one of the six eccentric Mitford sisters. A Bright Young Thing in the interwar years, she became famous for her biographies of upper-class subjects and comic novels, including *Love in a Cold Climate* (1949). CBE (1972). Subject of multiple books, including biographies by Laura Thompson (2003), Selena Hastings (1986) and Harold Acton (1979). Correspondence and papers at Chatsworth House.

Edwin Muir (1887–1959): Born Deerness, Orkney Islands, died Cambridge. Poet, novelist and translator, now being claimed, with his wife, for a Scottish modernism. He published seven volumes of poetry during his lifetime, in addition to novels and the controversial *Scott and Scotland* (1936). *The Complete Poems* appeared in 1991. There is an autobiography (1954) and memoir by his wife Willa Muir (1968). Biography by P. H. Butter (1966). Archives are in the National Library of Scotland's Manuscript Collection, the British Library Manuscript Collection, and St Andrews University Library, among other places.

Willa Muir (1890–1970): Born Island of Unst, Scotland, died Dunoon, on the West Coast of Scotland. Novelist, essayist, poet and translator best known for her mastery of European languages and translations, with her husband Edwin Muir, of Franz Kafka, among others. She adopted the pen name Agnes Neill Scott when translating on her own. Though author of only two novels, *Imagined Corners* (1931) and *Mrs Ritchie* (1932), she is considered an important contributor to the Scottish Renaissance and is now being claimed as a Scottish modernist. There is a critical biography by Aileen Christianson (2007). Archives are in the National Library of Scotland and St Andrews University Library.

George Orwell (Eric Arthur Blair, 1903–50): Born Motihari, India, died London. Novelist, journalist and critic, George Orwell is known for his international bestsellers, the satire *Animal Farm* (1945) and the dystopian *Nineteen Eighty-Four* (1949). Peter Davison has edited the *Complete Works* (finished in 2000). Biographies by Gordon Bowker (2003), D. J. Taylor (2003) and Bernard Crick (1980). Archives are in the University College Special Collections, London University.

Mollie Panter-Downes (1906–97): Born London, died Surrey. Correspondent and novelist. Best known for her column, 'Letter from London', published in *The New Yorker* (1939–84). Her first and bestselling novel, *The Shoreless Sea* (1923), was published when she was seventeen. *Good Evening, Mrs Craven: The Wartime Stories of Mollie Panter-Downes* (1999) is a collection of her short stories about life in England during World War II.

Anthony Powell (Anthony Dymoke Powell, 1905–2000): Born London, died Somerset. Novelist, literary critic and screenwriter best known for his satirical twelve-volume novel, *A Dance to the Music of Time* (1951–75). His famous four-volume memoir is *To Keep the Ball Rolling* (1976–82). In the 1930s he worked as scriptwriter for Warner Brothers (1936–7). CBE (1956); CH (1988). Biographies by Michael Barber (2004) and Nicholas Birns (2004). Papers are in the Lincolnshire Archives, the Manuscript Collection of the British Library and the University College London Special Collections.

Michael Powell (Michael Latham Powell, 1905–90): Born Bekesbourne, Kent, died Avening, Gloucestershire. British film-maker, director and writer. Worked for fifty years in the film industry, including as a still photographer for Alfred Hitchcock. With Emeric Pressburger, he founded Archers Film Production Company and made nineteen acclaimed feature films (1942–57).

Screen credits with Pressburger include *The Life and Death of Colonel Blimp* (1943) and *The Red Shoes* (1948). Autobiographies include *A Life in Movies: An Autobiography* (1986) and *Million Dollar Movie* (1992). Biography by James Howard (1996) and interviews collected by David Lazar (2003). Papers are in Special Collections of the British Film Institute.

Emeric Pressburger (Imre József Emmerich Pressburger, 1902–88): Born Miskolc, Hungary, died Saxstead, Suffolk. Screenwriter, producer, film director. With Michael Powell, he founded Archers Film Production Company and made nineteen acclaimed feature films (1942–57). In 1941, he won an Academy Award for best original story for the film, *The 49th Parallel*. Other screen credits include *Spy for a Day* (1940) and *Wanted for Murder* (1946). Novels include *The Red Shoes* (1978), based on his and Powell's best-known film. Biography by his grandson Kevin Macdonald (1994). Papers are in the Special Collections of the British Film Institute.

J. B. Priestley (John Boynton Priestley, 1894–1984): Born Bradford, Yorkshire, died Stratford-upon-Avon, Warwickshire. Prolific novelist, playwright, broadcaster and essayist. Notable novels include *The Good Companions* (1929), which won the James Tait Black Memorial Prize. His best-known play is *An Inspector Calls* (1946). His Sunday evening BBC broadcasts, 'Postscripts', won wartime audiences of up to sixteen million. Biography by Judith Cook (1997). Archives are in the Harry Ransom Center and in the J. B. Priestley Library, Bradford University.

V. S. Pritchett (Victor Sawdon Pritchett, 1900–97). Born Ipswich, Suffolk, died London. Prolific short story writer, novelist, journalist, critic, biographer and professor. *Clare Drummer* (1929) was his first novel. There are *Collected Stories* (1956, 1981), *More Collected Stories* (1982) and the massive *Complete Collected Stories* (1991). CH (1993). Biographies by Jeremy Treglown (2004) and Dean R. Baldwin (1987). Correspondence and papers are at the Harry Ransom Center.

Arthur Ransome (1884–1967): Born Leeds, buried Rusland, Lake District. Children's book author, foreign correspondent and socialist most famous for the Swallows and Amazons series (1930–47) which is set in a fictionalised Lake District. His autobiography was published posthumously in 1967. There is an Arthur Ransome Society and biography by Hugh Brogan (1984). Archives are in the Leeds University Library's Special Collections and Museum of Lakeland Life and Industry, among other places.

Herbert Read (1893–1968): Born Kirkbymoorside, North Yorkshire, died Stonegrave. Poet, memoirist, art critic and professor remembered for his poetry and memoir of World War I, *In Retreat* (1925), and his influential criticism, including *Form in Modern Poetry* (1932) and his edited volume on *Surrealism* (1936). The *Collected Poems* appeared in 1966. He was knighted by Churchill in 1953. Full autobiography (1963); biography by James King

(1990). Correspondence and papers in the McPherson Library of the University of Victoria and Churchill Archive Centre of Cambridge University.

I. A. Richards (Ivor Armstrong Richards, 1893–1979): Born Sandbach, Cheshire, died Cambridge. Scholar, professor, literary critic and theorist, famous for his *Principles of Literary Criticism* (1924) and *Practical Criticism* (1929). He developed Basic English with C. K. Ogden and co-authored with him *The Meaning of Meaning* (1923). Critical biography by Jean Paul Russo (1989). Papers at Harvard University's Houghton Library and Cambridge University's King's College Archive Centre and Department of Manuscripts and University Archives.

Dorothy Sayers (1893–1957): Born Oxford, died Wiltham, Essex. Novelist, translator, scholar and playwright best known for her Lord Peter Wimsey and Harriet Vane detective fiction, including *The Nine Tailors* (1934) and *Gaudy Night* (1935). Five volumes of letters, edited by Barbara Reynolds with biographies by Barbara Reynolds (1993, rev. 1998, 2002), David Coomes (1992) and James Brabazon (1980). Archives in the Harry Ransom Center, the Bodleian Library's Special Collections at Oxford University and Marion E. Wade Center, Wheaton College.

Dodie Smith (Dorothy Gladys Smith, 1896–1990): Born Whitefield, Lancashire, died Finchingfield, Essex. The 'Shopgirl' playwright who later became a novelist best known for *I Capture the Castle* (1948) and *One Hundred and One Dalmatians* (1956). Both works were made into films, the latter becoming a Walt Disney classic. Four-volume autobiography. Biography by Valerie Grove (1996). Papers are in the Howard Gottlieb Archival Research Center of Boston University.

Stevie Smith (Florence Margaret Smith, 1902–71): Born Hull, Yorkshire, died Ashburton, Devon. Poet, short story writer, critic and novelist who earned the Queen's Gold Medal for Poetry (1969). Her witty autobiographical *Novel on Yellow Paper* (1936), written while she was working as a secretary at Newnes Publishing Company, launched her career. Biography by Frances Spalding (1988). Papers at the University of Tulsa's McFarlin Library, Hull University Archives and the Washington University Library, among other places.

C. P. Snow (Charles Percy Snow, 1905–80): Born Leicester, died London. Novelist, physicist and government minister best known for his series of novels called Strangers and Brothers, of which *The Masters* (1951) and *The New Man* (1954) won the James Tait Black Memorial Prize. He is also remembered for his influential 1959 lecture, 'The Two Cultures', decrying the void between sciences and literature. There are critical biographies by Robert Gorham Davis (1965) and Jerome Thale (1964) and a bibliography by Paul W. Boytinck (1978). Papers at the Harry Ransom Center.

Freya Stark (1893–1993): Born Paris, died Asolo, Italy. British travel writer and cartographer fabled for her journeys through Iran and Arabia, where few

Westerners, let alone Western women, had ever ventured. Her first books were *Baghdad Sketches* (1932) and *The Valley of the Assassins* (1934). She was made DBE. Biographies by Jane Fletcher Geniesse (2002) and Caroline Moorhead (1985). Papers at the Harry Ransom Center, Harvard's Center for Italian Renaissance Studies and Edinburgh University's Special Collections, among other sites.

G. B. Stern (Gladys Bertha (later Bronwyn) Stern, 1890–1973): Born London, died Wallingford, Oxfordshire. Anglo-Jewish novelist, short story writer, dramatist, memoirist, biographer and critic most famous for her five volume novel series, The Rakonitz Chronicles (1924–42), which follow the adventures of a secular urban Jewish family much like her own. Her memoirs include *All In Good Time* (1954) and its sequel, *The Way It Worked Out* (1956). Virtually no criticism exists. Papers in Special Collections, Boston University Library and the Theatre Museum Archive, London.

Jan Struther (Joyce Anstruther Maxtone Graham Placzek, 1901–53): Born Whitchurch, Buckinghamshire, died New York. Novelist, poet, hymn writer and journalist most famous for her humorous portrayals of middle-class housewife Mrs Miniver, who first appeared in columns in *The Times* and later, the novel *Mrs Miniver* (1939). In 1942 MGM made a blockbuster, propagandistic movie from the novel. There is a biography by Ysenda Maxtone Graham (2001).

Angela Thirkell (1890–1961): Born London, died Bramley, Surrey. Journalist and children's story writer who became a prolific novelist, Thirkell is famous for her Barsetshire novels, set in a contemporary version of Anthony Trollope's fictional county. God-child to J. M. Barrie, granddaughter of Edward Burne-Jones, cousin of Rudyard Kipling and Stanley Baldwin, Thirkell enjoyed popularity in the 1930s and World War II years. There are Angela Thirkell societies in the UK and US. Uncomplimentary biography by Margot Strickland (1977). Archives in the Special Collections of the Leeds University Library.

J. R. R. Tolkien (John Ronald Reuel Tolkien, 1892–1973): Born Bloemfontein, Orange Free State, South Africa, died Bournemouth, England. Oxford scholar and professor, philologist, poet and novelist, internationally beloved for his classic fantasy series *The Hobbit* (1937), meant initially for children, and the three-volume *The Lord of the Rings* (1954, 1954 and 1955). He was designated CBE (1972). Recent biographies by Michael White (2003), Tom Shippey (2000) and Joseph Pearce (1998). Manuscripts are in the Special Collections of Marquette University's Raynor Library, Milwaukee, with additional papers at Oxford University's Bodleian Library.

P. L. Travers (Helen Lyndon Goff, 1899–1996): Born Maryborough, Australia, died London. Poet, actress and novelist most famous for *Mary Poppins* (1934), an immensely popular children's novel which was followed by five sequels, the last published in 1988. She was made OBE (1977). Biography by Valerie Lawson (1999, 2005).

Edward Upward (1903–2009): Born Romford, died Pontefract, aged 105, as this book went to press. Poet, novelist, short story writer, one-time Communist Party member famous for youthful fantasy about the village of Mortmere (collectively written with W. H. Auden and Stephen Spender). His novels, including *Journey to the Border* (1938), examine relations between literary and political commitments. Correspondence and papers in the Manuscript Collection, British Library.

Rex Warner (1905–86): Born Birmingham, died Wallingford, Oxfordshire. Poet, novelist, journalist, translator and professor of classics. Known for early political and allegorical novels, including *The Wild Goose Chase* (1937) and *The Aerodrome* (1941). Critical biography by Stephen E. Tabachnick (2002). Papers at the Harry Ransom Center and the libraries of the State University of New York, Buffalo and the University of Connecticut.

Sylvia Townsend Warner (1893–1978): Born Harrow on the Hill, Devonshire, died Frome Vauchurch, Dorset. Novelist, poet, biographer and translator who began her literary career as an editor of early music. A lesbian, member of the Communist Party, and leftist activist, Warner's successful novels include the fanciful *Lolly Willowes* (1926) and the historical novel *Summer Will Show* (1936). Biography by Clare Harman (1989). Correspondence and papers at the Harry Ransom Center; additional materials in the Sylvia Townsend Warner archive at the Dorset County Museum.

Evelyn Waugh (Arthur Evelyn St John Waugh, 1903–66). Born London, died Taunton, Somerset. Humorist and satirist most famous for his 1930s novels *Vile Bodies* (1930), *A Handful of Dust* (1934), *Scoop* (1938) and his more serious novels about World War II, *Brideshead Revisited* (1945) and the Sword of Honour trilogy (1952, 1955, 1961). Recent biographies by Alexander Waugh (2007), Douglas Lane Patey (1998), Selina Hastings (1994) and Martin Standard (in two volumes, 1987, 1994). Papers and manuscripts are in the British Library's Manuscript Collections, the Harry Ransom Center, the Rare Book and Manuscript Library of Columbia University, among other sites.

Rebecca West (Cicely Isabel Fairfield, 1892–1983): Born and died London. Journalist, critic, travel writer and novelist. Her work, including the novel *The Return of the Solider* (1918) and the massive history, ethnography and travel book of Yugoslavia, *Black Lamb and Grey Falcon* (1941), all show her signature qualities of critical insight, political nonconformity and savage wit. Awarded CBE (1949) and DBE (1959). Biographies by Carl Rollyson (1996) and Victoria Glendinning (1987). Correspondence and manuscripts in the McFarlin Library of the University of Tulsa and Beinecke Rare Book and Manuscript Library.

T. H. White (Terence Hanbury White, 1906–64): Born Bombay, India, died Athens, Greece. Writer best known for his series of novels about King Arthur (1938–40), published with the last and fourth instalment as *The Once and*

Future King (1958). This inspired the Broadway musical *Camelot* and Disney animated film *The Sword in the Stone*. Biography by Sylvia Townsend Warner (1967). Papers and archives in the Special Collections of Reading University Library and at the Harry Ransom Center.

Ellen Wilkinson (1891–1947): Born Manchester, died London. Novelist, journalist, activist and politician who was elected the Labour MP for Middlesbrough in 1924 and for Jarrow in 1935. One of the first female MPs in Britain, Wilkinson is known for her anti-fascist and feminist writings, as well as a novel *Clash* (1928), which is set against the 1926 General Strike. Biography by Betty D. Vernon (1982). Correspondence in the Labour History Archive and Study Center.

John Wyndham (John Wyndham Parkes Lucas Beynon Harris, 1903–69): Born Knowle, Warwickshire, died Petersfield. Science fiction writer known for his post-apocalyptic tales. His first and biggest success was *The Day of the Triffids* (1951). His next three novels, including *The Kraken Wakes* (1953), defined for many postwar science fiction. Consult Special Collections and Archives, Liverpool University.

E. H. Young (Emily Hilda Young, 1880–1949): Born Whitley, Northumberland, died Bradford-on-Avon, Wiltshire. Best-selling novelist known for her hopeful, interwar fictions of domestic realism including *Miss Mole* (1930), which won the James Tait Black Memorial Prize, and her contributions to a rural tradition, including *The Misses Mallett* (1922). Her papers are held privately by William Saunders of London.

SELECT BIBLIOGRAPHY

Note on sources: The authors contributing the chapters to this volume worked independently of each other and often in libraries situated in different continents. For this reason, they occasionally cite different editions of the same text. In part to honour the transatlantic character of their research, chapter bibliographies always cite the particular textual editions individual authors consulted. The main bibliography is both compilation of and compromise between these individual chapter bibliographies. It lists only one edition of any given text, even if different editions of that text are cited by various chapter authors.

PRIMARY SOURCES

Allingham, Margery. *Black Plumes*. 1940. New York: Bantam, 1983.
—. *Coroner's Pidgin*. 1945. London: Vintage, 2006.
—. *Traitor's Purse*. 1941. New York: Bantam, 1983.
Arendt, Hannah. *Eichmann in Jerusalem: A Report on the Banality of Evil*. 1963. New York: Penguin, 1994.
—. *The Origins of Totalitarianism*. 1948. New York: Harvest, 1973.
Auden, W. H. *The English Auden: Poems, Essays and Dramatic Writings 1927–1939*. Ed. E. Mendelson. London: Faber, 1977.
Bell, Adrian. *The Open Air: An Anthology of English Country Life*. London: Faber 1936; illustrated edition 1949.
Biddle, Francis. *In Brief Authority*. Garden City: Doubleday, 1962.
Bowen, Elizabeth. 'Advance in Formation'. Rev. of *New Writing in Europe*, by John Lehmann. *Spectator* 17 January 1941: 65.

—. *The Bazaar and Other Stories*. Ed. and intro. Allan Hepburn. Edinburgh: Edinburgh University Press, 2008.

—. 'Britain in Autumn'. Ten-page essay [1940]. HRC 2.2.

—. *Collected Impressions*. London: Longmans Green, 1950.

—. *The Collected Stories of Elizabeth Bowen*. Intro. Angus Wilson. New York: Ecco Press, 1981.

—. 'The Disinherited'. Bowen, *Collected Stories* 375–407.

—. 'The Dolt's Tale'. Bowen, *Collected Stories* 741–47.

—. 'Eire'. *New Statesman and Nation* 12 April 1941: 382–83.

—. 'English Fiction at Mid-Century'. *The Arts at Mid-Century*. Ed. Robert Richman. New York: Horizon, 1954. 209–13.

—. 'Folkestone: July, 1945'. Bowen, *Collected Impressions* 225–30.

—. 'Heart or Soul?' Rev. of *From the Heart of Europe* by F. O. Matthiessen. *Spectator*, 10 September 1948: 766.

—. *The Heat of the Day*. 1949. New York: Anchor, 2002.

—. 'The Heat of the Day'. Publicity note. HRC 5.5.

—. 'Hungary'. Ten-page essay dated 29 November 1948. HRC 6.2.

—. 'Impressions of Czechoslovakia'. Three-page essay dated 15 March 1948. Broadcast on BBC European Service 16 March 1948. HRC 2.3.

—. 'The Informer'. Rev. of *Witness* by Whittaker Chambers. *Observer* 19 July 1953: 9.

—. 'Interview, 1959'. Conducted by John Bowen, William Craig, and W. N. Ewer. Broadcast 11 September 1959 on BBC. Transcription. HRC 2.3.

—. Letter to Blanche Knopf. Dated Sunday, 2 April 1950. HRC 685.15.

—. Letter to Veronica Wedgwood. Dated 10 April 1952. Oxford University, Bodleian Library MS Eng. c. 6829, fols 2–49.

—. 'London, 1940'. Bowen, *Collected Impressions* 217–20.

—. 'Oh, Madam'. Bowen, *Collected Stories* 578–82.

—. 'Paris Peace Conference: 1946. An Impression.' Seven-page draft for subsequent published articles. HRC 8.7.

—. 'Paris Peace Conference – Some Impressions 1'. *Cork Examiner* 12 October 1946: 9.

—. 'Paris Peace Conference – Some Impressions 2'. *Cork Examiner* 15 October 1946: 7.

—. 'Paris Peace Conference – Some Impressions 3'. *Cork Examiner* 22 October 1946: 4.

—. 'Prague and the Crisis'. *Vogue* 1 April 1948: 156, 195–6.

—. 'The Unromantic Princess'. *The Bazaar and Other Stories*. Ed. and intro. Allan Hepburn. Edinburgh: Edinburgh University Press, 2008. 99–110.

—. 'Without Coffee, Cigarettes, or Feeling'. *Mademoiselle* February 1955: 174–75, 221–23.

Calder, Angus and Dorothy Sheridan, eds. *Speak for Yourself: A Mass-Observation Anthology, 1937–49.* London: Jonathan Cape, 1984.

Dane, Clemence. *The Arrogant History of White Ben.* London: William Heinemann, 1939.

Empson, William. *The Complete Poems of William Empson.* Ed. John Haffenden. Harmondsworth: Penguin, 2001.

—. *Poems.* London: Chatto and Windus, 1935.

—. *Selected Letters of William Empson.* Ed. John Haffenden. Oxford and New York: Oxford University Press, 2006.

—. *Seven Types of Ambiguity.* 1930. Harmondsworth: Penguin, 1961.

—. *Some Versions of Pastoral.* 1935. Harmondsworth, Penguin, 1995.

Forster, E. M. *Howards End.* Ed. Oliver Stallybrass. Harmondsworth: Penguin, 1975.

Fox, Ralph. *The Novel and the People.* London: Lawrence and Wishart, 1937.

Gallix, François. *T. H. White: Letters to a Friend: The Correspondence between T. H. White and L. J. Potts.* London: Alan Sutton, 1984.

Gibbons, Stella. *The Bachelor.* London: Longmans, 1944.

—. *Cold Comfort Farm.* 1932. Intr. Lynne Truss. Harmondsworth: Penguin, 2006.

—. *Miss Linsey and Pa.* London: Longmans, 1936.

—. *My American.* London: Longmans, 1939.

Gide, André. *Journal 1889–1939.* 1951. Paris: Pléiade, 1970. 345–46.

Gollancz, Victor. 'Foreword'. *The Road to Wigan Pier.* By George Orwell. London: Victor Gollancz, 1937. xi–xxiv.

Grierson, John. 'The G.P.O. Gets Sound'. *Cinema Quarterly* 2.4 (1934): 215–21.

—. *Grierson on Documentary.* Ed. Forsyth Hardy. London: Faber, 1979.

—. 'The Story of the Documentary Film'. *The Fortnightly Review* August 1939: 122–27.

Henderson, Philip. *The Novel Today: Studies in Contemporary Attitudes.* London: John Lane The Bodley Head, 1936.

Heslop, Harold. *The Crime of Peter Ropner.* London: The Fortune Press, 1934.

—. *The Earth Beneath.* London: T. V. Boardman, 1946.

—. *The Gate of a Strange Field.* New York: D. Appleton, 1929.

—. *Goaf.* 1926. London: The Fortune Press, 1934.

—. *Journey Beyond.* London: Harold Shaylor, 1930.

—. *Last Cage Down.* 1935. London: Lawrence and Wishart, 1984.

—. *Out of the Old Earth.* Ed. Andy Croft and Graeme Rigby. Newcastle: Bloodaxe Books, 1994.

—. 'The Working Class and the Novel'. *The Labour Monthly* 12 (1930): 689–92.

Huxley, Aldous. *After Many a Summer Dies the Swan*. New York: Harper and Row, 1939.

Isherwood, Christopher. *Kathleen and Christopher: Christopher Isherwood's Letters to his Mother*. Ed. Lisa Colletta. Minneapolis: University of Minnesota Press, 2005.

Jameson, Storm. *Before the Crossing*. London: Macmillan, 1947.

—. *The Black Laurel*. London: Macmillan, 1947.

—. *Civil Journey*. London: Cassell, 1939.

—. *Cloudless May*. London: Macmillan, 1943.

—. *Cousin Honoré*. London: Cassell, 1940.

—. 'Documents'. *Writing in Revolt*. Spec. issue of *Fact*. July 1937: 9–18.

—. *Europe to Let: The Memoirs of an Obscure Man*. London: Macmillan, 1940.

—. *Farewell, Night; Welcome, Day*. London: Cassell, 1939.

—. *The Fort*. London: Cassell, 1941.

—. *In the Second Year*. 1936. Ed. Stan Smith. Nottingham: Trent, 2004.

—. *The Journal of Mary Hervey Russell*. London: Macmillan, 1945.

—. *Journey from the North*. Vol. I, 1969. Vol. II, 1970. London: Virago, 1984.

—. Letter to Arthur Koestler. 1 March 1943 (2399/1). Koestler–Jameson Correspondence. Koestler Archive, University of Edinburgh Library.

—. The 'Mirror in Darkness' trilogy:
> *Company Parade*. 1934. London: Virago, 1982.
> *Love in Winter*. 1935. London: Virago, 1984.
> *None Turn Back*. 1936. London: Virago, 1984.

—. *The Moon is Making*. London: Cassell, 1937.

—. 'New Novels'. *The New English Weekly* 23 June 1932: 235–36.

— (as Hill, James). *No Victory for the Soldier*. London: Collins, 1938.

—. *The Novel in Contemporary Life*. Boston: The Writer, 1938.

—. Rev. of *The Waves*, by Virginia Woolf. *Fortnightly Review* Nov. 1931: 677–78.

—. *That Was Yesterday*. London: Heinemann, 1932.

—. *Then We Shall Hear Singing: A Fantasy in C Major*. London: Cassell, 1942.

—. The 'Triumph of Time' trilogy. 1932:
> *The Lovely Ship*. London: Heinemann, 1927.
> *A Richer Dust*. London: Heinemann, 1931.
> *The Voyage Home*. London: Heinemann, 1930.

—. Untitled essay. *What is Patriotism?* Ed. N. P. Macdonald. London: Thornton Butterworth, 1935. 123–33.

—. Untitled essay. *Adam International Review*. September 1941. Frontispiece.

—. 'Writing in Revolt, 1. Theory: Documents'. Spec. issue of *Fact*. July 1937: 9–18.

—. 'The Young Prisoner'. *Modern Reading* 9 (1944): 111–26.

Jennings, Humphrey and Charles Madge. 'Poetic Description and Mass-Observation'. *New Verse* Feb.–March 1937: 1–6.

Jennings, Humphrey and Charles Madge, T. O. Beachcroft, Julian Blackburn, William Empson, Stuart Legg and Kathleen Raine, eds. *May the Twelfth: Mass-Observation Day-Surveys 1937*. London: Faber and Faber, 1937.

Koestler, Arthur. *Darkness at Noon*. Trans. Daphne Hardy. 1940. London: Penguin, 1964.

Lawrence, D. H. *Phoenix*. London: Heinemann, 1970.

Leavis, F. R. and Denys Thompson. *Culture and Environment: The Training of Critical Awareness*. London: Chatto and Windus, 1933.

Leavis, Q. D. *Fiction and the Reading Public*. 1932. London: Chatto and Windus, 1968.

Le Carré, John. *The Spy Who Came in from the Cold*. 1963. London: Penguin, 1989.

Lehmann, Rosamond. *The Weather in the Streets*. 1936. London: Collins, 1968.

Leighton, Claire. *The Farmer's Year: A Calendar of English Husbandry*. London: Collins, 1933.

MacDiarmid, Hugh. 'A Poet Looks at the Cinema: Poetry and Film'. *Cinema Quarterly* 2.3 (1934): 146–49.

MacInnes, Helen. *Above Suspicion*. 1941. Boston: Little, Brown, 1942.

—. *Assignment in Brittany*. Boston: Little, Brown, 1942.

—. *While Still We Live*. 1944. New York: Crest/Fawcett Publications, 1964.

Madge, Charles. 'Press, Radio and Social Consciousness'. *The Mind in Chains: Socialism and the Cultural Revolution*. Ed. C. Day Lewis. London: Frederick Muller, 1937. 147–63.

Madge, Charles and Tom Harrisson, eds. *Britain by Mass-Observation*. Harmondsworth: Penguin, 1939.

Massingham, H. J. *English Downland*. London: Batsford: 'Face of Britain' series, 1936.

Mitchison, Naomi. 'The Fourth Pig'. *The Fourth Pig*. London: Constable, 1936.

Morton, H. V. *In Search of England*. London: Methuen, 1927.

Nairne, Campbell. 'The Writer's Approach to the Cinema'. *Cinema Quarterly* 3.1 (1935): 134–38.

Nietzsche, Friedrich. *Human, All Too Human*. 1886. Trans. Marion Faber and Stephen Lehmann. Harmondsworth: Penguin, 1994.

Orwell, George. *Animal Farm: A Fairy Story*. London: Gollancz, 1945.

—. *Nineteen Eighty-Four*. New York: Harcourt Brace, 1949.

—. 'The Proletarian Writer'. 1940. *The Complete Works of George Orwell*,

Volume XII: A Patriot After All 1940–1941. Ed. Peter Davison. London: Secker and Warburg, 2000. 294–99.

—. *The Road to Wigan Pier.* London: Gollancz, 1937.

Powell, Anthony. *Messengers of the Day.* London: Heinemann, 1978.

Priestley, J. B. *All England Listened: The Wartime Broadcasts of J. B. Priestley.* New York: Chilmark Press, 1967.

—. *Bright Day.* London: Heinemann, 1946.

—. *English Journey.* New York and London: Harper Collins, 1934.

—. *Margin Released: A Writer's Reminiscences and Reflections.* New York: Harper and Row, 1962.

—. *Midnight on the Desert.* 1937. London: Readers' Union Limited and Heinemann, 1940.

—. *Out of the People.* London: Heinemann, 1941.

—. *Rain upon Godshill: A Further Chapter of Autobiography.* London: Heinemann, 1939.

Raine, Kathleen. *The Land Unknown.* London: Hamish Hamilton, 1975.

Read, Herbert. 'The Poet and the Film'. *Cinema Quarterly* 1.4 (1933): 197–202.

Richards, I. A. *Principles of Literary Criticism.* 1924. London: Routledge and Kegan Paul, 1960.

—. *Science and Poetry.* London: Kegan Paul, Trench, Trubner and Co, 1926.

Ritchie, Charles. *Diplomatic Passport: More Undiplomatic Diaries, 1946–1962.* Toronto: Laurentian Macmillan, 1981.

Roberts, Michael, ed. *New Signatures.* London: Hogarth Press, 1932.

Rotha, Paul. *Documentary Diary: An Informal History of the British Documentary Film, 1928–1939.* New York: Hill and Wang, 1973.

—. *Documentary Film.* London: Faber, 1936.

Stonier, G.W. *Gog Magog.* London: Dent, 1933.

Sturt, George. *The Wheelwright's Shop.* Cambridge: Cambridge University Press, 1923.

Symons, Julian. *The Thirties: A Dream Revolved.* Rev. ed. London: Faber and Faber, 1975.

Warner, Sylvia Townsend. *After the Death of Don Juan.* London: Chatto and Windus, 1938

—. *The Corner That Held Them.* 1948. London: Chatto and Windus, 1977.

—. *Diaries of Sylvia Townsend Warner.* Ed. Claire Harman. London: Chatto and Windus, 1994.

—. *Dorset Stories.* Ed. Judith Stinton. Norwich: Black Dog Books, 2006.

—. 'The Historical Novel'. 1940. Reprinted in *Journal of the Sylvia Townsend Warner Society* (2007): 53–55.

—. *Letters.* Ed. William Maxwell. London: Chatto and Windus, 1982.

—. *Lolly Willowes: Or the Loving Huntsman*. London: Chatto and Windus, 1926.

—. *New Collected Poems*. Ed. Claire Harman. Manchester: Carcanet, 2008.

—. *Summer Will Show*. London: Chatto and Windus, 1936.

—. 'Sylvia Townsend Warner in Conversation'. *PN Review* 23 (Nov.–Dec. 1981): 35–37.

—. *T. H. White: A Biography*. London: Jonathan Cape and Chatto and Windus, 1967.

—. 'The Way I Have Come'. 1939. Reprinted in *Journal of the Sylvia Townsend Warner Society* (2007): 1–9.

Waugh, Evelyn. *The Diaries of Evelyn Waugh*. Ed Michael Davie. Boston: Little Brown, 1976.

—. *Vile Bodies*. 1930. Harmondsworth: Penguin, 1938.

West, Rebecca. 'The Birch Leaves Falling'. *New Yorker* 26 October 1946: 93–105.

—. *Black Lamb and Grey Falcon: A Journey through Yugoslavia*. 1941. New York: Penguin, 1982.

—. 'Extraordinary Exile'. *New Yorker* 7 September 1946: 34–46.

—. Foreword. *On Trial at Nuremberg*. By Airey Neve. Boston: Little, Brown, 1978. 5–9.

—. *The Meaning of Treason*. New York: Viking, 1949.

—. *The New Meaning of Treason*. New York: Viking, 1964.

—. *The Return of the Soldier*. 1918. New York: Penguin, 1998.

—. *Selected Letters of Rebecca West*. Ed. Bonnie Kime Scott. New Haven and London: Yale University Press, 2000.

—. *A Train of Powder*. New York: Viking, 1955.

White, T. H. (Terence Hanbury). *Burke's Steerage: The Amateur Gentleman's Introduction to Noble Sports and Pastimes*. London: Collins, 1938.

—. *England Have My Bones*. London: Collins, 1936.

—. *The Ill-Made Knight*. London: Collins, 1941.

—. *The Once and Future King*. 1958. Reprinted as *The Once and Future King: The Complete Edition* (including 'The Book of Merlyn' and an 'Afterword' by Sylvia Townsend Warner). London: Harper Collins, 1958.

—. *The Sword in the Stone*. London: Collins, 1938.

—. *The Witch in the Wood*. London: Collins, 1940.

Wilson, Norman. 'The Spectator'. *Cinema Quarterly* 1.1 (1932): 3–6.

Woolf, Virginia. *Three Guineas*. 1938. *A Room of One's Own and Three Guineas*. Ed. Morag Shiach. Oxford: Oxford University Press, 1992.

SECONDARY SOURCES

Aldgate, Anthony and Jeffrey Richards. *Britain Can Take It: The British Cinema in the Second World War*. Oxford: Blackwell, 1986.

Alldritt, Keith. *Modernism in the Second World War*. New York: Peter Lang, 1989.

Annan, Noel. *Our Age: English Intellectuals between the World Wars*. New York: Random House, 1991.

Ardis, Ann L. *Modernism and Cultural Conflict, 1880–1922*. Cambridge: Cambridge University Press, 2003.

Arnot, Robin Page. *The Miners: One Union, One Industry*. London: George Allen and Unwin, 1979.

—. *The Miners: Years of Struggle: A History of the Miners' Federation of Great Britain (from 1910 onwards)*. London: George Allen and Unwin, 1953.

Atkins, John. *The British Spy Novel*. London: John Calder, 1984.

Ayers, David. *English Literature of the 1920s*. Edinburgh: Edinburgh University Press, 1999.

Baker, Niamh. *Happily Ever After? Women's Fiction in Postwar Britain, 1945–1960*. New York: St Martin's Press, 1989.

Baughman, James L. *The Republic of Mass Culture: Journalism, Filmmaking, and Broadcasting in America since 1941*. Baltimore: Johns Hopkins University Press, 1997.

Bauman, Zygmunt. *Modernity and the Holocaust*. Ithaca: Cornell University Press, 1989.

Baxendale, John and Christopher Pawling. *Narrating the Thirties: A Decade in the Making: 1930 to the Present*. New York: Palgrave Macmillan, 1996.

Beauman, Nicola. *A Very Great Profession: The Woman's Novel 1914–39*. London: Virago, 1983.

Beddoe, Deirdre. *Back to Home and Duty: Women between the Wars, 1918–1939*. London: Pandora, 1989.

Belsey, Catherine. *Critical Practice*. London: Methuen, 1980.

Bergonzi, Bernard. *Reading the Thirties: Texts and Contexts*. Pittsburgh: University of Pittsburgh Press, 1978.

—. *Wartime and Aftermath: English Literature and Its Background, 1939–1960*. Oxford: Oxford University Press, 1993.

Berman, Marshall. *All That is Solid Melts into Air: The Experience of Modernity*. New York: Penguin, 1982.

Birchall, Danny. Notes on *Housing Problems*. In *Land of Promise: The British Documentary Film Movement*, booklet accompanying BFI DVD box set, p. 15.

Birkett, Jennifer. *Margaret Storm Jameson: A Life*. Oxford: Oxford University Press, 2009.

Birkett, Jennifer and Chiara Briganti, eds. *Storm Jameson: Writing in Dialogue*. Newcastle: Cambridge Scholars Publishing, 2007.

Bluemel, Kristin. *George Orwell and the Radical Eccentrics: Intermodernism in Literary London*. New York and Basingstoke: Palgrave Macmillan, 2004.

Blythe, Ronald. *Components of the Scene: Stories, Poems, and Essays of the Second World War*. Harmondsworth: Penguin, 1966.

Boehmer, Elleke. *Colonial and Postcolonial Literature*. 1995. New York: Oxford University Press, 2005.

Booth, Howard J. and Rigby Nigel, eds. *Modernism and Empire: Writing and British Coloniality 1890–1940*. New York: Palgrave, 2000.

Bracco, Rosa Maria. *Merchants of Hope: British Middlebrow Writers and the First World War*. Oxford: Berg, 1995.

Bradbury, Malcolm. *No, Not Bloomsbury*. New York: Columbia University Press, 1988.

Branson, Noreen and Margot Heinemann. *Britain in the Nineteen Thirties*. London: Weidenfeld and Nicolson, 1971.

Braudy, Leo. *The Frenzy of Renown: Fame and its History*. New York: Vintage, 1986.

Braydon, Gail and Penny Summerfield. *Out of the Cage: Women's Experiences in Two World Wars*. London: Pandora Press, 1987

Briganti, Chiara and Kathy Mezei. *Domestic Modernism, the Interwar Novel, and E. H. Young*. Burlington: Ashgate, 2006.

Britton, Wesley. *Beyond Bond: Spies in Fiction and Film*. Westport: Praeger, 2005.

Bryant, Marsha. *Auden and Documentary in the 1930s*. Charlottesville: University Press of Virginia, 1997.

Bürger, Peter. *The Decline of Modernism*. Trans. Nicholas Walker. University Park: Pennsylvania State University Press, 1992.

Byatt, A. S. (Antonia Susan). *On Histories and Stories: Selected Essays*. London: Chatto, 2000.

Caesar, Adrian. *Dividing Lines: Poetry, Class, and Ideology in the 1930s*. Manchester: Manchester University Press, 1991.

Calder, Angus. *The Myth of the Blitz*. London: Jonathan Cape, 1991.

—. *The People's War: Britain 1939–1945*. New York: Pantheon, 1969.

Carey, John. *The Intellectuals and the Masses: Pride and Prejudice amongst the Intelligentsia, 1880–1939*. London: Faber, 1992.

Caserio, Robert. *The Novel in England, 1900–1950: History and Theory*. New York: Twayne, 1999.

Chapman, James. *The British at War: Cinema, State and Propaganda, 1939–1945*. London: Tauris, 1998.

Cheyette, Bryan. *Constructions of the 'Jew' in English Literature and Society: Racial Representations, 1875–1945*. Cambridge: Cambridge University Press, 1993.

Clark, Jon, Margot Heinemann, David Margolis and Carol Snee. *Culture and Crisis in Britain in the 1930s*. London: Lawrence and Wishart, 1979.

Cohen, Debra Rae. 'Sheepish Modernism: Rebecca West, the Adam Brothers, and the Taxonomies of Criticism'. *Rebecca West Today: Contemporary Critical Approaches*. Ed. Bernard Schweizer. Newark: University of Delaware Press, 2006. 143–56.

Colletta, Lisa. *Dark Humor and Social Satire in the Modern British Novel: The Triumph of Narcissism*. New York: Palgrave, 2003.

Collier, Patrick. *Modernism on Fleet Street*. Burlington: Ashgate, 2006.

Connor, Steven. *The English Novel in History 1950–1995*. London and New York: Routledge, 1996.

Conrad, Peter. *Imagining America*. New York: Oxford University Press, 1980.

Cooke, Miriam and Angela Woollacott, eds. *Gendering War Talk*. Princeton: Princeton University Press, 1993.

Cowasjee, Saros. *Studies in Indian and Anglo-Indian Fiction*. New Delhi: Indus, 1993.

Crick, Bernard. *George Orwell: A Life*. Harmondsworth: Penguin, 1980.

Croft, Andy. *Red Letter Days: British Fiction in the 1930s*. London: Lawrence and Wishart, 1990.

Cross, Gary. *An All-Consuming Century: Why Commercialism Won in Modern America*. New York: Columbia University Press, 2000.

Cunningham, Valentine. *British Writers of the Thirties*. New York: Oxford University Press, 1988.

Davies, Andrew. *Where Did the Forties Go?* London: Pluto Press, 1984.

Deane, Patrick, ed. *History in Our Hands: A Critical Anthology of Writings on Literature, Culture and Politics from the 1930s*. New York: Leicester University Press, 1998.

de Certeau, Michel. *The Practice of Everyday Life*. Trans. Steven Rendall. Berkeley: University of California Press, 1984.

Deen, Stella, ed. *Challenging Modernism: New Readings in Literature and Culture, 1914–1945*. Burlington: Ashgate, 2002.

Denning, Michael. *Cover Stories: Narrative and Ideology in the British Spy Thriller*. London: Routledge and Kegan Paul, 1987.

DiBattista, Maria and Lucy McDiarmid, eds. *High and Low Moderns: Literature and Culture 1889–1939*. Oxford: Oxford University Press, 1996.

Donald, James, Anne Friedberg and Laura Marcus, eds. *Close Up 1927–1933: Cinema and Modernism*. Princeton: Princeton University Press, 1999.

Dowson, Jane. *Women, Modernism, and British Poetry 1910–1939: Resisting Femininity*. Burlington: Ashgate, 2002.

Dubord, Guy. *The Society of the Spectacle*. Trans. Donald Nicholson-Smith. New York: Zone Books, 1995.

Eagleton, Terry. *Exiles and Émigrés: Studies in Modern Literature*. New York: Schocken, 1970.

Edwards, Owen Dudley. *British Children's Fiction in the Second World War*. Edinburgh: Edinburgh University Press, 2007.

Elster, Jon, ed. *Retribution and Reparation in the Transition to Democracy*. Cambridge: Cambridge University Press, 2006.

Esty, Jed. *A Shrinking Island: Modernism and National Culture in England*. Princeton: Princeton University Press, 2004.

Eysteinsson, Astradur. *The Concept of Modernism*. Ithaca: Cornell University Press, 1990.

Fleishman, Avrom. *The English Historical Novel: Walter Scott to Virginia Woolf*. London and Baltimore: Johns Hopkins University Press, 1971.

Fordham, John. *James Hanley: Modernism and the Working Class*. Cardiff: University of Wales Press, 2003.

Fox, Pamela. *Class Fictions: Shame and Resistance in the British Working-Class Novel, 1890–1945*. Durham: Duke University Press, 1994.

Friedman, Susan Stanford. 'Definitional Excursions: The Meanings of Modern/Modernity/Modernism'. *Modernism/Modernity* 8 (2001): 493–513.

—. 'Periodizing Modernism: Postcolonial Modernities and the Space/Time Borders of Modernist Studies'. *Modernism/Modernity* 13 (2006): 425–43.

Frow, John. *Genre*. London and New York: Routledge, 2006.

—. '"Reproducibles, Rubrics, and Everything You Need": Genre Theory Today'. *PMLA* 122.5 (2007): 1626–34.

Fussell, Paul. *Abroad: British Literary Traveling between the Wars*. Oxford: Oxford University Press, 1980.

—. *Wartime: Understanding and Behavior in the Second World War*. New York: Oxford University Press, 1989.

Fyrth, Jim, ed. *Britain, Fascism and the Popular Front*. London: Lawrence and Wishart, 1985.

Gardner, Brian, ed. *The Terrible Rain: The War Poets 1939–45*. London: Methuen, 1966.

Garrity, Jane. *Step-Daughters of England: British Women Modernists and the National Imaginary*. New York: Manchester University Press, 2005.

Garside, W. R. *The Durham Miners, 1919–1960*. London: George Allen and Unwin, 1971.

Gasiorek, Andrzej. *Post-War British Fiction: Realism and After*. London: Edward Arnold, 1995.

Gervais, David. *Literary Englands: Versions of 'Englishness' in Modern Writing*. Cambridge: Cambridge University Press, 1993.

Gikandi, Simon. *Maps of Englishness: Writing Identity in the Culture of Colonialism*. New York: Columbia University Press, 1996.

Giles, Judy. *The Parlour and the Suburb: Domestic Identities, Class, Femininity and Modernity.* Basingstoke: Palgrave Macmillan, 2004.

Ginden, James. *British Fiction of the 1930s: The Dispiriting Decade.* New York: St Martin's Press, 1992.

Glancy, H. Mark. *When Hollywood Loved Britain: The Hollywood 'British' Film.* Manchester: Manchester University Press, 1999.

Gloversmith, Frank, ed. *Class, Culture and Social Change: A New View of the 1930s.* Brighton: Harvester Press, 1980.

Glucksmann, Miriam. *Women Assemble: Women Workers in the New Industries of Inter-War Britain.* London: Routledge, 1989.

Green, Martin. *Children of the Sun: A Narrative of 'Decadence' in England after 1918.* New York: Basic Books, 1976.

Gupta, Partha Sarathi. *Power, Politics, and the People: Studies in British Imperialism and Indian Nationalism.* New York: Cambridge University Press, 2000.

Hammill, Faye. *Women, Celebrity and Literary Culture between the Wars.* Austin: University of Texas Press, 2007.

Hapgood, Lynne. *Margins of Desire: The Suburbs in Fiction and Culture, 1880–1925.* Manchester: Manchester University Press, 2005.

Hapgood, Lynne and Nancy L. Paxton, eds. *Outside Modernism: In Pursuit of the English Novel, 1900–30.* New York and Basingstoke: Palgrave Macmillan, 2000.

Hardy, Forsyth. *John Grierson: A Documentary Biography.* London: Faber, 1979.

Hartley, Jenny. *Millions Like Us: British Women's Fiction of the Second World War.* London: Virago, 1997.

—, ed. *Hearts Undefeated: Women's Writing of the Second World War.* London: Virago, 1994.

Hartley, John. *Popular Reality: Journalism, Modernity, Popular Culture.* London: Arnold, 1996.

Hawthorn, Jeremy, ed. *The British Working-Class Novel in the Twentieth Century.* Baltimore: Edward Arnold, 1984.

Haywood, Ian. *Working-Class Fiction: From Chartism to Trainspotting.* Plymouth: Northcote House, 1997.

Head, Dominic. *The Cambridge Introduction to Modern British Fiction, 1950–2000.* Cambridge: Cambridge University Press, 2002.

Hepburn, Allan. *Intrigue: Espionage and Culture.* New Haven: Yale University Press, 2005.

Hewison, Robert. *Under Siege: Literary Life in London, 1939–45.* London: Weidenfeld and Nicolson, 1977.

Highmore, Ben. *Everyday Life and Cultural Theory: An Introduction.* London: Routledge, 2002.

Higonnet, Margaret Randolph, et al., eds. *Behind the Lines: Gender and the Two World Wars*. New Haven: Yale University Press, 1987.

Hipkins, Danielle and Gill Plain, eds. *War-Torn Tales: Literature, Film and Gender in the Aftermath of World War II*. New York: Peter Lang, 2007.

Hoggart, Richard. *A Sort of Clowning: Life and Times 1940–1959*. London: Chatto and Windus, 1990.

—. *The Uses of Literacy: Changing Patterns in English Mass Culture*. 1957. Boston: Beacon Press, 1961.

Holsinger, M. Paul and Mary Anne Scholfield, eds. *Visions of War: World War II in Popular Literature and Culture*. Bowling Green: Bowling Green State University Popular Press, 1992.

Hopkins, Chris. *English Fiction in the 1930s*. London: Continuum, 2007.

Horsley, Lee. *Twentieth-Century Crime Fiction*. Oxford: Oxford University Press, 2005.

Howarth, Peter. *British Poetry in the Age of Modernism*. New York: Cambridge University Press, 2005.

Hubble, Nick. 'Intermodern Pastoral: William Empson and George Orwell'. *New Versions of Pastoral: Post-Romantic, Modern, and Contemporary Responses to the Tradition*. Ed. David James and Philip Tew. Madison: Fairleigh Dickinson University Press; London: Associated University Press, 2009. 125–35.

—. *Mass-Observation and Everyday Life: Culture, History, Theory*. London: Palgrave, 2006.

—. 'The Origins of Intermodernism in Ford Madox Ford's Parallax View'. *Ford Madox Ford: Literary Networks and Cultural Transformations*. Ed. Andrzej Gasiorek and Daniel Moore. Amsterdam and New York: Rodopi, 2008. 167–88.

Hughes, Helen. *The Historical Romance*. London: Routledge, 1993.

Humble, Nicola. *The Feminine Middlebrow Novel, 1920s to 1950s: Class, Domesticity and Bohemianism*. Oxford: Oxford University Press, 2001.

Hussey, Mark, ed. *Virginia Woolf and War: Fiction, Reality and Myth*. New York: Syracuse University Press, 1991.

Huyssen, Andreas. *After the Great Divide: Modernism, Mass Culture, Postmodernism*. Bloomington: Indiana University Press, 1986.

Hynes, Samuel. *The Auden Generation: Literature and Politics in England in the 1930s*. Princeton: Princeton University Press, 1972.

—. *The Soldiers' Tale: Bearing Witness to Modern War*. New York: Penguin, 1997.

Ingman, Heather. *Women's Fiction between the Wars: Mothers, Daughters and Writing*. New York: St Martin's, 1998.

Ingram, Angela and Daphne Patai, eds. *Rediscovering Forgotten Radicals:*

British Women Writers, 1889–1939. Chapel Hill: University of North Carolina Press, 1993.

Innes, C. L. *A History of Black and Asian Writing in Britain, 1700–2000*. New York: Cambridge University Press, 2002.

Jaffe, Aaron. *Modernism and the Culture of Celebrity*. Cambridge: Cambridge University Press, 2005.

James, Clive. *The Meaning of Recognition: New Essays 2001–2005*. London: Picador, 2005.

Jameson, Fredric. *Postmodernism or the Cultural Logic of Late Capitalism*. London: Verso, 1991.

Jeffery, Tom. *Mass-Observation: A Short History*. Birmingham: Centre for Contemporary Studies, 1978.

Joannou, Maroula. *'Ladies, Please Don't Smash These Windows': Women's Writing, Feminist Consciousness, and Social Change, 1914–1938*. Oxford and Providence: Berg Press, 1995.

—, ed. *Women Writers of the 1930s: Gender, Politics, and History*. Edinburgh: Edinburgh University Press, 1999.

Johnston, Dillon. *Poetic Economies of England and Ireland, 1912–2000*. New York: Palgrave Macmillan, 2001.

Johnstone, Richard. *The Will to Believe: Novelists of the Nineteen-Thirties*. New York: Oxford University Press, 1982.

Joshi, Priya. *In Another Country: Colonialism, Culture, and the English Novel in India*. New York: Columbia University Press, 2002.

Kalliney, Peter J. *Cities of Affluence and Anger: A Literary Geography of Modern Englishness*. Charlottesville: University of Virginia Press, 2006.

Kent, Susan Kingsley. *Making Peace: The Reconstruction of Gender in Interwar Britain*. Princeton: Princeton University Press, 1993.

Kershaw, Angela and Angela Kimyongür, eds. *Women in Europe between the Wars: Politics, Culture, Society*. Aldershot and Burlington: Ashgate, 2007.

Kirkham, Pat and David Thoms, eds. *War Culture: Social Change and Changing Experience in World War II*. London: Lawrence and Wishart, 1995.

Klaus, H. Gustav. *The Socialist Novel in Britain: Towards the Recovery of a Tradition*. Brighton: Harvester, 1982.

Klaus, H. Gustav and Stephen Knight, eds. *British Industrial Fictions*. Cardiff: University of Wales Press, 2000.

Klein, Holger, John Flower and Eric Homberger, eds. *The Second World War in Fiction*. London: Macmillan, 1984.

Knight, Stephen. 'The Golden Age'. *The Cambridge Companion to Crime Fiction*. Ed. Martin Priestman. Cambridge: Cambridge University Press, 2003. 77–94.

Knowles, Sebastian D. G. *A Purgatorial Flame: Seven British Writers in the Second World War*. Philadelphia: University of Pennsylvania Press, 1990.

Kushner, Tony. *The Persistence of Prejudice: Antisemitism in British Society during the Second World War*. Manchester: Manchester University Press, 1989.

Larson, Neil. *Modernism and Hegemony: A Materialist Critique of Aesthetic Agencies*. Minneapolis: University of Minnesota Press, 1990.

Lassner, Phyllis. *Anglo-Jewish Women Writing the Holocaust: Displaced Witnesses*. New York and Basingstoke: Palgrave Macmillan, 2008.

—. *British Women Writers of World War Two: Battlegrounds of Their Own*. London: Macmillan, 1998.

—. *Colonial Strangers: Women Writing the End of Empire*. New Brunswick: Rutgers University Press, 2004.

Lefebvre, Henri. *The Production of Space*. Trans. Donald Nicholson-Smith. Oxford: Blackwell, 1991.

Lewis, Pericles. *Modernism, Nationalism, and the Novel*. New York: Cambridge University Press, 2000.

Light, Alison. *Forever England: Femininity, Literature and Conservatism between the Wars*. New York: Routledge, 1991.

Lucas, John. *Moderns and Contemporaries: Novelists, Poets, Critics*. New York: Barnes and Noble, 1985.

—, ed. *The 1930s: A Challenge to Orthodoxy*. Brighton: Harvester, 1979.

Lukacs, Georg. *The Historical Novel*. 1961. Trans. Hannah and Stanley Mitchell. London and Lincoln: University of Nebraska Press, 1983.

MacKay, Marina. *Modernism and World War II*. Cambridge: Cambridge University Press, 2007.

— and Lyndsey Stonebridge, eds. *British Fiction after Modernism: The Novel at Mid-Century*. New York: Palgrave Macmillan, 2007.

Madden, David. *Proletarian Writers of the Thirties*. Carbondale: Southern Illinois State University Press, 1968.

Marcus, Jane. *White Women Writing Race*. New Brunswick: Rutgers University Press, 2004.

Marcus, Laura. *The Tenth Muse: Writing about Cinema in the Modernist Period*. Oxford: Oxford University Press, 2007.

Marcus, Laura and Peter Nicholls, eds. *The Cambridge History of Twentieth-Century English Literature*. Cambridge: Cambridge University Press, 2004.

Margolis, David, ed. *Writing the Revolution: Cultural Criticism from 'Left Review'*. London: Pluto Press, 1998.

Marrus, Michael, ed. *The Nuremberg War Crimes Trial 1945–46: A Documentary History*. Boston: Bedford, 1997.

Marx, John. *The Modernist Novel and the Decline of Empire*. Cambridge and New York: Cambridge University Press, 2005.

Maslen, Elizabeth. *Political and Social Issues in British Women's Fiction, 1928–1968*. London: Palgrave Macmillan, 2001.

Matless, David. *Landscape and Englishness*. London: Reaktion Books, 1998.

McHale, Brian. *Constructing Postmodernism*. New York: Routledge, 1992.

McKibbin, Ross. *Classes and Cultures: England 1918–1951*. Oxford: Oxford University Press, 1998.

Mehrotra, Arvind Krishna, ed. *History of Indian Literature in English*. New York: Columbia University Press, 2003.

Mengham, Rod and N. H. Reeve, eds. *The Fiction of the 1940s: Stories of Survival*. New York: Palgrave, 2001.

Miller, Tyrus. *Late Modernism: Politics, Fiction, and the Arts between the Wars*. Berkeley: University of California Press, 1999.

Minns, Raynes. *Bombers and Mash: The Domestic Front 1939–45*. London: Virago, 1980.

Montefiore, Janet. *Men and Women Writers of the 1930s: The Dangerous Flood of History*. London: Routledge, 1996.

Morgan, David and Mary Evans. *The Battle for Britain: Citizenship and Ideology in the Second World War*. New York: Routledge, 1993.

Morgan, Fidelis, ed. *The Years Between: Plays by Women on the London Stage 1900–1950*. London: Virago, 1994.

Morley, Sheridan. *Tales from the Hollywood Raj: The British, the Movies, and Tinseltown*. New York: Viking Press, 1983.

Mulhern, Francis. *The Moment of Scrutiny*. London: New Left Books, 1979.

Munton, Alan. *English Fiction of the Second World War*. London: Faber and Faber, 1989.

Nesbitt, Jennifer Poulos. *Narrative Settlements: Geographies of British Women's Fiction between the Wars*. Toronto: University of Toronto Press, 2005.

Nicholas, Siân. *The Echo of War: Home Front Propaganda and the Wartime BBC, 1939–45*. New York: Manchester University Press, 1996.

Nicholls, Peter. *Modernisms: A Literary Guide*. Berkeley: University of California Press, 1995.

North, Michael. *Henry Green and the Writings of his Generation*. Charlottesville: University of Virginia Press, 1984.

Owen, Stephen. 'Genres in Motion'. *PMLA* 122.5 (2007): 1389–93.

Parry, Benita. *Delusions and Discoveries: India in the British Imagination 1880–1930*. London: Verso, 1998.

Parsons, Deborah L. *Streetwalking the Metropolis: Women, the City and Modernity*. New York: Oxford University Press, 2000.

Paxton, Nancy. 'Eclipsed by Modernism'. Hapgood and Paxton 3–12.

Peach, Linden. *Masquerade, Crime and Fiction*. Basingstoke: Palgrave, 2006.

Perkins, David. *Is Literary History Possible?* Baltimore: Johns Hopkins University Press, 1992.

Piette, Adam. *Imagination at War: British Fiction and Poetry 1939–1945*. London: Papermac, 1995.

Plain, Gill. *Twentieth-Century Crime Fiction: Gender, Sexuality and the Body*. Edinburgh: Edinburgh University Press, 2001.

—. *Women's Fiction of the Second World War*. New York: St Martin's Press, 1996.

Pugh, Martin. *Women and the Women's Movement in Britain, 1914–1959*. London: Macmillan, 1992.

Quinn, Patrick, ed. *Recharting the Thirties*. Selinsgrove: Susquehanna University Press, 1996.

Radway, Janice. *A Feeling for Books: The Book-of-the-Month-Club, Literary Taste, and Middle-Class Desire*. Chapel Hill: University of North Carolina Press, 1997.

Rainey, Lawrence. *Institutions of Modernism: Literary Elites and Public Culture*. New Haven: Yale University Press, 1998.

Rawlinson, Mark. *British Writing of the Second World War*. Oxford: Clarendon Press, 2000.

Reilly, Catherine. *Chaos of the Night: Women's Poetry and Verse of the Second World War*. London: Virago, 1984.

Richards, J. M. *The Age of the Dream Palace: Cinema and Society in Britain, 1930–1939*. London: Routledge and Kegan Paul, 1984.

Richardson, Brian. 'Remapping the Present: The Master Narrative of Modern Literary History and the Lost Forms of Twentieth-Century Fiction'. *Twentieth-Century Literature* 43 (1997): 291–309.

Roberts, John. *The Art of Interruption: Realism, Photography and the Everyday*. Manchester: Manchester University Press, 1998.

Roberts, Michael, ed. *New Country*. London: Hogarth Press, 1933.

Rollyson, Carl. *Rebecca West: A Life*. New York: Scribner, 1996.

Rose, Jonathan. *The Intellectual Life of the British Working Classes*. New Haven: Yale University Press, 2001.

Rowland, Susan. *From Agatha Christie to Ruth Rendell: British Women Writers in Detective and Crime Fiction*. Basingstoke: Palgrave, 2001.

Royal Commission on Capital Punishment 1949–1953 Report. London: Her Majesty's Stationery Office, 1953.

Saler, Michael T. *The Avant-Garde in Interwar England: Medieval Modernism and the London Underground*. New York: Oxford University Press, 1999.

Samuels, Raphael. *Patriotism: The Making and Unmaking of British National*

Identity. 3 vols. Vol. 1. *History and Politics.* Vol. 2. *Minorities and Outsiders.* Vol. 3. *National Fictions.* London: Routledge, 1989.

Scannell, Paddy and David Cardiff. *A Social History of British Broadcasting.* Cambridge: Blackwell, 1991.

Scannell, Vernon. *Not Without Glory: Poets of the Second World War.* London: Woburn Press, 1976.

Schneider, Karen. *Loving Arms: British Women Writing the Second World War.* Lexington: University of Kentucky Press, 1997.

Schweizer, Bernard. *Radicals on the Road: The Politics of English Travel Writing in the 1930s.* Charlottesville: University of Virginia Press, 2001.

Shelden, Michael. *Friends of Promise: Cyril Connolly and the World of Horizon.* 1989. London: Minerva, 1990.

Sheridan, Dorothy, Brian Street and David Bloome. *Writing Ourselves: Mass-Observation and Literary Practices.* Cresskill: Hampton Press, 2000.

Shires, Linda M. *British Poetry of the Second World War.* London: Macmillan, 1985.

Shuttleworth, Antony, ed. *And in Our Time: Vision, Revision, and British Writing of the Thirties.* Lewisburg: Bucknell University Press, 2003.

Sinclair, Andrew. *War Like a Wasp: The Lost Decade of the Forties.* London: Hamish Hamilton, 1989.

—, ed. *The War Decade: An Anthology of the 1940s.* London: Hamilton, 1989.

Skelton, Robin. *Poetry of the Thirties.* Harmondsworth: Penguin, 1964.

Smith, Anthony D. *Modernism and Nationalism.* London: Routledge, 1998.

Stansky, Peter and William Abrahams. *London's Burning: Life, Death and Art in the Second World War.* London: Constable, 1994.

Stetz, Margaret. *British Women's Comic Fiction, 1890–1990: Not Drowning, But Laughing.* London: Ashgate, 2001.

Stevenson, John and Chris Cook. *Britain in the Depression: Society and Politics, 1929–1939.* 1977. New York: Longman, 1994.

Stewart, Victoria. *Narratives of Memory: British Writing of the 1940s.* Basingstoke: Palgrave Macmillan, 2006.

Summerfield, Penny. *Women Workers in the Second World War.* London: Routledge, 1984.

Symons, Julian. *The Thirties: A Dream Revolved.* London: Cresset Press, 1960.

Taylor, A. J. P. *English History 1914–1945.* New York: Oxford University Press, 1965.

Taylor, John Russell. *Strangers in Paradise: The Hollywood Emigres, 1933–1950.* New York: Holt, 1983.

Tolley, A. T. *The Poetry of the Forties.* Manchester: Manchester University Press, 1985.

—. *The Poetry of the Thirties*. London: Gollancz, 1975.

Trodd, Anthea. *Women's Writing in English: Britain 1900–1945*. Harlow: Addison, 1998.

Tuan, Yi-Fu. 'Place: An Experiential Perspective'. *The Geographical Review* 65 (1975): 151–65.

Tylee, Claire. *The Great War and Women's Consciousness: Images of Militarism and Womanhood in Women's Writings, 1914–1964*. Iowa City: University of Iowa Press, 1990.

Visram, Rozina. *Asians in Britain: 400 years of History*. Sterling: Pluto Press, 2002.

Walkowitz, Rebecca L. and Douglas Mao. 'The New Modernist Studies'. *PMLA* 123 (2008): 737–48.

Wallace, Dina. *Sisters and Rivals in British Women's Fiction, 1914–1939*. New York: Palgrave, 2000.

Wallace, Jane and Michael Vaughan-Rees. *Women in Wartime: The Role of Women's Magazines 1939–1987*. London: Macdonald Optima, 1987.

Waugh, Patricia. *Practicing Postmodernism/Reading Modernism*. London: Edward Arnold, 1992.

West, Nigel. *Secret War: The Story of SOE, Britain's Wartime Sabotage Organization*. London: Hodder and Stoughton, 1992.

Wild, Jonathan. *The Rise of the Office Clerk in Literary Culture, 1880–1939*. New York: Palgrave Macmillan, 2006.

Williams, Keith and Steven Matthews, eds. *Rewriting the Thirties: Modernism and After*. London: Longmans, 1997.

Williams, Raymond. 'The Bloomsbury Fraction'. *Contemporary Marxist Literary Criticism*. Ed. Francis Mulhern. London: Longmans, 1992. 125–45.

—. *The Politics of Modernism: Against the New Conformists*. Ed. Tony Pinkney. London and New York: Verso, 1989.

Wolfe, Peter. *Rebecca West: Artist and Thinker*. Carbondale: Southern Illinois University Press, 1971.

Žižek, Slavoj. *The Parallax View*. Cambridge and London: MIT Press, 2006.

NOTES ON CONTRIBUTORS

Kristin Bluemel is Professor of English at Monmouth University in New Jersey. She is author of *George Orwell and the Radical Eccentrics: Intermodernism in Literary London* (2004) and *Experimenting on the Borders of Modernism: Dorothy Richardson's Pilgrimage* (1997). She edits the interdisciplinary journal *The Space Between: Literature and Culture 1914–1945*.

Debra Rae Cohen is Assistant Professor of English at the University of South Carolina. She is author of *Remapping the Home Front: Locating Citizenship in British Women's Great War Fiction* (2002) and co-editor of the collection *Broadcasting Modernism* (2009). Her next book will use Rebecca West as a limit case for modernist historiography.

Lisa Colletta is Associate Professor of English at the American University of Rome. She is the author of *Dark Humor and Social Satire in the Modern British Novel* (2003), editor of *Kathleen and Christopher: Christopher Isherwood's Letters to his Mother* (2005), and co-editor of *Wild Colonial Girl: Essays on Edna O'Brien* (2006). She is currently writing a book on the life and work of British novelists in Hollywood. Research for the chapter included in this collection was funded by the Babson College Faculty Research Fund.

John Fordham has lectured in higher education since 1993 and currently teaches twentieth-century literature at the Open University. He is the author of *James Hanley: Modernism and the Working Class* (2003) and has written a number of articles on modernism, class and regionalism.

Faye Hammill is Senior Lecturer in English at the University of Strathclyde.

She is co-editor of *The Encyclopedia of British Women Writers 1900–1950* (2006) and author of *Women, Celebrity and Literary Culture between the Wars* (2007), *Canadian Literature* (2007) and *Literary Culture and Female Authorship in Canada 1760–2000* (2003). She is currently working on a project about sophistication.

Allan Hepburn is Associate Professor of English at McGill University in Montreal. He is the author of *Intrigue: Espionage and Culture* (2005) and editor of *Troubled Legacies: Narrative and Inheritance* (2007). He has also edited two volumes of material by Elizabeth Bowen: *The Bazaar and Other Stories* (2008) and *People, Places, Things: Essays by Elizabeth Bowen* (2008). He has finished writing a book called *Enchanted Objects: Visual Art in Contemporary Literature*. His next book project concerns Elizabeth Bowen and modernity.

Nick Hubble is Lecturer in English at Brunel University. He is the author of *Mass-Observation and Everyday Life: Culture, History, Theory* (2006), and in addition to articles on various twentieth-century and contemporary English writers, has published two foundational articles on intermodernism. He is now at work on an article on Katherine Mansfield and intermodernism.

Phyllis Lassner teaches Holocaust Studies, Gender Studies and Writing at Northwestern University. She is the author of two books on Elizabeth Bowen (1990, 1991), *British Women Writers of World War II: Battlegrounds of Their Own* (1998) and *Colonial Strangers: Women Writing the End of the British Empire* (2004). Her latest book is *Anglo-Jewish Women Writing the Holocaust: Displaced Witnesses* (2008).

Laura Marcus is Regius Professor of Rhetoric and English Literature at Edinburgh University. She is the author of many books and articles on British modernism, cinema, early film writing, the novel, autobiography, feminist theory, women's writing and psychoanalysis. Her most notable publications include *The Tenth Muse: Writing about Cinema in the Modernist Period* (2007) and *Virginia Woolf: Writers and Their Work* (1997, 2004). She is editor with Peter Nicholls of *The Cambridge History of Twentieth-Century English Literature* (2005) and with James Donald and Anne Friedberg of *Close Up 1927–1933: Cinema and Modernism* (1998).

Elizabeth Maslen taught for many years at Westfield College, University of London, and then at Queen Mary, University of London. She is now a senior research fellow at the Institute of English Studies, University of London. Her publications include books on Doris Lessing and on women writers between 1928 and 1968, and she is at present writing a book on Storm Jameson.

Janet Montefiore is Professor of Twentieth-Century English Literature at the University of Kent at Canterbury, where she is director of the Centre for Gender, Sexuality and Writing in the School of English. She is the author of *Feminism and Poetry* (1989, 3rd ed. 2004), *Men and Women Writers of the 1930s* (1996), *Arguments of Heart and Mind* (2002) and *Rudyard Kipling* (2007).

INDEX